APM

Social Engagement

The Challenge of the Social in Missiological Education

The 2013 Proceedings of

The Association of Professors of Mission

2013 APM Annual Meeting, Wheaton, IL
June 20-21, 2013

First Fruits
THE ACADEMIC OPEN PRESS OF ASBURY SEMINARY

ISBN: 9781621711148 (print), 9781621711179 (digital)

Social Engagement: The Challenge of the Social in Missiological Education
The 2013 Proceedings of the Association of Professors of Mission
First Fruits Press, c2013

Digital version at http://place.asburyseminary.edu/academicbooks/3/

Questions, contact:
Association of Professors of Mission
108 W. High St.
Lexington, KY 40507
http://www.asmweb.org/content/apm

Social engagement: the challenge of the social in missiological education.
        xvi, 339 p. : ill. ; 23 cm.
        Wilmore, Ky. : First Fruits Press, c2013.
        The 2013 proceedings of the Association of Professors of Mission.
        Includes bibliographical references.
        ISBN: 9781621711148 (pbk.)
        1. Missions – Study and teaching – Congresses. 2. Missions – Theory – Congresses. 3. Social action – Religious aspects – Christianity – Congresses. I. Title. II. Proceedings of the Association of Professors of Mission. III. Association of Professors of Mission annual meeting (2013 : Wheaton, Ill.) IV. Association of Professors of Mission.
BV2090 .S624 2013 / BV2020 .A876 2013
266/.007

Cover design by Kelli Dierdorf

asburyseminary.edu
800.2ASBURY
204 North Lexington Avenue
Wilmore, Kentucky 40390

First Fruits
THE ACADEMIC OPEN PRESS OF ASBURY SEMINARY

About the Association of Professors of Mission

ROBERT DANIELSON, ADVISORY COMMITTEE MEMBER

The Association of Professors of Mission (APM) was formed in 1952 at Louisville, Kentucky and was developed as an organization to focus on the needs of people involved in the classroom teaching of mission studies. However, the organization also challenged members to be professionally involved in scholarly research and share this research through regular meetings. In the 1960's Roman Catholic scholars and scholars from conservative Evangelical schools joined the conciliar Protestants who initially founded the organization.

With the discussion to broaden membership to include other scholars from areas like anthropology, sociology, and linguistics who were actively engaged in mission beyond the teaching profession, the decision was made to found the American Society of Missiology (ASM) in 1972. Since the importance of working with mission educators was still vital, the APM continued as a separate organization, but always met in conjunction with the ASM at their annual meetings.

The APM continues as a professional society of those interested in the teaching of mission from as wide an ecumenical spectrum as possible. As an organization it works to help and support those who teach mission, especially those who often lack a professional network to help mentor and guide them in this task. Through its influence, the APM has also helped establish the prominence and scholarly importance of the academic discipline of missiology throughout theological education.

Table of Contents

Conference Papers

Opening Plenary Address

Group A: Participatory Learning

Group B:
Curriculum Models for Missional Education

Group C:
Missiology in the Social-Cultural Context

Group D:
Issues in Social Engagement

Closing
Plenary Address

Conference Proceedings

Index of Figures
and Appendix

Foreword

GREGORY P. LEFFEL, PRESIDENT

For many years—a decade-and-a-half, ending in 1974—the Association of Professors of Mission mimeographed (these were the days before copiers!) and bound the papers and reports presented at our annual meetings. These were made available and mailed to the members at a low cost for circulation within the missiological community. This year we renew our tradition by making the proceedings of our 2013 annual meeting available in this permanent on-line and print volume for the benefit of our members and the wider community of mission scholars—and as a record of this particular moment in APM's history.

In one way or another the papers that follow respond to our 2013 conference theme highlighting missiology's growing engagement with social issues. This marks a "social turn" of sorts that expands missiological reflection in the direction of social change, social justice, activism, advocacy, and related research. Such emphasis is hardly new but taking it with renewed seriousness raises fresh questions for professors of mission. Of primary importance to our members are questions about how we equip our students to concretely and practically engage social realities while reflecting on them theologically and theoretically. And in keeping with APM's mission to advance the teaching of mission studies, such educational questions were brought to the center of our discussions this year.

With this pedagogical emphasis in mind, our collection of papers begins and ends with the plenary papers presented by David Fenrick, from Northwestern College, and Al Tizon, from Palmer

Theological Seminary. Both papers concentrate on service-learning or "engaged" scholarship as they explore new ways to move beyond the classroom to train missioners as scholar-practitioners. David presented a vital (even path-breaking) model for experience-based education; Al described the challenges of creating an entire graduate program rooting classroom instruction in social advocacy and activism. Both are instructive as we envision new curricula and new programs for effectively training the next generation of missioners and missiologists. In between these plenaries, twelve other papers were presented in workshops. Several of these also touch on pedagogical issues related to engaged scholarship and service-learning. Others explore theoretical, historical and social-cultural issues in missiological perspective.

Taken together, this collection of papers reflects the emerging interests of our members. Even more, the quality of research and reflection in them demonstrates the creative scholarship emerging within our discipline. And as a sign of missiology's growing vitality, many of the papers included here were written by young, emerging scholars and doctoral students. Looking at this work, any of us could be forgiven for believing that missiology's best days are yet to come!

A few things could not be included in this volume. Three of the workshop papers have been accepted for publication in professional journals and for copyright reasons cannot be reproduced here. Their titles and authors' names are listed for reference on the section title pages in the text. Congratulations are in order for the authors, of course, but we will miss them in the "Proceedings."

Unfortunately, two other presentations are missing from the "Proceedings" including Gary Simpson's (Luther Seminary) energetic plenary session entitled "Missional Congregations, Civil Society and Social Theory: How a Turn to the Social Helps Widen Our Vision for Research, Teaching and Guidance for Mission." This was an electronic rather than a written presentation and for technical reasons we are unable to publish it here. Also not included is Kendi Howells Douglas's (Great Lakes Christian College) short discussion and question and answer interaction, "Undergraduate Service Learning: Urban Mission Minor Program," presenting an innovative year-long, engaged learning program placing undergraduate students on-site in an urban Bangkok squatter neighborhood. This informative interactive discussion was not recorded.

For the record: In 2013 the APM met at Wheaton College, Wheaton, Illinois from Thursday evening, June 20 through Friday afternoon, June 21. In all, 116 registered for the meeting, making it the largest APM gathering, we believe, in its 61 year history. Other records from the meeting including business meeting reports and minutes are documented here and provide additional details related to the meeting's proceedings.

Finally, our thanks are due for the hard work of the executive committee in organizing and directing our meeting this year. The work that happens behind the scenes from year to year is seldom noticed but greatly appreciated. So, many thanks to Sr. Madge Karecki, Ben Hartley and David Fenrick for their dedication and commitment in support of this year's meeting. Thanks also to Sean Gladding who inspired us in worship on Thursday evening and Friday morning. Special thanks to Robert (Robbie) Danielson for preparing the "Proceedings" for publication, and thanks as well to Asbury Theological Seminary for making "First Fruits Press," its online, open source publishing service, available to APM to enable us to preserve and distribute the fruits of our meeting.

Next year we gather at Northwestern College in St. Paul, Minnesota. I look forward to seeing all of you there!

Conference Theme

2013 Conference Theme Announcement

Social Engagement: The Challenge of the Social in Missiological Education

The gospel's social dimensions have been integral to Christian mission from the beginning. Caring for the poor, naked, homeless, starving, oppressed, and abandoned; "seeking the welfare of the city"—these concerns always have accompanied faithful witness. They also have animated generations of missioners who established schools and universities, hospitals, orphanages, agricultural programs, and relief programs for the poor with great impact throughout the world. Indeed, while the first great commandment, "You shall love the Lord your God . . . ," might be (and often is) addressed in individual terms, the second great commandment, "You shall love your neighbor as you love yourself," is inherently a social one. Who is my neighbor? How are we related? What do we owe one another? How do we live together, work, and shape our communities and societies for the common good?

The voice of the "social" in missiology often, however, is a tentative one. Throughout the twentieth century tension between evangelism and the social gospel polarized Christian witness. In recent decades, missiologists sought to overcome this tension with proposals for "holistic" mission, "integral" mission, mission as "transformation," and theologies of liberation. Such comprehensive paradigms are not new, nor are they without controversy, though they occupy an important place in contemporary missiology. What is new is the rising generation's ambivalent commitment to social involvement. Recent research in the United States suggests that young adults are less interested in civic engagement than at any time in the last half-century (while paradoxically being *more* likely to volunteer for community service in high school and college). At least some younger Christians, though, have made a decisive "turn to the social" in renewed concern for social justice, advocacy for the disadvantaged, social service and social renewal in cross-cultural ministry. This "turning" is reflected in emerging Christian renewal movements such as the "missional-incarnational church" as well as mission focused upon the poor in North America and abroad, and has energized the prophetic voices of traditional churches and missions. It is also reflected in career choices to pursue fields in the non-profit "social enterprise" sector such as community development, development economics and social advocacy, and these choices are sometimes at the expense of traditional missionary service. Such renewed social interest among the young is reinforced (or perhaps even created) by colleges, universities and seminaries which increasingly stress community involvement in their admissions criteria and curricula. For some young Christians today (perhaps those entering selective colleges or self-selecting for the ministry?), simply believing the gospel is not enough. "Doing" the gospel through service to others has become essential to authentic and faithful life and witness. But for most others, moving beyond individualism to embrace a broad-based concern for the world and its needs requires deliberate nurturing through a process of education and spiritual formation. The emerging challenge to missiological instruction is to frame a comprehensive understanding of the gospel and provide guidance for socially-engaged mission, and also to awaken and shape the interests and passions of the next generation of missioners and missiologists.

To meet this challenge thoughtful attention must be given to course content, curricular objectives and effective service-learning requirements. As a community of educators we will seek together to discern emerging best practices, share expertise and draw from the experiences of our colleagues. Attention must also be given to the nature of faith-inspired social influence itself and the objects of Christian social involvement. Much as the 1970s "cultural turn" enriched our field with anthropological insight, a conceptual "social turn" also confronts us with the challenge to assimilate additional domains of insight and application, and to reflect anew on the social-theoretical dimensions of mission. Traditionally, theology and the social sciences have not easily coexisted. Some argue that they are incommensurable. Yet Christianity is scarcely recognizable without its social forms and influence. Work must continue at the conceptual level to envision the missiology of Christian social encounter, and beyond this to visualize mission's role in social change and transformation. At the same time, a wider framing of mission theory and practice is also needed in order to include other fields—such as community development and social science research itself—more integrally within missiological reflection. Such a framing will provide scholars in cognate fields with a theological home that unites us all in our vocation to see the transforming witness of the gospel advance in the world. For Christian scholars who (implicitly, anyway) may practice "missiology by other names and identities" this can provide, perhaps, a refreshing participation with the broader mission tradition and a new source of vitality for missiology.

To sharpen the point a bit, as many missiologists turn their gaze to the question of mission in and to North America they confront a social and cultural context of bewildering complexity at a time of historic transformation and restructuring. Questions about demographics, social class, structures of power, collective action, human identity, migration, political economy, social theory, and so on, perhaps once considered marginal to missiological reflection, are now central to understanding the environment in which mission confronts the contemporary West. Missiology's vital, interdisciplinary historical dialogue with the humanities and the social sciences will no doubt be stretched as it considers Modernity/Postmodernity not just in the West but wherever it shapes the missional context across the globe as it is doing with accelerating force.

APM's own mission to strengthen and advance the teaching of mission is a complex faithfulness. And it is to the demands of teaching a challenging interdisciplinary missiological curriculum in a world of growing complexity that we will turn in 2013. We will think together about mission's "Social Engagement" with one eye on the development of course content and research agendas and with the other on the formation of our students. In the background lie questions of curriculum development and the shapes of our faculties. We also recognize that a large proportion of our members labor alone in the academy without the fellowship of a wider missiological faculty. Nothing is more central to APM's ethos than encouraging mutual support among our members. To this end we will, in 2013, unveil new web-based member services to encourage greater sharing of resources and to facilitate collegial interaction.

"Social Engagement," APM 2013! We look forward to another great year of exciting conversation, fellowship and fresh vision. See you this June at Wheaton!

APM

Conference
Papers

APM

Opening Plenary Address

Missional Education for Social Action

DOI: 10.7252/Paper.000022

About the Author:
David E. Fenrick is the Director of the Center for Global Reconciliation and Cultural Education, and teaches Intercultural Studies and Communication at Northwestern College in St. Paul, MN. David earned his Ph.D. in Intercultural Studies from Asbury Theological Seminary. David has lived and studied in Zimbabwe, Palestine and Israel, and has led numerous educational travel seminars around the world. He also served as a United Methodist minister in Virginia, receiving Excellence in Ministry Awards from both the Commission on Race and Religion, and the Board of Global Ministry.

Abstract

The world is in the midst of rapid change due to powerful forces such as globalization. Although these changes have led to a greater sense of interdependence and interconnectedness than ever known before and tremendous advances on many fronts, the prevalence of conflict, injustice, and environmental degradation around the globe has also heightened people's awareness of their differences and the need for all Christians to be actively engaged in God's mission. In light of these concerns, the need for a missional level of social action and intercultural competence is of critical importance. The predominant models of education alone are no longer the optimal means for addressing the emerging missiological realities of the 21st century. Missiological education at all levels needs to focus on a learning process that serves a missional purpose and will provide Christians with new experiences, in addition to new skills and knowledge, to be responsibly engaged in missional social action. This paper analyzes the degree to which the principles of experiential education theories and practices can inform and enhance missiological education. "Essential Ingredients" for a "Missional Education" (ME) are presented, providing insights for an educational praxis.

Introduction

A few years ago I attended an international conference of missiologists. This was a "working" conference. Our specific task was to address the issue of effective education for world mission in an age of globalization. From the beginning of our collaborative work it became apparent that there was a division within our group. The majority of the contributors focused their research and discussion on the *content* of missiological education, elements such as the "right" course topics and academic disciplines, particularly within formal settings such as Bible schools and theological seminaries. Only a few people were discussing the learning *process*, i.e., pedagogy. Consequently, the greater part of our discussion focused on formal educational models and the content – courses, topics, theology, etc. – necessary for missiological education in the church and school.[1] Only a few participants raised the issue of creating a pedagogy for mission to assist in fulfilling the *purpose* of missiological education, i.e., exploring the *process* by which *all* Christians can most effectively learn how to be participants in God's global mission within their cultural, or multicultural, context.

Educational experiences leading up to the conference had reinforced my thinking that the learning *process* was of equal importance as the content of the education, if not more so, in achieving the *purpose* of missiological education, which is equipping all Christian disciples for participation in God's mission in the world. These experiences also reinforced my belief that missiological, and for that matter, theological education is not a higher level of Christian education (exclusive to academic qualifications, residency programs, and graduation into "professional" careers), but a dimension of everyone's Christian formation, depending on their stage in life and calling.

While working at Augsburg College in Minneapolis, MN, I assisted in coordinating numerous short-term intercultural experiential educational programs through the Center for Global Education (CGE). All of the educational experiences occurred outside of traditional (formal) Bible school or seminary settings, instead including combinations of both formal and non-formal settings and educational processes. In many of the programs there was little or no reference to missiological literature or disciplines, yet results were produced in the lives of many participants that I had rarely seen in my peers who attended seminary and studied missiology or other theological disciplines.

A "metamorphosis" happened with the learners during and in the weeks that followed these intercultural immersion experiences. Both "students" and "teachers" came away from these intercultural learning programs transformed. This was not evident simply in the participants' testimonies of having "a life-changing experience." Instead, the transformations were made evident by what happened with them *after* the program ended. Although none of the programs were explicitly missiological in their focus, these "life-changing experiences" were most profoundly expressed in an awareness of their responsibility as "global citizens" engaged in issues of social justice, the transformation of their worldviews, a greater understanding of their personal and communal vocation as participants in God's mission in the world, and, most importantly, their *actions*. Upon further inquiry, I discovered that all of the participants connected their present actions to an awakening of their Christian faith as a result of the intercultural educational experiences.

These phenomena began to raise questions for me concerning the nature of missiological education – pedagogy, process, and vocational formation leading to action. My initial observations revealed that each of the "life-changing" educational programs had three ingredients in common: They involved (1) an experiential pedagogy that endeavored to engage the "whole" person (emotion, mind, behavior, etc.); (2) an intercultural immersion experience; and (3) a multicultural learning community (See Figure 1). Consequently, I began to ask, "Does the field of experiential education, particularly within a multicultural context, have implications for developing a missional pedagogy - actively centered on God's mission in the world - which will lead to an awakening of the missionary vocation in Christian disciples and active participation in God's global mission?" I think this is a critical question. The following are my insights following several years of research, particularly at the University of Northwestern (UNW), Center for Global Education (CGE), and School of Urban Ministry (SUM), toward discovering a learning *process* – a missional pedagogy – to more effectively prepare and engage Christian disciples toward fulfilling God's mission in the world today.

Figure 1: Missional Education

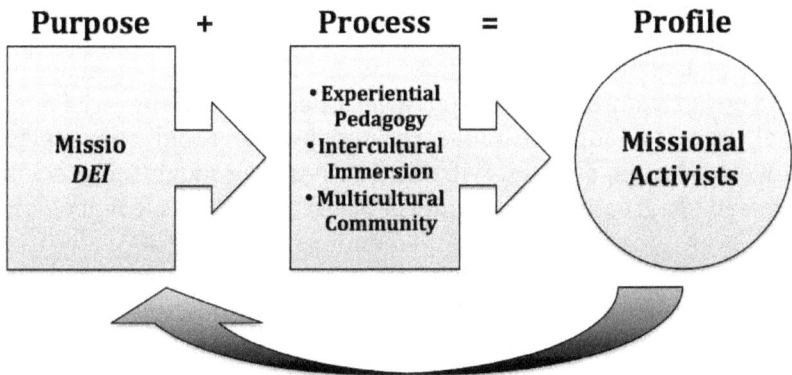

Purpose + Process = Profile

Missio DEI

• Experiential Pedagogy
• Intercultural Immersion
• Multicultural Community

Missional Activists

A Missional Approach to Education for Social Action

For many, the teacher's primary task is to *form* people *for* the service of God's kingdom via a *cognitive* and *problem-oriented* approach, not *engage* people *in* it through actual missional action (Costas 1986; Woodberry, et al. 1996; Alvarez 2004). The primary "missiological contribution to theological education has been *formal teaching*, rather then *in-service instruction*" (Banks 1999:132). Missiologists have predominantly focused on the content (course topics, academic disciplines, etc.), innovations, such as distance learning, and the missiology of theological education in *preparation for* future mission rather than *reflective experience of* mission. This current approach is missiological rather than missional.

A missional approach to education is undertaken with a view of where the Holy Spirit is graciously at work from a local and global perspective. It emphasizes the essential missionary nature and vocation of the community of Jesus, the church, as God's called and sent people actively participating in God's mission. It is education that wholly, or partly, involves an intercultural immersion experience – overseas or locally – and involves a measure of doing and reflecting upon what is being studied. It is a pedagogical approach that moves from a mode of action, instead of the predominant (formal) pedagogies that move from a passive/receptive mode. In other words, a missional pedagogy finds its roots in a life-oriented faith focused on concrete actions and relationships.

Although the communities in which we live are increasingly interdependent and culturally diverse, and the need for a Christian understanding of a missional vocation for social action, what I call "missional activism" - is vital for mission. Yet scant attention has been paid by Christian educators to creating a pedagogy for the missiological challenges and opportunities created by the rapid changes from powerful forces, such as globalization. And although these changes have led to a greater sense of interdependence and interconnectedness than ever known before and tremendous advances on many fronts, the prevalence of conflict, injustice, and environmental degradation around the globe has also heightened people's awareness of their differences. In light of these concerns, a missional level of social action and intercultural competence is of critical importance. Consequently, the need is not simply for educational innovations, better methods, or the inclusion of missiological disciplines, such as the behavioral sciences and world religions. The need is for a transformation in our concept of education: learning as reflective experience versus gathering content, a body of information; a movement toward a wholistic and practical approach, what Samuel Escobar calls a "post-Enlightenment missiology" (1996:111). The rational intellectual approach we have used for so long brings only new information and, at best, a new way of thinking. What is needed is a missional pedagogy that brings about a new way of thinking that leads us out to a new way of living. Thus, the goal of a missional approach to education needs to be the preparation of *every* Christian disciple with both the knowledge *and* experiences to *do* and to *be* missional activists and multicultural witnesses to God's actions in the world.

Essential Ingredients that Emerge for Developing a Missional Pedagogy

Over the past several years, I have conducted research in order to investigate the degree to which the principles of intercultural communication and experiential education theories and practices can inform and enhance missiological education for assisting Christian disciples in the discovery of their personal and communal missionary vocation, and equipping and empowering them as missional and social activists participating in God's mission to all creation in an increasingly interconnected, interdependent, and multicultural world.[2] Drawing from these educational principles and the discoveries from my research, this paper introduces nine "essential ingredients" for a "Missional Education" (ME) toward the development of missional activists, i.e., Christians with global awareness, intercultural competence, and an apostolic imagination rooted in missiological values. These are strongly inter-connected principles that should guide the design and implementation of educational programs that are missional, multicultural, and experiential.

1. Integrated Learning for Personal Growth

One of the core values of ME is the development of a wholistic educational framework. Thus the first key ingredient in developing ME is rooted in the suggestion by experiential pedagogies that the most effective kind of learning is "connected," that is, coupled to an awareness of how one learns and integrated into one's own life. Perhaps one of the most important things to be learned in ME is how to become open to a process of transformation, both within oneself and in the world. Hence, an experiential approach to missional education should be attentive to the learner's personal growth and ability to integrate the educational experience into his or her own life (Dewey 1997; Freire 1970; Gochenour and Janeway 1993; Groome 1999; Hertig 2002; Wallace 1993).

Gordon Murray, who has directed intercultural programs in Nepal for many years, refers to this principle as the "inner side of experiential learning." He states:

> "I start with the assumption that everything the [learners] observe about Nepal is equally an observation about themselves and that every observation about themselves—their behaviors, feelings, values, likewise reflects Nepal. In this way I try to help them see their experiences not as exotic adventures but as integral parts of their lives, a chapter in their own broader evolution. I am often reinforced by the observation that when they feel good about that inner quest, they are more receptive to and involved in the outer world" (1993:27).

In this regard, missiologist Darrell Whiteman goes so far as to state that the greatest value of intercultural education "is not what we learn about exotic cultures that are different from our own, but rather, in what we discover about ourselves" (1996:137). Christian religious educator Thomas Groome refers to this process as the discovery of "self-identity," namely, the awareness of one's self-image, one's worldview, and one's value system (Groome 1999:109). This discovery of self-identity is central to the well-being of both individuals and communities. Research on learning outcomes in intercultural education suggest that learners often develop a deeper self-understanding and succeed in meeting personal challenges through living and learning in a different culture. Moreover, Christian disciples and communities of faith need a sense of identity before they can be engaged in God's mission. Therefore, the discovery of self-identity through intercultural experiences should be embraced as one of the articulated goals of ME and incorporated into the design of a ME program (See Figure 2).

Figure 2: ME Praxis: Experience

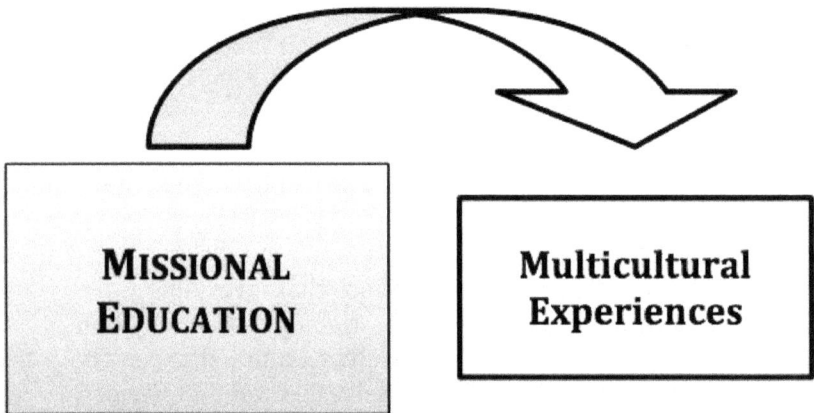

| MISSIONAL EDUCATION | Multicultural Experiences |

My research on the use of experiential pedagogies within the Center for Global Education (CGE), the University of Northwestern (UNW), and School of Urban Ministry (SUM) reveals that students' ability to connect the learning experiences to their personal lives was one of the most important learning characteristics reported. In response to a post-program question regarding the most significant experiences of a cross-cultural program, one UNW student commented:

"I think the most important thing from this semester is the reflection and the connections to me - personally. [...] I'm sure the many of us have thought about these issues before, but I think the important part of the class was connecting [it] to me. I have a better understanding of myself and my own culture and a new perspective from which to view others and cultural values. [...] My experience changed the way I look at life and my role as a Christian in the global body of Christ. It directed me down a future path I would not have explored otherwise."

When connecting the learning to the individual, experiential educators utilize direct experience as a means to develop the whole person and present opportunities for self-discovery (Citron and Kline 2001:18-26; Gochenour and Janeway 1993:1-9). The experiential approach to intercultural education has been chosen by CGE precisely because "...the whole person is being engaged in the process and the very identity of the person may be fundamentally challenged. In other words, all aspects of the person – spiritual, mental, emotional, physical – can be affected" (McBride 2005). At the same time, the knowledge-based cognitive study in experiential education plays a supportive role by providing learners with the framework for interpreting what they see and experience. However, many educators consider the affective realm of experiential learning to be one of its most important values (Wallace 1993:11-16).

Research indicates that students learn best when they make emotional connections with the course material being studied through concrete experiences or form relationships with people who make the readings, lectures, and other formal learning methods come alive. Mark Warren calls these emotional and relational connections are "seminal experiences," i.e., profound emotional and moral "shocks" accompanied by powerful emotions (2010:27). Seminal learning experiences often represent abrupt events or a series of events and factors, a crystallization of awareness in time, which spark a process of growing transformation and commitment (Daloz 1996:71). William Gamson calls this "hot cognition," not just an intellectual judgment (1992:32). This is an awareness where the affected person, faced with direct experiential evidence, begins to make a real shift in challenging dominant ideologies and choosing alternative views (Warren 2010:

34). In other words, it is the integration of an emotional and cognitive experience rooted in a moral impulse, which is a critical step toward missional commitment and eventual action.

In his term paper reflecting on service-learning with World Relief Minnesota, undergraduate student Jesse Schustedt contrasts two of his own educational experiences: The first involved taking a course in Christian mission in which he learned about the plight of refugees without being changed in any significant way, while the second involved nurturing a relationship with a young refugee man his age in which his intellectual knowledge was transformed into emotional awareness, which became a seminal experience for him.

> "What new insights [were] gained? Through [my friend], I was able to see a little more of what it is like to be a refugee. [...] It was not their greatest desire to move to this country. Many refugees would like to live in their home country, but they are forced to move because of terrible circumstances. [...] Many refugees carry a lot of pain and 'baggage' from their past. [Before] this was hard for me to imagine, even as I passed someone on the sidewalk, that they have been through a war. It was hard for me to imagine that I am walking among people who have experienced death, torture and rape because of the war going on in their home country. However... I have seen a little more of what it is like to be a refugee. I think I can empathize and should be sensitive to peoples' experiences. [...] Many times God calls us to do things that do not make us feel comfortable. This project [was] a great learning experience." (2006:1-2).

In addition to the affective nature of experiential learning, which helps connect it to the personal life of the learner, ME ought to involve some kind of personal challenge that supersedes the outcomes demonstrated in typical papers, reports, or exams. In fact, research suggests that the more intense and less routine the intercultural educational experience, the greater the impact toward personal integration and growth (Chickering 1997; Peterson 2002; Steinberg 2002; Hull 2004). In his essay "Educational Values of Experiential Education," John Wallace suggests that the outcomes of such challenges include

"...an increased self-confidence, a deeper awareness of one's own strengths and weaknesses, and a heightened knowledge of effective approaches to other human beings - all of which come from having functioned successfully in a strange environment and under a different set of ground rules from those found in one's own culture" (1993:13).

This also has significant implications for spiritual growth. In his extensive research with short-term mission teams, John Hull discovered that spiritual growth can occur when people are separated form their normal life through cross-cultural immersion and community interaction. "Individuals are in an environment where they find themselves stripped of status, property, rank, role, or anything that may distinguish them and define their identity" (2004:133). This is a process of transformation called a "Faith-Centered Liminal Interaction" that serves to deepen faith and encourage growth (2004:22). This transformation is not simply cognitive understanding; it is all encompassing. It is personal and intimate. It is relational and wholistic. "It is a dynamic that reaches into every aspect of our lives" (2004:70, 72). For as learners move beyond their "comfort zones," they are open to a process of discovery and absorbing new knowledge and experiences that will be the basis for their new identity and role in life as responsible missional activists. Such experiences, as well as empowering students to share in the responsibility of their own educational process assists them in integrating learning into their own lives and, thereby, more effectively opens them up to the process of transformation leading to personal growth.

2. Problem-Posing Content

A second essential ingredient for ME is directly connected to the first ingredient: The content of the curriculum should relate to real-life problems. Learning takes root and becomes transformative when it is situated in the real-life issues and felt needs of both the learner and the community. Dewey asserts that "problems are the stimulus to thinking" (1997:79). In addition, the student evaluations in my research confirmed that more formal educational materials can be made real through direct experience so that students can develop and test theories based upon their personal experiences.

Experiential educators propose replacing "banking education," in which students are seen as empty accounts into which knowledge is deposited by an "expert," with "problem-posing education," defined by Freire as "the posing of the problems of [human beings] in their relations with the world" (1970:66, 168). This type of problem-posing education, which is also referred to as "problematizing," does not just mean "problem-solving," but rather "critical analysis of a problematic reality." For example, when a class in a particular community problematizes a livability issue such as the lack of affordable housing that is affecting local residents, the discussion focuses not only on an immediate solution to the problem but also on analyzing the root causes of the problem and exploring a myriad of potential solutions. For example, in the context of ME, the UNW Intercultural Communication class in my research, addressed a conflict a student team encountered with their World Relief host family. However, reflection upon the conflict included an analysis of the broader intercultural context and underlying differences in values, gender roles, communication styles, and behaviors in which the conflict emerged.

In a program which frames course content in terms of problems, the experiential educator needs to first investigate the concerns and "felt needs" of the learners—what Freire terms the "people's 'thematic universe' - the complex of their 'generative themes' " - that is, the principal themes which preoccupy them (1970:86). These generative themes then become the starting point for critical analysis and dialogue which relates to the overall subject being studied and a greater potential for transformation leading to missional activism.

For example, students in the UNW program expressed a growing awareness of racism within the greater community and their own personal prejudices as they assisted refugee and immigrant families through their service-learning with World Relief Minnesota. For nearly all of the students, this was their first exposure to explicit personal and structural racism. Although they understood the concept of individual prejudice, they were not aware of, and thus not equipped to deal with, the complexities of prejudice enforced through power – both on the individual level and (especially) at the institutional level. Many of the students were both troubled and frustrated by the racism they witnessed, particularly among Christians. Seminal experiences of racism through the real life experiences of refugee and immigrant families created "moral shocks" and moments of "hot cognition." Likewise, racism became a perceived problem or "generative theme" that was embraced as a starting point for discussion. Selected reading materials, a documentary, personal stories from international and immigrant students (their own peers), and a guest speaker who could address issues of racism and biblical reconciliation from his own cultural perspective as an African American inner-city minister, were included in the course.

The challenge for the educator is to make the links between the students' concerns and the course material. This may require additional work on the part of the missional experiential educator, whose task, according to Dewey, is "to select the kind of present experiences that live fruitfully and creatively in subsequent experiences" (1997:27-28). However, by beginning with the problems and felt needs about which students are already troubled, the instructor can emotionally engage the students in the topic and use the students' experiences in the community as a point of departure for analysis and reflection.

Because problem-posing education starts with problems identified by the learners, it involves the whole student on both the affective and cognitive level, engaging the student in the learning process by connecting the subject matter to the life of the student. Hence, Ira Shor asserts, "Through problem-posing, students learn to question answers rather than merely to answer questions. In this pedagogy, students experience education as something they *do*, not as something done to them" (1993:26).

Although problem-posing education begins with the generative themes of the students, it must not end there when leading toward missional activism. Rather, if two of the goals of missional education are to stimulate multicultural thinking and awareness for social action, then it must broaden students' horizons by helping them to identify the problems and concerns of others within the "glocal" community. Dewey states that a system of education based upon the connections of education with experience must, to be faithful to its principle, take into account the conditions of the local community, physical, historical, economic, occupational, etc., in order to utilize them as educational resources (1938:40). This is particularly true in the multicultural and cross-cultural context, as local conditions pose new problems for students to analyze while providing different cultural perspectives on the nature of and potential solutions to such problems.

3. Reflection and Critical Analysis

As noted earlier, ME *requires* reflection and critical analysis of experiences in order to make the experiences educational (Freire 1970; Banks 1999; Groome 1999; Silcox 1993; Mintz and Hesser 1996; Welch 1999; Hull 2004). In other words, we do not learn from experience alone, rather we learn from actively reflecting on experience. (See Figure 3.) The necessity of this ingredient was reinforced upon analysis of the post-program evaluations and students' reflections on the learning experiences within the programs of this study. Furthermore, it becomes self-evident in problem-based education because it is impossible to solve a problem without first analyzing and understanding the nature of the problem. The initial analysis leads to the development of a thesis that must be tested, in other words, to some kind of *action,* which then requires further analysis and reflection as it is reflection that enables learners to make sense out of the new information and experiences (Silcox 1993). Dewey writes: "To reflect is to look back over what has been done so as to extract the net meanings which are the capital stock for intelligent dealing with further experiences. It is the heart of intellectual organization and a disciplined mind" (1997:87).

While it is clear that critical analysis and reflection are essential ingredients and, in fact, defining characteristics of experiential education, it is not enough to simply ask students who participate in ME programs to engage in critical analysis and reflection on their own. Rather, this is something they must engage in with others. By engaging in this process together, learners are often "pushed" by other group members to ask deeper-level questions, confront their own personal prejudices, and consider other insights and interpretations from one another's experiences. They also lose a sense of isolation as they reflect together and encourage one another. Consequently, students develop a growing sense of community.

Figure 3: ME Praxis: Reflection and Analysis

MISSIONAL EDUCATION

Multicultural Experiences

Reflection & Analysis

While this process of reflection and critical analysis is an essential ingredient for ME, in several respects it needs strengthening. For instance, a more objective criterion than simply reflection on personal experiences is required. Alongside reflection on one's personal situation, other critical questions must be considered. In order to accomplish the goal of empowering and educating learners to become missional activists, and thereby effective cross-cultural witnesses, it is also appropriate for critical analysis and reflection within ME programs to include social analysis that problematizes questions about the economic, political, cultural, and religious or ideological aspects of the society (Holland and Henroit 1983). For example, what is the dominant economic model? What are the relations of production and distribution? How is the government organized? What is the role of the military? How are education, health-care, and other social services organized and provided? What is the nature of the media? What are the principal centers of power and community institutions, including local churches? What constraints does the present cultural, sociological, or ecological context place on one's actions? What are the dominant cultural groups? What are the concrete rule and roles that should be followed? When problems are being studied, whose voices are heard? And whose voices are excluded? The latter questions are particularly important, as critical pedagogies highlight the fact that particular ways of knowing and sources of knowledge that come from socially marginalized positions, such as women, indigenous peoples, cultural and racial minorities, and poor people, are often invalidated (Evans et al. 1986; Freire 1970; Giroux 1996; Gore 1993; Holland and Henroit 1983; Lee 1995; McLaren and Leonard 1993; Segunado 1976; Shor 1987, 1992, 1993). Educators should then encourage and guide learners to consider the nature and consequences of their own behaviors, and their subsequent feelings and emotions in relation to the social analysis and emergent questions.

After these important questions have been asked and a solid understanding of the situation has begun to take shape, biblical and missiological reflection must be integrated into the process (Hull 2004). In ME, critical analysis in conjunction with biblical and theological reflection within the context of ongoing mission in the world is vitally important toward the nurture of missional activists. The work of the Uruguayan Jesuit Juan Luis Segundo provides some valuable insights into the importance of this critical praxis of reflection in ME. Serving at the grassroots level with "Base Christian Communities" in working for social change, Segundo based his work on the praxis of Freire in developing a method of doing "liberating theology." He calls this method of biblical and theological reflection the hermeneutic circle - "the continuing change in our interpretations of the Bible which is dictated by the continuing changes in our present-day reality, both individual and societal" (1976:8).

This method of theology begins with ideological suspicion: "Anything and everything involving ideas, including theology, is intimately bound up with the existing social situation in at least an unconscious way" (1976:8). In other words, culture and lived experience always influences the way people think and must be taken into account when doing theology, reflecting, or analyzing. *All theology is contextual.* Therefore in Segundo's process, liberation theology consciously tries to combine the disciplines that open up the past (such as biblical and historical studies) with the disciplines that help to explain the present (such as sociology and anthropology). The circular nature of his methodology stems from the fact that "each new reality obliges us to interpret the Word of God afresh, to change reality accordingly, and then to go back and reinterpret the Word of

God again, and so on" (1976:8). This is doing theology by praxis, i.e., reflecting on the Word of God amidst the ongoing process of action and reflection.

Segundo's methodology and hermeneutic is significant to the task of developing a missional pedagogy because it takes seriously the understanding of current reality in order to transform it and bring about a more just order manifest in the reign/kingdom of God. Both Freire and Segundo make clear that there is no such thing as purely "objective" understanding of reality; one's worldview - the filters through which experience is interpreted - inevitably color the way reality is seen. Teachers and students alike are prisoners of their own worldviews and cultural backgrounds. And because the worldview perspectives of the politically, economically, and culturally powerful are too often considered "objective reality," liberation theology tries to understand "reality" from the perspective of the oppressed by allowing them to be interpreters of their own experiences. A liberating theology allows the experience of the marginalized, silenced, or "invisible" communities (such as the poor, indigenous peoples, women, people of color, and children) to be taken seriously in doing theological reflection and biblical studies. It does not deny the experience of those who have traditionally held power, but says that theirs is not the *only* experience, and therefore consciously tries to do theology "from the underside," from the perspective of the traditionally excluded and marginalized.

In the UNW and CGE programs, where biblical and missiological reflection incorporating Segundo's hermeneutic circle was integral to the process of critical analysis, students stated (during class discussions and in final evaluations) that such guided reflection sessions were among the most significant learning experiences.[3] The sessions were especially "helpful in showing different interpretations to questions and situations encountered." They provided "a better understanding of my own cultural lens in interpreting Scripture" and "a new perspective from which to see others and how cultural values influence [the] interpretation of Scripture." Several students stated that interactions with people of other cultures, and "hands-on experiences and biblical reflection challenged [their] thinking" and "serve[d] its purpose in broadening [their] understanding of the Bible and learning from Christians of other cultures." Others found their "worldview being challenged" as they began to learn the cultural "lenses" of Jesus and the biblical writers, and, consequently, "reflect on the meaning of Scripture from a different cultural perspective." The value and necessity of an integrated approach to critical analysis and reflection for ME was succinctly stated by one student who noted that the cultural immersion coupled with biblical reflection served "as a catalyst... for a new understanding of global mission and the role of the entire Christian community in the struggle for global justice." [4]

Kathy McBride, CGE Central America Director, shares Freire's perceptions regarding the empowering nature of critical analysis and reflection. She states:

> "As students come to recognize that certain features of their 'reality' – their worldview - is not 'natural' but is socially and historically constructed, they can act on these to change them. In this process they learn more about these structures and about themselves within them" (2005).

Clark Smith, a participant in a CGE travel seminar to Nicaragua concerning issues of fair trade initiatives and community development with Lutheran World Relief and Equal Exchange, illustrates the enlightening and empowering nature of this praxis of facilitated group reflection and analysis. While staying with a family in a small village in the mountains of Nicaragua he shared:

> "Then it hit me that while the gracious people of La Reyna carry 100-pound bag after 100-pound bag of coffee cherries on their backs down these steep mountain paths, we carry the responsibility of valuing their labor and their coffee at a handful of nickels and dimes. For coffee sold on the 'open' market, small farmers, especially the many who are not part of a cooperative, often receive less than the cost of planting, let alone what they need to support their families. We are the ones, through consuming and accepting the market price as 'fair,' who dangerously undervalue the hard, hard work of the farmers in La Reyna" (CGE 2006:1).

If this process of reflection and critical analysis appears to be too one-sidedly cognitive, one should remember that the process of considering the ethical and missional questions mentioned above has its counterpart at the level of personal integration and growth. Experiences, followed by intense reflection and analysis, allow participants to process their emotions in a way that lectures cannot. There is a depth and emotion that often surfaces as a result of experiential learning, which then becomes a powerful catalyst for reflection and application to real life. In the insightful words of one teacher, "...classroom knowledge without an experiential foundation does little to create a spiritually based (non-dogmatic liberating spirit) activism intended to alter unjust structures that are the root cause of human conflict and suffering."[5] And as the following ingredients of ME will reveal, this revelation is significant because it is vitally important that students "act out," not just "learn from," the educational process. In this way, educators are not only *preparing* Christian disciples for missional social action but also *inserting* them into it. This is why ME is truly learning by "praxis."

4. Cooperative Learning

The wise teacher of Ecclesiastes said that two are better than one... and three better still (Ecclesiastes 4:8-12). Thus cooperative learning is the heart of problem-posing learning. As evident in the previous section on reflection and critical analysis, experiential educators believe that collaboration and dialogue within community are essential ingredients to authentic reflection and critical analysis in problem-posing education, for individuals are rarely if ever capable of perceiving all angles of a problem or grasping all aspects of an issue alone (Dewey 1997; Freire 1970; Holland and Henroit 1983; Hooks 1994). Reflection and critical analysis involve a collective process that helps learners move beyond their own perspectives to new understandings created through dialogue with others, and hence, cannot be carried out exclusively by individuals alone.

Dialogue, defined by Freire as "the encounter between [people], mediated by the world, in order to name the world," is not a new phenomenon (1970:64). Rather, it has played an important role in education since the time of Socrates, who began with his students' starting point and then asked questions, engaging them in the art of discourse. In the same way, Jesus, the "rabbi," often began with his disciples' (students') starting point for asking questions: "Who do people say that I am? [...] Who do you say that I am?" (Matthew 16:13-20.) Similarly, Jesus often began with the listener's own questions to engage them in a dialogical learning process:

> "A certain ruler asked Jesus a question. 'Good teacher, what must I do to have eternal life?' Jesus answered... 'You know what the commandments say.' [...] 'I have obeyed all of the commandments since I was a boy,' the ruler replied. When Jesus heard this, he said to him, 'You are still missing one thing. Sell everything you have and give the money to those who are poor so you will have treasure in heaven. Then come follow me.' When the ruler heard this he became very sad for he was very rich. Jesus looked at him and said, 'How hard it is for rich people to enter God's kingdom...'" (Luke 18:18-24).

As illustrated in Jesus' teaching conversations, dialogue, at times, has the potential to lead to conflict. However, healthy conflict can occur when individuals cooperate, allowing conflict to create "cognitive disequilibrium, which in turn stimulates perspective-taking ability and cognitive development" (Johnson 1998:29).

Within the context of ME, which seeks to promote an understanding of God's mission in a multicultural world, cooperative learning, dialogue, and constructive conflict cannot be restricted only to the community of learners themselves but must involve diverse members of the community, as people from the local community are the true experts regarding their own lives and culture. Hence, collaborative learning in the multicultural context should mean the inclusion of diverse members of the host community—including people with opposing or conflicting viewpoints—in both the definition of problems that serve as the core of the learning and in the critical analysis of such problems.

Religious educator, Thomas Groome, points out the dialectical dynamics embedded in the "controversy theory." Such a learning process involves a conversation, a dialectical relationship between the learner and the social context. In such a relationship between a learner and the social environment, the learner "accepts and affirms some of the social influence and refuses and rejects some," and from this comes a movement beyond the limitations of the learner's worldview (Groome

1999:113). When learners encounter opposing worldviews through discussion and critical analysis, they have the potential to discover new truth, even as their identity is challenged, thus moving beyond the limitations of their cultural and religious socialization. A "shared praxis" opens Christian disciples up to new truth, which in turn opens them up to new patterns of living and cooperation. In this way, truth is between us, in relationship, to be found in dialogue between "knowns" and "knowers" who are understood as independent but accountable selves (Palmer 1983:55-56). This dialectic relationship "promotes both the autonomy of the individual and the restructuring of society" (Groome 1999:115). It saves personal truth from subjectivism, for a relationship of genuine collaboration and dialogue is possible only as an integrity in the other is acknowledged that cannot be reduced simply to individual perceptions and needs (Palmer 1983:55-56). And when this relationship is properly promoted and facilitated, it is one of creative tension rather than opposition between two protagonists.

This process of collaboration, dialogue, and cooperative learning are especially important for building Christian community across cultures and mutual partnerships in missional social action. Because the Christian faith each person possesses and practices has been profoundly shaped by his or her sociocultural situation, ME needs the context of the entire global Christian community in order to more fully understand the dimensions of God's character, become the community of Christ, and understand and participate effectively together in God's mission. This is why listening within community and to other communities is so vital to ME praxis. Listening as part of learning provides a diversity of perspectives, interests, insights, concerns, questions, and ideas. Listening as part of community also offers each person a mirror on himself or herself and enhances the possibility of reflection (Saengwichai 1998:242). And learning as part of a community furnishes spiritual, emotional and intellectual support as we struggle through the process of self-discovery, transformation, and mutual participation in God's mission.

Our individual Christian life is always related to the lives of others in community because the Christian life is relational. Christianity is life together. And in a very real sense, we "become Christian together" (Groome 1999:126). "Only in community does a person appear in the first place, and only in community can the person continue to become (Palmer 1983:57). For in a learning community we come to know ourselves as we are known by God (Kang 2004b:166).

"Christianity means community through Jesus Christ and in Jesus Christ" (Bonheoffer 1954:21). As best expressed in an African phrase, "I am" is always also "because we are" (Lee 1995:8; Lingenfelter and Lingenfelter 2003:80). Thus our ability to struggle through controversy, resolve conflict, learn cooperatively, and work together, thus preserving our unity in Christ, is directly related to people's coming into a relationship with God (Elmer 1993:27). The Church's owned lived experience indicates that becoming Christian requires an educational process within a community capable of listening and learning together, working constructively through conflict, and "lift[ing] human life above its present standards and attainments" (Elliot 1953:219). For this reason, ME is profoundly aware of the need to continually listen and learn in openness to God's Spirit and the world for the sake of the Gospel of Jesus Christ. Otherwise, "both education and religion leave individuals as good or as bad as the present level of society" (1953:225). In this way our relationships, our living, learning, loving, and working together affect God's mission. Only a community practicing dialogue and cooperation in the pursuit of learning and understanding is ready to actively engage in God's mission. In this context, then, ongoing dialogue and cooperation is nothing less than the gracious gift of God through the work of the Spirit within community.

5. Community

Since we have established that collaboration and dialogue are essential to ME, it follows naturally that community is also a key ingredient in developing ME since dialogue and collaboration are by definition collective and imply the existence of others. Education for participation in God's mission in the world includes the formation of communities of learners, immersion in the local community and in partnership with the local Christian community, as well as reflection upon one's connections to the global community. (See Figure 4) In ME, the formative power of the social-cultural context, particularly within Christian community, is foundational for Christian formation (Groome 1999:107; Kang 2004a:100).

Figure 4: ME Praxis: Community

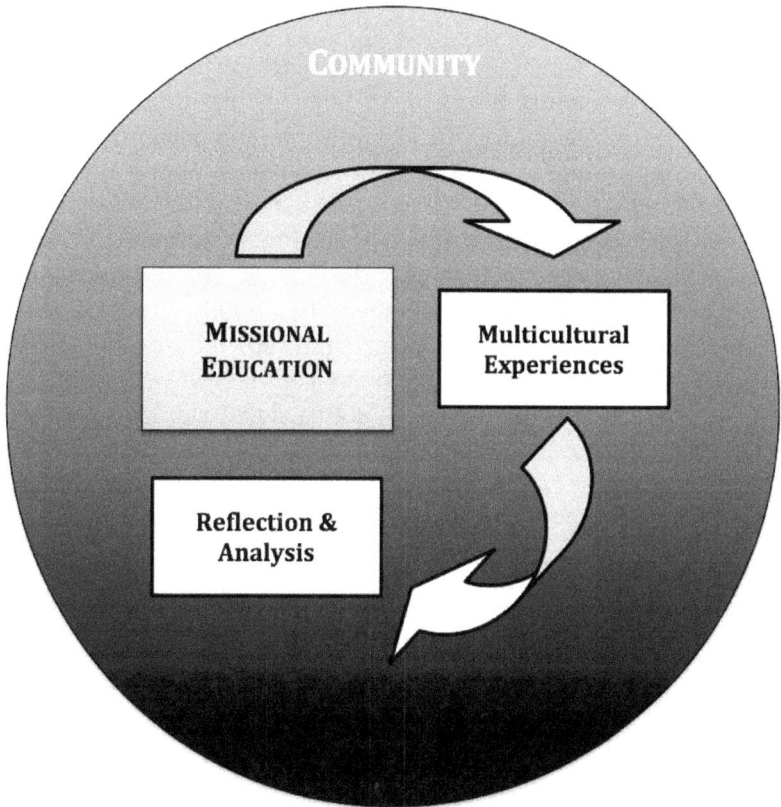

First of all, as students reflect upon experiences prior to a ME program, it is important for them to recognize that much of what they have learned in life up to now has been profoundly shaped by the particular contexts and communities in which they have lived. Their self-identity has been shaped in large part by their social and cultural context, including their Christian social context, which has been significant in the process of coming to Christian self-identity (Groome 1999:108). Moreover, the Christian faith community itself has been systematically shaped by the same factors that shaped each person, as well as by the people themselves. For this reason, students are encouraged to reflect upon the communities from which they come and the ways in which these communities have been shaped, and simultaneously shaped their own values and perceptions of the world. Sparrow writes: "Self-awareness is crucial to intercultural learning. Our predispositions, expectations, and reactions affect our perceptions. Our perceptions affect our judgments, how we solve problems and make decisions, and ultimately how we are perceived and trusted by others" (1993:155).

Secondly, since teachers and teaching are central to ME, special attention must be given to what a missional praxis means for teachers and teaching. In ME, missional experiential educators must strive to build a community of learners among the students who are learning together. This is consistent with both theological and feminist pedagogies that see learning communities as vital to transformative education (Conde-Frazier 2004; Groome 1999; Hooks 1994; Lingenfelter and Lingenfelter 2003). In these learning communities, education is learner-centered, not teacher-centered, and the teachers work to create an environment in which instructors and students work together as "co-learners" or "co-investigators in dialogue" (Freire 1970:68; McBride 2005). In other words, this relationship between teacher and students is based upon "cognitive equality" – the idea that all people involved in the educational process are participants of social conversations; "differences in expertise and experience have to do with time, location, dedication, and method." Teachers and students are partners in the educational process (HECUA 2006).

Missiological educators, Judith and Sherwood Lingenfelter, call this approach "incarnational teaching." This is a model of engagement in which the teacher is willing to give up aspects of the teacher role, particularly that which fits his or her cultural background, and to take on a new "incarnational" role (2003:83). In this role, Jesus sets for us an example of engagement. And it is precisely here that divine wisdom is most fully revealed. Jesus' focus was on establishing relationships, as an insider. This incarnational model of teaching was evident in his teaching and learning relationships with his disciples, the people he encountered in his ministry, and the Pharisees - a group of "teachers" from which he was excluded. Jesus accepted invitations to eat with them and to engage them in dialogue on issues of life and faith. He respected people, allowing them to share their stories and perspectives while at the same time challenging them in areas where there behavior was in contradiction to their expressed values and God's "kingdom values." Jesus often did this simply by asking questions or encouraging people to reflect on the very questions they had asked him (2003:84).

Jesus also modeled this incarnational approach by telling his disciples, "I no longer call you servants, but friends" (John 15:14). Perhaps, no teacher can be a true teacher unless to some degree the teacher becomes a friend (Nouwen 1971:11). In this way, Jesus became the real teacher because the fear of the teacher as judge was overcome, allowing the real learning to begin (1971:12).

Finally, the culmination of Jesus' teaching in and through the cross reminds us that transformation that leads to missional action comes primarily through self-sacrifice on the world's behalf. Ideas, no matter how profound or persuasive, are not enough: it is only in lives that embody and on occasion risk all for the truth that this happens (Banks 1999:172). Jesus did not have an impact on people's lives simply because he was a good teacher, but only as he poured out his life for them.

The Apostle Paul illustrates from his own life, and thereby reminds us all, of the immense importance of being incarnational for the purpose of missional ministry.

> "To the Jews I became like a Jew, to win Jews. To those under the law I became like on who is under the law, even though I myself am not under the law. That was to win those under the law. To those not having the law I became like one not having the law... so as to win those not having the law. To the weak I became weak in order to win the weak. I have become all things to all people so that in all possible ways I might save some. I do this all for the sake of the gospel, that I may share in its blessings" (1 Corinthians 9:20-23).

Reflecting on the immeasurably powerful example of Jesus and Paul, the Lingenfelters go so far as to state that the most important element in missional education for the "incarnational teacher" is "to recognize that as teachers we need to be learners" (2003:84). ME for missional action is a mutual learning process for both teacher and students. "They are fellow pilgrims in a journey of discovery and intentional practice of God's kingdom in this world" (Kang 2004b:155). One way teachers model an incarnational approach is in trust-building behavior, i.e., by sharing their own experiences with students in such a way that their experiences are not seen as superior to but rather equal in value to those of the students. In this way, the incarnational teacher creates a learning environment where students feel safe to be stretched beyond their previous experiences. Henri Nouwen calls this process the "redemptive model" of teaching (1971:10). A central characteristic of a redemptive teaching relationship is that it is "bilateral." By this Nouwen means that the student not only learns from the teacher but, conversely, the teacher has to learn form the student (1971:12). Education is never a redemptive process until such time as the teacher is willing to become a student and allow the student to become a teacher.

This "incarnational" or "bilateral" process of teaching is essentially an open-ended process. Discussion, then, is no longer a means of getting a well-prepared opinion across students, but "an exchange of experiences and ideas whose outcome is not determined" (1971:12). In this way, discussion creates the possibility for discovery of new perspectives and insights. "When teacher and students are willing to be influenced by each other, learning can become a creative process that can hardly be boring or tiring. It is only through a relationship of this sort that learning can take place" (1971:13).

In a post-program evaluation for the UNW course on intercultural communication, a student noted that one of "the most significant learning experiences" was the professor sharing his own "cross-cultural mistakes" and "valuing the [intercultural] experiences of others," which "helped the class feel free to open up and share." Groome affirms the importance of the teacher's attitude in creating a healthy learning environment for ME.

> "The educator's underlying attitude is perhaps the most crucial variable in shaping the activity of Christian religious education. The teacher's attitude shapes, in large part, the teacher's way of being with students, and ultimately education is a way of being with people. [...] If Christian religious education is to lead people out in response to the Kingdom of God in Jesus Christ toward lived Christian faith and human freedom, then our most appropriate underlying attitude is to see ourselves as brother or sister pilgrims in time *with* our students" (Groome 1999:137).

In the same vein, in order for missional experiential educators to create the conditions for critical analysis and reflection, they must also devote time and energy to developing a healthy learning community. One of the goals of the incarnational teacher is to create a learning community and context that is familiar to students yet stretches them beyond their previous experiences. This is especially critical in a multicultural learning community. Central to this task is a respect for diversity and a sense of trust that one will not be verbally or physically assaulted for expressing a different point of view. Without this respect and trust, cooperative learning, controversy-based learning, and critical analysis and dialogue are impossible, because as Freire says, "trust is basic to dialogue" (1970:169). A UNW student affirmed the importance of the teacher nurturing a learning community with respect and trust when reflecting on a difficult and emotional discussion regarding racism.

> "[Our professor's] attitude encouraged listening... showing sincere interest in different points of view and being patient... even as emotions were expressed. [He] encouraged us to listen to the international and minority students in our class – to hear their stories of racism, what they experience every day. There could have been a lot of conflict in class, but [his] attitude created an atmosphere in the class where we could be vulnerable... and it was okay. I've been in a lot of programs and workshops on racism lately. Emotions always flare up and things get really negative... people just shut down... but this [class] was the best. We could be vulnerable because we learned to really listen to each other...and empathize" (Kraus 2006).

It is crucial that students are assisted in building a learning community from the start of the multicultural experience by getting students to reflect upon the communities from which they come and choosing orientation exercises that begin building respect and trust between students. As time progresses, it is important for teachers to help students address issues of power, privilege, and diversity within the group, particularly if some voices seem to dominate over others. This is crucial if a learning community is to exist in which there is a sense of equality. In the end, when careful attention is paid to nurturing a multicultural learning community, the educational experience will be enhanced from *within* the learning community.

Likewise, it is important that learning communities be immersed within the local host community. (See Figure 4) This serves to further the goal of learning from and within the local community because if students were to remain isolated in "island" communities of their peers, then their learning would be incomplete and they would fail to meet this goal of ME. As stated earlier, students must engage in dialogue with local people in the host community regarding the content of their education in such a way that their education is truly community-based. In doing so students have direct encounters with different family structures, work environments, social attitudes and values, gender relationships, organizational structures, moral norms, and many other patters of behavior, communication, and organization. The community then becomes the classroom, and people within neighborhoods, churches, and local organizations become the primary teachers, as students engage in problem-based learning within the local community. And this process of dialogue for partnership is vital for both the effectiveness of the learning experience and the health of the host community.

Finally, the importance of community as an ingredient in ME becomes even more evident when considering why the pedagogy takes root in some learners and not in others. In fact, community is the indispensable ingredient *following* a missional education experience. Former UNW and CGE students all testified to the necessity of community in taking the new discoveries and energy from their learning experiences and putting them into action.[6] This is true essentially for two reasons: accountability and partnership.

First, because, as Bonheoffer said, "we belong to one another only through and in Jesus Christ" (1954:21), community creates a structure of accountability whereby students are held to the expressed discovery of their vocation as missional activists, and the resultant promises made to God and one another. In other words, "we need each other because of Jesus Christ" (1954:21). As ME moves learners from reflection to action, community is needed to hold learners accountable to the critical movement in the learning process: active participation in God's mission. Action is what brings the learning process "full circle" and moves students to the next cycle of learning. As one participant of several CGE short-term programs stated:

"I discovered I needed others to make the learning experience 'stick.' [After other CGE travel seminars] God had opened my eyes, but the promises I made never turned into real action.... But this time [the class] promised to hold each other accountable. [...] We need each other to remind us of our promise to God and one another."[7]

Second, students not only need community for accountability, but also for partnership in fulfilling the vocational task to which they have been called. One's missional vocation can never be fulfilled alone. Again, Bonheoffer reminds us that, "a Christian comes to others only through Jesus Christ" (1954:21). And one only comes to Jesus Christ through community (Hunter 2003:54-55). God's mission in the world is never done alone, but always in partnership with other members of the Christian community. And those partnerships are what sustain missional activists.

A former student who serves as an inner-city minister in Minneapolis shared that the only reason he has been able to continue in urban mission is because he has partners in ministry to help sustain him. "I have a circle of brothers and sisters that share a common passion... creating energy to sustain me in urban ministry. They are my partners in ministry... strength when I want to 'throw in the towel.' [...] I would have quit if I had to do this alone." Another student said she discovered, "Community enlarges our capacity to be a Christian. We need each other to be the person and community that God intends us to be.... Even as we struggle together... our hope is contagious."

The power of Christian community, community that learns together, discovers missional vocation together, and serves together as missional social activists was very real for one former CGE student:

"Luckily... I was surrounded by a network of people who were able to aid me in my growing process. The group was such an essential part of the experience, as each person had unique personal histories and goals from which to view and sort out all we learned during our travels.... Of course, there are problems that arise from being in a group, but overall these men and women provided me with inspiration, intellectual ideas, and hope in making our world a more just and sustainable place. [...] However, an equally powerful experience was coming together [after the program] with people from my previous travel/study groups. [...] Coming together from places so far away to take part in things that manifested what we learned on our trips was an experience too great for words.... All of the [former CGE participants] reminded me of the fight for justice that we are struggling with, but also that we have each other to share these struggles with on our journeys" (Falbo 2005:6).

ME that includes full participation of the people in the learning community is the beginning of the process of community organization for social action. (Hertig 2002:63).[8] When students change by becoming less passive and more the primary actors in their own learning and personal growth, learning becomes community empowerment for participation in God's mission. Moreover, learning from and within the context of community involves and deepens our understanding of God's missional activity in the world, enhances awareness of one's own culture and other cultures, raises issues that require serious reflection, nurtures partnerships for missional ministry, and sustains us in obediently fulfilling the promises we have made to God and one another to be missional activists in the kingdom of God.

6. Transformation in Missional Action

One of the goals of ME is teaching students how to learn so that future reflection and analysis on experiences will lead to continual growth and missional action. Consequently, ME places greater emphasis on action than most other educational models, even those using the language of praxis. Therefore, it is critical to understand that praxis in ME refers not simply to actions but to the reflection that lies behind and within actions. Too often praxis is simply a synonym for action rather than for reflection on life oriented towards and involved in missional action. For ME, the "praxis of God" is the primary text for learning. To understand what God is presently doing in the world we must bring the biblical narrative into dialogue with our situation, for Scripture tells the story of God's "missional activism" in the world. Moreover, if a core missiological value of ME is to actively engage the Christian community in God's mission in the world, thus equipping

Christian disciples to become responsible missional activists and multicultural thinkers, we must more fully explore the praxis of "reflection-in-action" in experiential pedagogies.

As previously noted, intercultural and experiential education share common goals with ME of increasing students' global awareness and intercultural competence, thereby empowering them to become missional activists. Most international experiential educators share the sentiment of CGE Central America Director Kathy McBride, who states, "In CGE programs we seek to influence students in the direction of becoming committed agents of change" (2005). This is a natural expectation because critical analysis and reflection, which plays a central role in experiential education, leads to "conscientization"—

> "...an awakening of the conscience, a shift in mentality involving an accurate, realistic assessment of one's locus in nature and society, a capacity to analyze the causes and consequences of that, the ability to compare it with other possibilities, and finally a disposition to act in order to change the received situation" (Boston 1973:28).

Experiential education is grounded in action and leads to new action after critical analysis and reflection. In fact, education has not really taken place unless it shapes commitment that leads to action (McBride 2005). Freire writes that "reflection—true reflection – leads to action..." because "thought has meaning only when generated by action upon the world" (1970:52, 64). When education is centered on problems that require solving, it is natural for learners to want to take action. Freire's problem-posing strategy empowers students to either accept their life situation, or challenge and change it. This is evident in the following journal entry written by a CGE student of a seminal experience in Central America:

> "In some ways I feel like my experience here in El Salvador was an awakening, but in other ways I feel like I have just been given an enormous amount of responsibility. [...] If anything, this trip has given me something to dream for. I'm not sure if it's for peace, utopia, the kingdom of God on earth, or the fall of globalization. But what I do know is that it's a good dream. A dream that calls for me to act with

everything I've been given in this life and shine it bright for everyone else to see. I can't exactly say what the change will be, but 'a new world is possible' if we all decide to do something about it. Poco a poco" (Jungerberg 2002).

And herein lies the power of experiential education: having learners reflect on experiences and through that reflection make decisions about changing their thinking *and* behavior. Changes in thinking and behavior requires learners to "create new forms, new methods, new structures; and it requires them to find new content, new ideas, new truths, and new meaning to bear on the new challenges" (McLaren 2004:192). From a missional perspective, this means coming to awareness that Jesus' call to the Kingdom of God is a call to transformation from one way of life to another. And such an awareness leading to transformation only takes place as a learning community and its individuals open themselves to the Holy Spirit; for in community learners are joining together to help one another experience transformation.

Missiologist Robert Tuttle, Jr. states that to grow in Christian faith and life is to be open to the "converting work of the Holy Spirit that takes place through faith and trust in Jesus Christ." This means that our Christian life will be a series of conversions because "we remember then forget, remember then forget, but we mostly forget..." what we have learned about God's work in our lives and the world. This is why we need community. Community helps us to remember God's narrative in our lives and the lives of the community past and present. This is how we open ourselves up to the experience of being "converted again and again."

As the learning community prayerfully reflects upon and analyzes problem-based content together with the members of the greater community in the multicultural setting, engaging in dialogue, and collaborating with them, learners can become empowered and, in turn, develop the skills they need in order to take action that makes a difference in God's world. (See Figure 5.) This is because some of the skills needed for mission are precisely an awareness of cultural differences, the ability to listen to others, to engage in respectful and vulnerable dialogue, to analyze problems critically from multiple angles and perspectives, and to foster reciprocal partnerships within the community (Whiteman 1996:138).

Figure 5: ME Praxis: Action

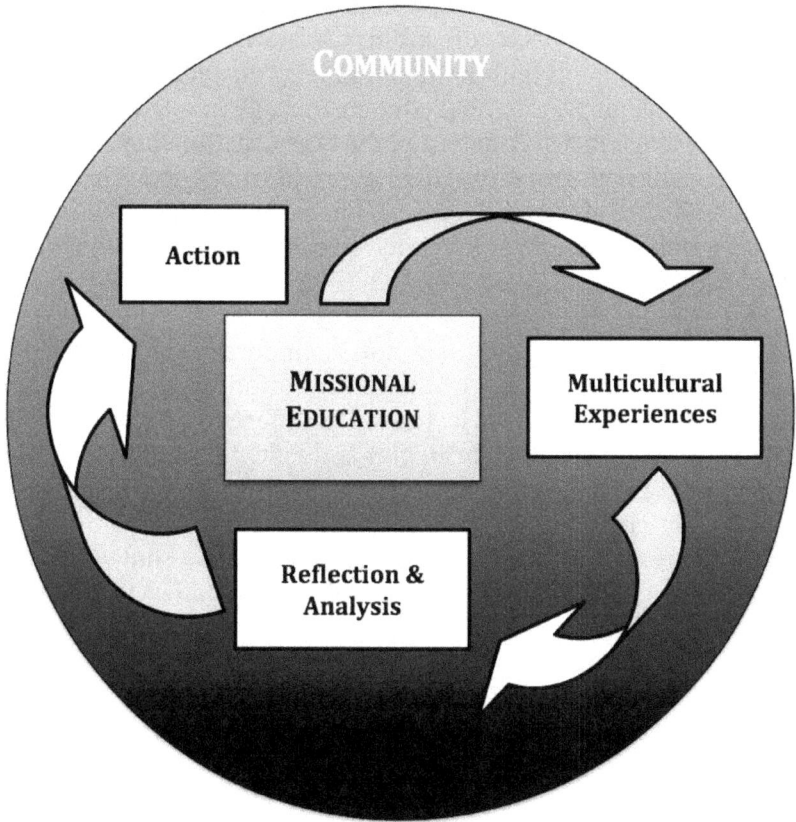

ME can also expose students to diverse cultural understandings of mission and responsible missional activism, as well as to diverse cultural approaches to social transformation being taken by leaders within their spheres of influence within the host community. For example, nursing students can conduct research regarding important work and critical care issues related to HIV/AIDS addressed by healthcare workers in the host community, while business and economic students can meet with local business leaders to search for new approaches to ethical leadership in the context of globalization. Ministerial students can learn about different cultural approaches to evangelism and church planting among diverse people groups, while social workers research indigenous approaches to community development. And so on.

Students who possess adequate language and/or intercultural communication skills may collaborate with members of the host culture in local projects of social transformation as considered appropriate by people within the community. In addition, teacher and community members can help students engage in ongoing reflection upon their missional vocations and the type of action they may take in the future. In such situations, field notes, journals, and other writing assignments are also excellent tools for reflection upon the meaning of God's global mission, and action for on-going personal and social transformation.

True transformation is a not a temporary change, a feeling, or "mountain top experience" that wears off in time. It is a change within a change that causes us to see life differently, to change values and perspective, to change priorities and motives, to change thinking and actions (Hull 2004:72). It is an on-going process. What we will be is not yet clear. God is constantly transforming us from what we were and are into what we are becoming, not just as individuals, but as participants in the transforming realities of families, communities, cultures, and the world. In this way, new transformation does not nullify former experiences, but rather reshapes them for growth. This reinforces the need for constant reflection and analysis on our experiences, particularly within the context of Christian community, so that we remind each other of God's gracious work in our lives and our commitments to participate together in God's mission in the world. In this way the learning community "acts out," not just "learns from" in the ME process, for ultimately the importance of learning is living out our missional vocation as a transformed and transforming community. This is a praxis that can truly be called missional activism!

7. Reciprocity

Because a distinctive of God's mission in the world is one of relational reconciliation – about creating a new community, ME programs ought to be based on reciprocity with the communities in which we live, learn, and serve. Therefore, the design and implementation of ME programs, as stated earlier, involve collaboration and dialogue with community constituents regarding the ways in which educational programs can be mutually beneficial. Roland Wells, founding director of the School of Urban Ministry, calls attention to the needs of the local community as well as students, and highlights the problem of "using the community to provide an education for the participants" (2005:6). Similarly, in her analysis of the impact of U.S. students on Indian society, Jennifer Ladd asks,

> "How are they [the Indians] affected by our process of growth and learning? Are we in danger of using other cultures... for our own... needs, this time taking personal growth and cross-cultural awareness instead of cotton and tea? Are we exploiters or imperialists unconscious of the consequences of our learning?" (1990:123).

John Wallace phrases the ethical questions regarding reciprocity in intercultural education as follows:

> "How much obligation do we assume toward the host culture in which these experiences are offered? When we enroll students in a laboratory course on campus, we are placing them in an educational setting that is completely under our control. When we encourage them to engage in experiential education, we are implicitly urging them to use a particular culture as their laboratory. Is this fair to the hosts? How would you and I react if a young Saudi Arabian, for example, were to visit our communities and our homes and ask us to assist him with a study in which he proposed to find out American attitudes toward cleanliness in public toilets? It is in many cases just such individual studies that we are inflicting upon our overseas hosts. Should there be a line drawn beyond which activity would be considered objectionable, intrusive? Who draws such a line, and how can it be justified to the students whose education will be inhibited thereby?" (1993:16).

Given the goal of educating for missional *action* and multicultural *competence*, missional experiential educators must grapple with these ethical questions regarding their relationship to the communities in which students are placed, ensuring that their educational programs and social actions are not undermining their goals of increasing understanding and promoting justice by instead engaging in acts of cultural invasion. Freire writes:

"In this phenomenon, the invaders penetrate the cultural context of another group, in disrespect of the latter's potentialities; they impose their own view of the world upon those they invade and inhibit the creativity of the invaded by curbing their expression. All domination involves invasion - at times physical and overt, at times camouflaged, with the invader assuming the role of a helping friend" (1970:150).

Most missional educators and advocates for justice would argue that their purpose is not cultural invasion but rather the nurturing of harmonious and non-exploitative relationships between people of different cultures. Therefore, they have a responsibility to work collaboratively with the local community to ensure that their relationships are built on reciprocity and not on any kind of exploitation.

In her research regarding both educators' and community partners' attitudes toward the benefits that the latter may receive from intercultural experiential education, Amy Greeley identifies two primary types of reciprocity. The first is "specific reciprocity," which involves "giving back directly to those who have served them," whereas the second is "generalized reciprocity," in which the experiential education program and the community "believes that someone or some group, be they from the host community or not, will benefit from what participants contribute to society someday" (2004). The latter may be the most common in experiential education and is clearly the most difficult to assess. Thus a few strategic questions for those involved in the design and implementation of ME programs are: "What type of reciprocity, if any, is involved? Does the larger community benefit from the students' learning; if so, how?" (2004).

Service-learning, short-term missions, and internships are often seen as forms of direct reciprocity because it is hoped that participants make valuable contributions to the communities where they work, giving back to the host communities while also learning from them. These kinds of programs are becoming increasingly popular with an ever-increasing number of students participating in internships and cross-cultural service programs. Nonetheless, special concerns about "cultural imperialism" are raised by this demand for international service-learning, short-term missions, and internship programs, because students who are not fluent in the required foreign language and who do not have the proper attitude toward and a full appreciation of the host culture may unwittingly act as cultural imperialists and do more damage than good. In the now famous words of Monsignor Ivan Illich, "To hell with good intentions. (This is a theological statement.) You will not serve anybody by your good intentions... the road to hell is paved with good intentions... (1968). Therefore, ME programs must evaluate students' suitability for service-learning, short-term missions, and internship projects, provide sufficient training and preparation, as well as assess the desire for and potential effectiveness of such projects in the host community so the working and learning relationship will be truly reciprocal.

8. Celebration

While in El Salvador on a CGE travel seminar, our class stayed in the agricultural community of Nueva Esperanza – "New Hope."[9] There we lived with, worked alongside, and learned from the members of this Christian cooperative community. Sister Naomi was our cultural guide and teacher, and the spiritual leader of the entire community.

One day over 1,000 people from the surrounding rural communities came together to rebuild a dike that had been destroyed by a powerful hurricane. Although international aid had been given to the Salvadoran government specifically for rebuilding the dike, the government failed to act and during several rainy seasons the communities along the river flooded. So on this day, Sister Naomi had brought the people together to do "God's work" by rebuilding the dike. In sweltering (115 degree) heat and humidity, we worked together filling bags with sand and rebuilding the dike. The work was grueling, yet no one seemed to complain. After 12 hours of backbreaking work, we gathered at the church in the center of Nueva Esperanza to celebrate the Mass. Hot, sweaty, smelly, dirty and exhausted, we sang praises to God at the top of our lungs. As we prepared for the Holy Eucharist, the "Great Thanksgiving," Sister Naomi stood before us, and with arms reaching to heaven exclaimed, "Today we celebrate the work of the Holy Spirit among us! Today we celebrate the new thing God has taught us! We have learned that together, united in Christ's Spirit and Body, we can do what no government or mighty army can do to us or for us. In this Mass, we celebrate the work of Jesus, His presence, in our community!"

On the final evening of our stay in Nueva Esperanza, during a community Bible study, Sister Naomi led us in joyful celebration and thanks to God for the new things each of us was learning, even giving thanks for our struggles and questions. She also gave thanks for the new experiences we would have in service to God as we lived in solidarity with the people of Nueva Esperanza.

Following our final "fiesta" together, a student asked Sister Naomi why she placed so much emphasis on celebration.

> "It is the Latin way," she replied. "It is also the biblical way... to celebrate new learning and God's revelation in our lives. Jesus said, 'I have taught you these things so that my joy may be in you, and that your joy may be full.' Joyful celebration is both the outcome and the fuel that provides the energy for service and learning, which in turn keeps the cycle going." (See Figure 6.)

Sister Naomi told us that education has not occurred until a new action step has been taken, until we take what God has revealed to us and obediently put it into a new action – a new way of living. Real learning is evident in a life transformed by God's Spirit, and that is worth celebrating. Celebration also serves as a ceremony, a rite of passage,[10] which acknowledges our transformation as new creations in Christ. In the same way, Kathy McBride, of CGE, says that celebration serves to imprint what we have learned, evidenced in our new actions, on our hearts and minds. Whether these are "big" or "tiny" actions steps, they must be celebrated because they are important (McBride 2005).

Figure 6: ME Praxis: Celebration[11]

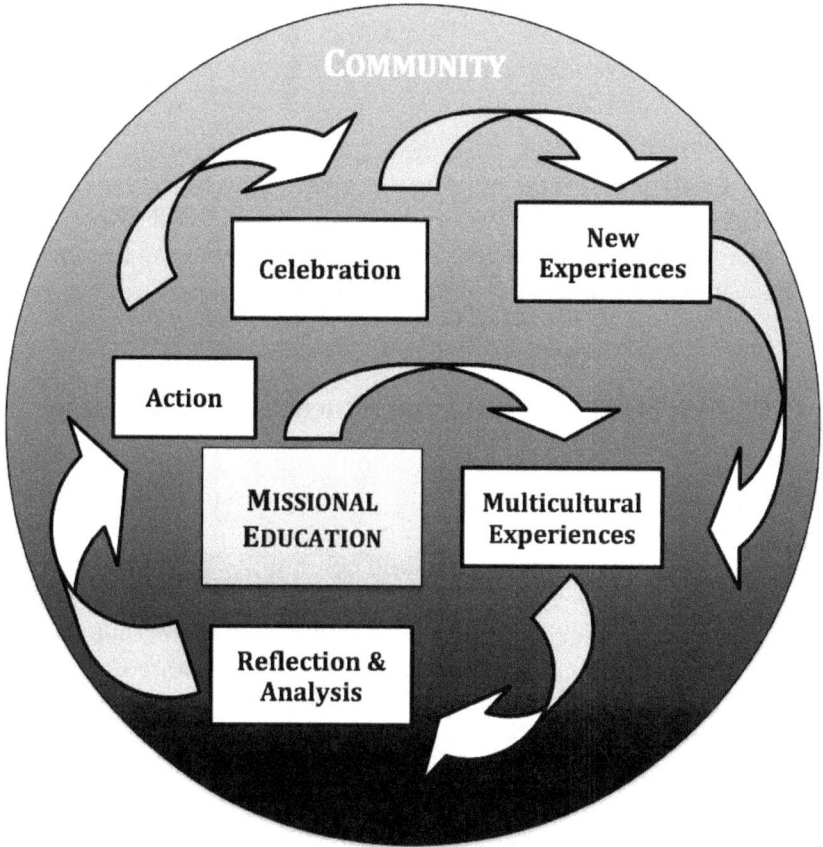

Richard Foster, in *Celebration of Discipline: The Path to Spiritual Growth,* states that since most action steps are taken within the context of or relation to community, they should be celebrated with the community. We should celebrate the work of God's Spirit among us as the body of Christ no matter which part does the work; it is still together. New actions are signs of openness to the Holy Spirit and God's transforming work within us. And this work of God has missional implications; it is a living testimony! New learning, evident in life transformation, no matter how small, encourages others in the community – those who have been partners in our learning and those to whom we can be a witness (Foster 1998:191).

"Celebration brings joy to life, and joy makes us strong" (Foster 1998:191). Our work in God's mission can be exhausting and make us weary. But Scripture tells us, "The joy of the Lord is our strength"

(Nehemiah 8:10). Celebration restores our whole being! It restores our strength to press on in God's strength (1998:191). Learning leads to action, and action leads to celebration, but we will not know the genuine joy of celebration until there is a transforming work in our lives and communities.

Perhaps this is the missing ingredient in so much of education. Ultimately, joyful celebration is what will keep the ME praxis going. For celebration produces energy that gives us strength to live in joyful service in God's world!

9. Program Evaluation and Educational Assessment

Missional experiential education requires ongoing community-based program evaluation and educational assessment to ensure that the stated objectives are accomplished and to continuously improve the overall quality of the educational and community program. Perhaps, this is the most overlooked ingredient in educational programs, as well as missional social activism. But it is critical for determining if learning and transformative outcomes match stated goals and objectives. Consequently, two types of assessment are necessary: first, the assessment of student learning, and second, the assessment of the missional program or action itself. In fact, the evaluation process is also a critical part of practicing an experiential pedagogy (Gingerich and Lutterman-Aguilar 2002:75; McBride 2005).

In the evaluation and assessment process, both missional activists/learners and community members should return to the stated learning and social justice objectives to evaluate the extent to which those outcomes have been achieved. To aid in this evaluation process, missional activists and experiential educators are also encouraged to conduct a self-assessment, which reflects upon program and community objectives and can assist people in their own critical analysis regarding the quality of their work and the degree to which they have accomplished their objectives.

In addition to assessing missional activism and learning, it is essential to engage in continual assessment of program effectiveness related to goals that are explicitly incorporated into the program design (Wallace 1993; Wyatt 1993; Jaenson 1993; Citron and Kline 2001). Overall program evaluations should remind missional learners of the stated program goals so that programs can be evaluated on that basis. Just as student learning should be evaluated on the basis of clearly articulated learning objectives, ME programs themselves should be evaluated on what they say about themselves, their implementation of experiential learning pedagogies, and the extent to which they are truly rigorously academic, experiential, intercultural, wholistic, transformative, and missional.

If Christian disciples are going to be prepared for the missiological realities in this era of globalization, they will need to learn how to *think and act* both globally and multiculturally (Smith 1999:132). Consequently, missiologists have a special role in casting a new vision for missiological education, i.e., creating a missional pedagogy that will help all disciples think multiculturally and act globally. This topic is of vital importance. "More of the same kinds of missiological education will put us further behind. The church needs new paradigms of missiological education freshly drawn from both the text and the contexts of ministry" (Elliston 1996:232). The time has come to redefine the *purpose* of missiological education and discover a new learning *process* – a missional pedagogy – to more effectively prepare and engage missional activists toward fulfilling God's mission in the world today.

The "essential ingredients" articulated in this paper may serve as a helpful starting point for the implementation and assessment of ME programs toward effectively fulfilling the stated objective to provide a distinctive missional pedagogy, which awakens the apostolic imagination of Christian disciples and prepares them to competently participate as missional activists in God's mission to all creation.

Notes

1   Traditional forms of formal education in a classroom setting, particularly in higher education, i.e., Bible college or seminary, were the dominant models that were presented for learning. In addition, the "professional" educator, e.g., pastor or theological professor, were considered the primary models for teaching and mentoring. It should be noted, though, that there were challenges to these "traditional," and primarily "Western," models of education. Participants who serve "illiterate" populations, people in remote areas without access to "higher" education, members of oral cultures, etc., expressed concern at the narrow definition and model of theological education being proposed by the majority of the group.

2   The National Society for Experiential Education (NSEE) has proposed the following basic "Principles of Good Practice" for experiential education: Intention, authenticity, planning, clarity, monitoring and assessment, reflection, evaluation, and acknowledgment (NSEE 1998). I have drawn from the NSEE principles, in addition to three of the fundamental principles of service-learning—collaboration, reciprocity and diversity (Mintz and Hesser 1996), key principles in the experiential educational philosophy of CGE, and critical elements discovered in my research to propose what I think are the "essential ingredients" of "Missional Education" (ME).

3   Not all CGE programs include biblical reflection as several programs are in partnership with secular colleges and universities.

4   These comments were drawn from the following post-program evaluations: UNW 2006, CGE 2004 and 2005. They represent a sampling of (anonymous) student comments related to the value of critical analysis in conjunction with biblical reflection.

5   Larry Hufford, PhD., is the Graduate Director of International Relations at St. Mary's University, San Antonio, TX. He participated in his first CGE travel seminar in 1986 to El Salvador and Nicaragua. He states that the experience was "spiritually transformative." He has since taken students on over twenty CGE travel seminars.

6   For those who have shared in a transformational journey of learning, a pilgrim experience, a pilgrimage experience, a strong bond of communitas is formed (Zahniser 1997). In ME, the shared realities

of a "faith liminal experience" combined with the absence of normal cultural identities, statuses, and roles, draw participants together in an uncharacteristic, yet deeply meaningful way (Hull 2004:21).

7   This comment was made on the last day of class, during the final reflection session, following a short-term immersion experience in El Salvador embedded in the middle of a Spring 2005 course entitled, "Latin American Liberation Theologies."

8   By community organizing, Hertig is referring to a community that comes together to take action on issues that are vital to their community and the world.

9   The people of Nueva Esperanza (New Hope) chose this name in hopeful thanks to God for God's presence with them during the Civil War in El Salvador, in their experience as refugees in Nicaragua, and the hopeful future for them and the generations to come. Upon returning to El Salvador in 1991, the people cooperatively purchased a farm and established their new home. 104 families live in a community that is founded on the Christian principles practiced by the early church in the book of Acts - unity, solidarity, democracy, sharing, and sufficiency.

10   Rites of passage are rituals and ceremonies that facilitate and recognize the transition of an individual or community from one stage of life to another. The process results in the old status being replaced by a new status (Hull 2004:19).

11   As the figure illustrates, the MEE praxis is a continuous cycle; it is not a circle. It is a helical – an ascending and widening spiral in which each new stage covers the same 360 degrees of territory as its predecessors but in a larger way. Each stage in the praxis enfolds, embraces, integrates, and revalues the gains of previous stages in the learning process, and, in doing so doing, rises to a higher level. So if this figure continued through multiple stages of MEE praxis, the helical would be one of emergence, that is, the outer ring embracing everything within it; and it needs everything within it. Without the previous learning praxis, it wouldn't exist.

Works Cited

Alvarez, Miguel
    2004   "The New Context of Missiological Education." *Journal of Asian Mission* 6(2):167-181.

Banks, Robert
    1999   *Reenvisioning Theological Education: Exploring a Missional Alternative to Current Models.* Grand Rapids, MI: William B. Eerdmans Publishing Company.

Bonheoffer, Dietrich
    1954   *Life Together.* San Francisco: Harper & Row, Publishers.

Boston, Bruce O.
    1973   "The Politics of Knowing: The Pedagogy of Paulo Freire." *New Catholic World.* January-February:26-29.

Center for Global Education
    2006   "Planting Seeds for Fair Trade." *Global News and Notes.* Fall 2006.
    2005   *Cross-Cultural Connections: Teaching and Learning Cross-Culturally.* David E. Fenrick, ed. Minneapolis: Center for Global Education.

Chickering, Arthur W.
    1997   *Experience and Learning: An Introduction to Experiential Learning.* West Lafayette, IN: Change Magazine Press.

Chickering Arthur W., and Linda Reisser
    1993   *Education and Identity.* Second Edition. San Francisco: Jossey-Bass Publishers.

Citron, James L. and Rachel Kline
    2001   "From Experience to Experiential Education: Taking Study Abroad Outside The Comfort Zone." *International Educator* 10(4):18-26.

Conde-Frazier, S., Steve Kang, and Gary A. Parrett, eds.
2004   *A Many Colored Kingdom: Multicultural Dynamics for Spiritual Formation.* Grand Rapids, MI: Baker Academic.

Costas, Orlando
1986   "Theological Education and Mission." *New Alternatives in Theological Education.* C. Rene Padilla, ed. Pp. 4-9. Oxford: Regnum.

Dewey, John
1971   "My Pedagogic Creed." In *Dewey on Education.* Martin S. Dworkin, comp. Classics in Education No. 3. New York: Teachers College Press.
1997 [1938]   *Experience and Education.* Touchstone Edition. New York: Simon and Schuster.

Daloz, Laurent A. Parks, et al.
1996   *Common Fire: Leading Lives of Commitment in a Complex World.* Boston: Beacon.

Elliston, Edgar J.
1996   "Moving Forward From Where We Are in Missiological Education." In *Missiological Education for the 21st Century.* J. Dudley Woodberry, et al. Pp. 232-256. Maryknoll, NY: Orbis Books.

Elmer, Duane H.
1993   *Cross-Cultural Conflict: Building Relationships for Effective Ministry.* Downers Grove, IL: InterVarsity Press.

Escobar, Samuel
1995   "The Training of Missiologists for a Latin American Context." In *Missiological Education for the 21st Century.* J. Dudley Woodberry, et al. Pp. 101-111. Maryknoll, NY: Orbis Books.
1992   "The Elements of Style in Crafting New International Mission Leaders." *Evangelical Mission Quarterly* 28(1):6-15.

Falbo, Julie
   2005   "Reflections on Coming Home." *Global Connections.*
          Winter 2004-2005:6-7.

Foster, Richard J.
   1998 [1978]   *Celebration of Discipline: The Path to Spiritual
          Growth.* San Francisco: HarperSanFrancisco.

Freire, Paulo
   1970   *Pedagogy of the Oppressed.* New York: Continuum
          Publishing Company.

Gamson, William A.
   1992   *Talking Politics.* New York: Cambridge University
          Press.

Gingerich, Orval and Ann Lutterman-Aguilar
   2002   "Experiential Pedagogy for Study Abroad." *Frontiers:
          The Interdisciplinary Journal of Study Abroad.* Winter:
          41-82.

Giroux, Henry A.
   1996   *Living Dangerously.* New York: Peter Lang.

Gochenour, Theodore, and Anne Janeway
   1993   "Seven Concepts in Cross-Cultural Interaction:
          A Training Design." In *Beyond Experience: An
          Experiential Approach to Cross-Cultural Education.* 2nd
          edition. Theodore Gochenour, ed. Pp.1-9. Yarmouth,
          ME: Intercultural Press.

Gore, J. M.
   1993   *The Struggle for Pedagogies.* New York: Routledge.

Greeley, Amy and David E. Fenrick
   2004   "Reciprocity Leads to Culture Learning." 15 November.
          NAFSA: Association of International Educators, Sioux
          Falls, SD.

Groome, Thomas H.
1999 [1980] *Christian Religious Education: Sharing Our Story and Vision.* 2nd Edition. San Francisco: Jossey-Bass.

Hertig, Paul
2002 "Transforming Theological Education Through Experiential Learning in Urban Contexts." *Mission Studies* 109(2-38):56-76.

Holland, Joe and Peter Henroit
1983 *Social Analysis: Linking Faith and Justice.* Maryknoll, NY: Orbis Books.

Holm, Bill
1992 *Coming Home Crazy.* Minneapolis, MN: Milkweed Editions.

Hooks, Bell
1994a *Outlaw Culture: Resisting Representations.* New York: Routledge.
1994b *Teaching to Transgress: Education as the Practice of Freedom.* New York: Routledge.

Hull, John Kenneth
2004 *Faith Development Through Cross-Cultural Interaction and Liminality: Bonding to the Meaning of Scripture in a Short-Term Mission Experience.* Doctor of Missiology dissertation, Asbury Theological Seminary, Wilmore, KY.

Hunter, George G., III
2003 *Radical Outreach: The Recovery of Apostolic Ministry & Evangelism.* Nashville: Abingdon Press.

Illich, Ivan
1968 "To Hell with Good Intentions." 20 April. Conference on InterAmerican Projects, Cuernavaca, Mexico.

Jaenson, Carol
1993   "Sample Formats from Experiment Programs: Evaluation." In *Beyond Experience: An Experiential Approach to Cross-Cultural Education.* 2nd edition. Theodore Gochenour, ed. Pp.175-195. Yarmouth, ME: Intercultural Press.

Johnson, David W., Roger T. Johnson, and Karl A. Smith
1998   "Cooperative Learning Returns to College: What Evidence Is There That It Works?" *Change.* July/August: 27-35.

Jungerberg, Nat
2002   A journal entry. Cuernavaca, Mexico. July 2.

Kang, S. Steve
2004a   "Salient Theoretical Frameworks for Forming Kingdom Citizens." In *A Many Colored Kingdom: Multicultural Dynamics for Spiritual Formation.* Elizabeth Conde-Frazier, et al. Pp. 79-104. Grand Rapids, MI: Baker Academic.
2004b   "The Formation Process in a Learning Community." In *A Many Colored Kingdom: Multicultural Dynamics for Spiritual Formation.* Elizabeth Conde-Frazier, et al. Pp. 151-166. Grand Rapids, MI: Baker Academic.

Kraus, Betty
2006   Personal interview by author. November 1.

Ladd, Jennifer
1990   *Subject India: A Semester Abroad.* Yarmouth, ME: Intercultural Press.

Lee, Jung Young
1995   *Marginality: The Key to Multicultural Theology.* Minneapolis: Augsburg Fortress Publishers.

Lingenfelter, Judith E., and Sherwood G. Lingenfelter
2003   *Teaching Cross-Culturally: An Incarnation Model for Learning and Teaching.* Grand Rapids, MI: Baker Academic.

McBride, Kathy
2005   "Presentation on Experiential Pedagogy." July 25. Managua, Nicaragua.

McLaren, Brian D.
2004   *Generous Orthodoxy.* Grand Rapids, MI: Zondervan

McLaren, Peter, and Peter Leonard, eds.
1993   *Paulo Freire: A Critical Encounter.* New York: Routledge.

Mintz, Suzanne, and Garry Hesser
1996   "Principles of Good Practice in Service-Learning." In *Service-Learning in Higher Education.* Barbara Jacoby, et al. Pp. 26-54. San Francisco: Jossey-Bass.

Murray, Gordon
1993   "The Inner Side of Experiential Learning." In *Beyond Experience: An Experiential Approach to Cross-Cultural Education.* 2nd edition. Theodore Gochenour, ed. Pp.27-43. Yarmouth, ME: Intercultural Press.

Nouwen, Henri J.M.
1971   *Creative Ministry.* Garden City, NY: Doubleday and Company, Inc.

Palmer, Parker J.
1982   *To Know as We are Known: Education as a Spiritual Journey.* New York: HarperCollins.

Peterson, Chip F.
2002   "Preparing Engaged Citizens: Three Models of Experiential Education for Social Justice." *Frontiers: The Interdisciplinary Journal of Study Abroad.* Winter: 165-206.

Saengwichai, Dadee-en
1998   *Khit-Pen Theological Education Model: A Methodology for Contextualizing Theological Education in Thailand.* Doctor of Missiology dissertation, Asbury Theological Seminary, Wilmore, KY.

Schustedt, Jesse
2006   "World Relief Project." Term paper, Northwestern College, St. Paul, MN.

Segundo, Juan Luis
1974   *The Liberation of Theology.* Maryknoll, NY: Orbis Books.

Shor, Ira
1987   *Critical Teaching and Everyday Life.* Chicago: University of Chicago Press.
1993   "Education is Politics: Paulo Freire's Critical Pedagogy." In *Paulo Freire: A Critical Encounter.* Peter McLaren and Peter Leonard, eds. New York: Routledge.

Silcox, H.
1993   *A How to Guide to Reflection: Adding Cognitive Learning to Community Service Programs.* Philadelphia: Brighton Press.

Smith, Efrem
2006   "A Biblical Theology of Reconciliation." 29 November. Northwestern College, St. Paul, MN.

Smith, Robert C.
1999   "Training College Students for Urban Ministry." In *A Heart for the City: Effective Ministries to the Urban Community.* John Fuder, ed. Pp. 125-140. Chicago: Moody Bible Institute.

Sparrow, Lise
1993   "Examining Cultural Identity." In *Beyond Experience: An Experiential Approach to Cross-Cultural Education.* 2nd edition. Theodore Gochenour, ed. Pp.155-166. Yarmouth, ME: Intercultural Press.

Steinberg, Michael
2002 "Involve Me and I Will Understand: Academic Quality in Experiential Programs Abroad." *Frontiers: The Interdisciplinary Journal of Study Abroad.* Winter:208-222.

Wallace, John A.
1993 "Educational Values of Experiential Education." In *Beyond Experience: An Experiential Approach to Cross-Cultural Education.* 2nd edition. Theodore Gochenour, ed. Pp. 11-16. Yarmouth, ME: Intercultural Press.

Warren, Mark R.
2010 *Fire in the Heart: How White Activists Embrace Social Justice.* New York: Oxford University Press.

Wells, Roland J., Jr.
2005 *Handbook for the School of Urban Ministry.* Minneapolis: St. Paul's Evangelical Lutheran Church.

Whiteman, Darrell L.
1996 "The Role of the Behavioral Sciences in Missiological Education." In *Missiological Education for the 21st Century.* J. Dudley Woodberry, et al. Pp. 133-143. Maryknoll, NY: Orbis Books.

Woodberry, J. Dudley, Charles Van Engen, and Edgar J. Elliston, eds.
1996 *Missiological Education for the 21st Century: The Book, the Circle, and the Sandals.* Maryknoll, NY: Orbis Books.

Wyatt, Bruce
1993 "Assessing Experiential Learning Overseas." In *Beyond Experience: An Experiential Approach to Cross-Cultural Education.* 2nd edition. Theodore Gochenour, ed. Pp. 171-174. Yarmouth, ME: Intercultural Press.

Zahniser, A. H. Mathias
1997 *Symbol and Ceremony: Making Disciples Across Cultures.* Monrovia, CA: MARC.

APM

Group A: Participatory Learning

Catching Missional

Shaping a Participatory Environment in Missiological Education (A Case Study)

Karen E. Parchman

DOI: 10.7252/Paper.000021

About the Author:
An Adjunct Instructor in Christian Formation and Intercultural Studies at Fuller Theological Seminary, Karen Parchman teaches courses in missiology, missional leadership, and practical theology. Her dissertation focuses on the effects of missional change on communication in local churches. Karen is always looking for ways to engage students in the learning task, and is always looking to foster innovation through reflection in the classroom.

Abstract

A recent gathering at Fuller Theological Seminary framed its discussion with the following provocative title: "The End of Missiological Education (as we know it): The Path Thus Far" (April 10, 2012). The panel discussed the need for innovative, novel approaches to the learning task in order to renew missiological education. Traditional education frames the process of learning in a theory-praxis model, where student's lived experiences are rarely considered or critiqued in light of missiological or theological reflection. Active learning, where students combine activities with reflection upon them, presents an innovative opportunity for missiological education. This case study explores the effects of an active learning environment for the course "Congregations in the World" at Fuller Theological Seminary's Houston Campus in the Fall of 2012. In the paper, I outline the theoretical and practical frameworks of adult learning and practical theology and introduce the pedagogical goals for the learning environment. I then provide three learning tasks that the participants engaged in, and how they led to opportunities for deeper learning. Finally, some broad and general questions for consideration are made regarding an active learning environment for future missiological education.

"We all live within the stories we tell, for these tales fashion a coherent direction and identity out of the discontinuities of our past, present, and future" -Caroline Fehl

Introduction

It was 9:30 on a Friday night, when this weekend class was supposed to end for the evening. Earlier, a learning activity meant to engage people in one-to-one conversation on their cultural heritage had broken open to reveal significant stories of pain, longing, hope, and adaptation. The subsequent spirited conversation engaged everyone in a journey of theological and cultural reflection. Though they would be back in this classroom in 11 short hours, the students assembled had no interest in leaving; one remarked, "but what's the answer?! How can we leave without knowing how to fix this in our churches?"

Looking back on the notes from this evening and subsequent learning exercises meant to challenge their habits and practices of 'missional', there was a moment at which it became clear that the learning activities significantly challenged the expectations and norms of the classroom culture. And while the mediated interaction held a firm resolution at bay, the encounter compelled everyone in the room to be fully present and engaged.

Communication and social interaction are important for corporate sensemaking, particularly in situations when there are gaps in knowledge or distinctions between normative perspectives. The potential for deep learning happens in the space between persons as they interact. Any time there is naturally occurring interaction in the classroom, there is the possibility for both deep learning and deep anxiety. Educators have the responsibility during times of active reflection to dislodge assumptions and raise questions about what people know and how they come to know. Discourse scholars Ann Cunliffe and John Shotter address the challenges of the lecture hall, suggesting that educators "have completely ignored the kind of knowledge or knowing-within-the-moment" (2004:226) that derives from novel perspectives and information, informed by the multiples and varied experiences of family and culture, and from failures and successes.

This case study will introduce the outcome of several learning tasks in the course, "Congregations in the World" (See Appendix A for syllabus, created by Mark Lau Branson) at Fuller Seminary's Houston Campus. The intention is to explain and explore the deep learning and possible transformative moments that emerged in a participatory learning environment focused on leading and creating mission-shaped congregations. The course objectives were largely influenced by the task of developing proficiency with the praxis-theory-praxis of Practical Theology through action and reflection. Principles of Adult and Active Learning were engaged, which acknowledge that students are active subjects in the learning task. There was also recognition that students bring specific lived experiences into the learning environment that shape mental models, actions, and relationships in and about the world. Finally, it was assumed that knowledge creation takes place through a discovery of lived experiences in communication with cultural, contextual, theological, and biblical narratives.

As Christian educators, we are interested in the task of understanding truth, garnering knowledge, and developing wisdom. Through our processes of instruction, we might see our subject expertise informing how and what we wish to pass on to the next generation of leaders. Some curricular designs anticipate that the information transfer will lead students to incorporate the new ideas into daily practices. Current critiques of higher education, however, would argue that these 'technical-functional' (Neville 2008:32) approaches to learning do not help students to actively critique or engage the postmodern culture.

In contrast, the participative learning environment is meant to engage the lived stories of students in association with the cultural, contextual, theological and scriptural narratives that are reflexively influencing what they notice about the world. Students are dancing between action and reflection, or "doing things and thinking about what they are doing" (Bonwell and Eison 1991:2). In this course, the classroom was not isolated from the scripts and stories of daily life; rather those stories were integral to the educational experience itself. As the instructor, my goal was to foster habits of faithful presence to what God is doing in the world through solid content and inductive experiences.

The content of this paper is practical rather than theoretical, though these two principles of educational design function in concert. Section One explores the theoretical frameworks that are assumed as part of the course: Adult Learning, Practical Theology as a core requirement of the Ministry Division at Fuller Theological Seminary, and practical considerations regarding Just In Time learning. Section Two will highlight three specific learning tasks during which just-in-time teaching and interactive reflection occurred. Finally, Section

Three will draw conclusions about the efficacy of interactive learning environments for missiological education, and raise questions for future conversation.

Section 1: Theoretical and Practical Frameworks

Theological education as it relates to the *missio Dei* has been informed by Christendom models of the Western culture(s). Leaders in congregations, the academy, and on the mission field critique seminary education, stating that our systems do not train and educate leaders for the people of God who live in a changed and adaptive context.[1] The task of theological education, they suggest, has a deeply important task in preparing people for serving as witnesses to the missionary God we serve, and contribute to developing habits of faithfulness fundamental to missional living.[2]

Critical Pedagogy and Adult Learning

We are living in a changing world that is becoming more complex, requiring skillful critical thinking to solve difficult problems. The concern with higher education has moved from a single focus on what people learn, to how and to what end they learn. In studying higher education Richard Paul acknowledged this concern, and suggested that developing habits of the mind would require different type of learning frameworks, specifically targeting reasoning, reflection, and personal responsibility in the learning task (Fink 2001:13). Instruction-based pedagogy, with the emphasis on transferring information from teacher to student, supposes the student to be a passive and ready container to be filled by the information supplied in the classroom through lecture and assigned tasks. Paul's study indicated that, while most professors in higher education affirm their intent to create learning experiences to engage critical thinking, they are often unable to describe what critical thinking is, and how to introduce students to it. As a result the learning task is equated with teacher-based curriculum design.

Adult learning principles recognize that knowledge creation occurs in the space where people make sense of their actions together. Paolo Friere notes that adults have stories they bring to the learning environment that must be acknowledged and used in order to create new habits and actions. As it relates to learning, people are more likely to default to hold habits, not adapt to new learning. Freire explains that no "reality transforms itself" (1970:53); instead, people are more likely to exhibit deep commitment to equilibrium. All social systems are autopoetic in that they are preconditioned reproduce themselves nearly exactly (Luhman 2005), and the actions they engage in support reproduction, not adaptation. In order to incorporate new knowledge or understanding, Freire notes that action and reflection are intimately intertwined and necessary for change (Freire 1970:53). Dialogue is not information exchange, it is corporate reflection that assumes the right and responsibility of the learner to participate in making sense of the activities and practices in the task of learning. In her work with adults throughout the world, Jane Vella has explored the dimensions of adults as learners. As active subjects of their own learning she has discovered that "[p]eople are naturally excited to learn anything that helps them understand their own...lives" (Vella 2002:6).

In participatory learning, the educational experience is different in another respect: it mines the experiences of daily life as data to guide future action. Every day, the students that attend our classes are bombarded with messages from a diverse set of public and private narratives: from the movies they choose to watch to the news they ingest, to the type of civic and social activities they engage in *and also resist*. For missiological education, the complexity engaging the task of knowing how (Cunliffe and Shotter 2006:231) must incorporate lived experience with the learning endeavor.

Practical Theology and the Goals of the Fuller Theological Seminary Ministry Division

The core requirements of the Master of Divinity include 8 different arenas for learning. For each division, there are expected learning outcomes related to the core requirements. This course is housed in the Ministry Division (MIN1), and as such must "specify the course as one that teaches a practical theology method" (Branson 2010:2) of praxis-theory-praxis.

Practical Theology presumes that learners arrive at the task of learning with built-in assumptions, and have been influenced by informal and formal relationships in the wider cultures where people gain identity. In his volume on Practical Theology, Thomas Groome suggests that the task of theological education must move beyond its concern for knowledge acquisition to a "person's whole way of being" (1991:7). Fundamentally he argues, that a knowing faith must encompass not only what people know, but how they come to know it. Whereas much of our theological education is concerned with the cognitive and rational aspects of theological truths in doctrine, practical theology's contribution brings the truth of experience into the theological task (Anderson 2001:23).

To introduce practical theology to the class, students reflected on their experiences as Christians in the world: their interaction with neighbors and co-workers, how they received instruction for the task of 'witness' in the world, and their own interaction with congregational mission and ministry. In the first week of class, the students were involved in the process of learning Practical Theology's interactive steps through practice, interaction, and reflection.

Figure 1: Practical Theology Cycle (Branson 2011:45)[3]

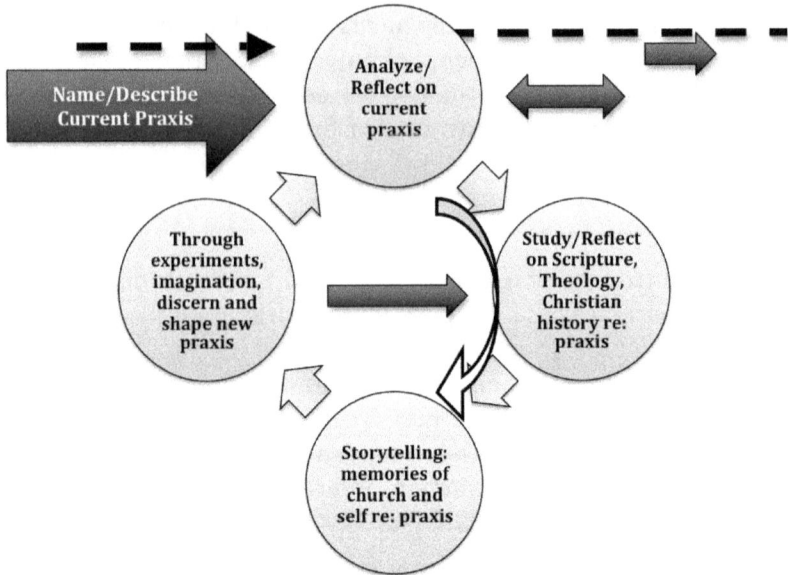

As each of the learning activities was reflected upon, the students were consistently drawn toward the praxis-theory-praxis dimension of the course to analyze, reflect, and learn.

Just-In-Time Learning

I discovered just-in-time learning through the work of Ronald Heifetz, whose leadership classes at Harvard are often oversubscribed. Also known as 'case in point learning, Heifetz explains that he sees the classroom as a case itself, "a social system inevitably made up of a number of different factions and acted upon by multiple forces" (Parks 2005:7). The educator task not only includes disseminating the information from the course documents, but focusing on what is happening in the classroom at that moment to illustrate the content.

From the perspective of the educator, just-in-time is a work of interpretation. It requires educators to listen and be fully present to the activities of the classroom. Heifetz uses the metaphor of a ballroom to get this point across (1994). He suggests of the important qualities of educators is to get off the field of play, where the action is going on, and try to see the larger patterns of activity and interaction from the metaphoric balcony. Parks addresses this less metaphorically and more succinctly, asking the educator to reflect on how "I can use what is happening right here and now to illustrate the content I want the class to learn" (Parks 2005:7).

Section 2: Foundations of the Course

The discipline of Practical Theology is an integral part of missiological education, for it seeks to interpret human activity, tradition, and culture through the praxis of the missional God of Scripture. From an ecclesiological perspective, the mission of the church must be grounded in and responsive to God's ultimate care for all of creation. The church's purpose is found in this bedrock theological and mission-focused direction as the foundation and the future horizon of its ministry.

Learning Task 1: Cultural Autobiography
Small Group Session

One of the first learning tasks of the course incorporated a small group event. Identity is assumed to be a combination of nature, context, nurture, and culture, and students enter the learning experience with attitudes that have been shaped by a variety of life experiences. From this perspective, theological education honors the "wholeness" of people's experience, rather than casting experience aside during the learning task. The following represents the small group experience.

1. Students were invited to find two others in the class with whom to share their backgrounds. They were then given 30 minutes to share their "Cultural Autobiography" through a series of questions provided.[4] The racial, ethnic, and cultural diversity in the classroom was felt in these triads, where native African, Indian, and Egyptian students were learning together with African-American, Latino(a), and Caucasian Americans.

2. During the corporate reflection period, multiple experiences were noted and then discussed as a group. It allowed for the educator to begin to develop the practical theology cycle of current praxis (life experiences), the way culture influenced those experiences, how Scripture informed individual and corporate praxis.

The sociological exploration that occurs during a narrative reflection requires the educator to remain fully present to what is being said, and the "song beneath the words" (Parks 2005:99). If we pay attention, our students are peppering us with data about what and how they see the world. As interpreters of the classroom, educators must be attentive to the unfolding awareness taking place individually and corporately as students begin to explore the boundaries and horizons of their experience. These boundaries represent "fault lines" where fixed meaning structures break down, providing opportunity for new practice and new relationships.[5] During this assignment, students were introduced to each other's lifeworlds and experiences, often disrupting their understanding of the culture and context in which they live.[6] Opportunities exist for transformation in this space, because every participant experiences vulnerability and dislocation. As an educator, holding this space is important, for it is in vulnerability and dialogic consciousness of one another that new avenues of understanding can be reached.

In the exercise above, students were engaging in deep conversation about race, congregational stereotypes, and the cultural dissimilarities of their life experiences. When the class returned from their triads, a spirited conversation about color, race and relationships turned on the interaction between a white student and a black student. The two were eager to display their connectedness. Rather than moving off of this assignment and on to the 'real work' of the class, this experience brought forward the opportunity to discuss reconciliation as a fundamental intention of God's restoration project through the ministry of Jesus. Students shared episodes of congregational health, dysfunction, and their own stories in them. Because the content focused on introducing the Practical Theology cycle, the students were directed once again to the cycle of action and reflection, bringing together the praxis they identified and reflecting on scripture and theology relating to God's reconciling work in the world and through the people of God.

Learning Task 2a: The Exploration of
Missional: Making the Familiar Strange[7]

The term 'missional' has become a familiar language tool in our congregations, but in many cases it lacks a fundamental attitude connected to the *missio Dei*. Van Gelder and Zscheile note a tendency in many congregations to validate an "instrumental view of mission" that focuses on providing religious goods and services through the church in order to bring more people into its community (2011:113). The repeated use of the language of missional, with little analysis or reflection, has subtly been drained of its ability to transform congregations.[8] The language of missional must be disturbed in order to allow for novel meanings to be introduced. That is the basis for "making the familiar strange." It is what Fink notes as one of the basic tenets of the educational process: to "get students to see that there are some unexpected phenomena" that might be contrary to their understanding (2005:72).

In order to create new habits and capacities relating to the concept of *missional*, the students were encouraged to engage in an experiment outside the classroom, and keep a journal of their experience and how it might influence their behaviors in the future. The assignment required students to actively look for where the Spirit of God might be at work as they went about their daily lives during one week. They were asked to be fully attentive in their going and note their responses in their journals. Prior to the day's activities, students were tasked with reflecting on Luke 10:1-12,[9] and journal what struck them from that passage. This was meant to develop a deeper awareness of how God might be active in their daily lives and in the world around them. Students were then asked to reflect on what they saw, what God made them attentive to, and then provide some insights on God's larger activity in the world.

The experience of journaling is an individual one: it is personally reflective, and can be important for transformation. As an active learning strategy, journaling presents little risk for the educator. Class time is not used, and it is a relatively structured assignment with definite outcomes (Bonwell and Eison 1991). However, if the strategy is to be employed for more enduring learning, the journal exercise becomes a space for disturbing the taken-for-granted assumptions about the practice of missional living.

Several students willingly allowed their journal entries to be used for the classroom learning after the journal exercise was complete. For the purposes of this paper, I will highlight two and demonstrate how they were used in the classroom discussions that bracketed the lecture(s). The two students were both male. Their cultural and social experiences were different, as were their theological standpoints. They both were and are active leaders in their congregations. The first journal entry came from a student who was in his first quarter of seminary:

> "As I began to walk through the mall simply enjoying being aware of God's presence, there was a young teenage girl who happened to be on the phone in a near corner. She was crying and looked as if something terrible had just happened. I walked passed her twice and the Holy Spirit told me to go back.... I watched everyone as they walked passed her looking at her as they continued to shake their heads in disbelief.... The Lord reminded me of verse 9 of Luke 10. I immediately began to intercede on her behalf. As the spirit led me over to her, I asked her if she would allow me to pray with her. She welcomed me as I introduced myself and she began to tell me that her father had just been diagnosed with cancer. I began to pray for healing, for restoration, for peace, and for God's Will to be done.... After the prayer, we just began to share our testimonies and life stories. She is a new believer and had just given her life to Christ a week ago, literally. She asked if I wanted anything from her job, which was in the food court. As I told her that I had already eaten, I immediately thought of verse 7 of Luke 10. This experienced really allow my heart to be tender and receptive to all that God was saying and doing. It was such a powerful day. I am so grateful for the privilege to be apart of God's mission." (Journal Response, Student K)

Bonwell and Eison (1991) note that active learning strategies place greater emphasis on developing skills and assessing attitudes and values; for this exercise it was necessary to go beyond the textual data a student wrote, and engage in social interaction around the exercise itself. In a classroom setting, educators often use provisional objects, such as learning exercises, to demonstrate what they mean. Just in time learning dispels the myth that there are taken-for-granted standpoints, using the interactive space to reflect as the action is happening in the moment. By the time of this exercise, everyone in the classroom had been made aware of the tapestry of multiple social memories that affected learning and interaction. They had been exposed to just in time learning, and had begun to assess their interpretations of the stories they heard and acknowledge the cultural forces that made those interpretations 'true.' In this case, students began a discussion about the cultural understanding of personal space, drawing from their own experiences. Through a guided discussion on congregational space and interaction, they reflected on the theological and missiological significance of community, raising questions about the nature of the church as it relates to the fellowship within the Trinity. The notion of engagement gave rise to a conversation about 'sentness' and the example of this student's willingness to be present to another's suffering.

Learning Task 2b: The Exploration of Missional: Making the Invisible Visible

Any discussion about cultural awareness necessitates using language. For better or worse, language is embedded in the very culture being discussed, and therefore is limited. Ann Swidler (2001) remarks that the cultural and interactive repertoires that people use to describe their world constrain the type of action that is available, and reflexively organizes the language used to describe those actions. As a result, culture is largely invisible to us because what we know about our environment is simply "the way we do things around here." When something disturbs the pattern of assumptions in one's practice of daily life, it makes paradigms visible, but also creates uncertainty about what actions are appropriate. During uncertainty, when the patterns of behavior don't seem to make sense, interaction may need to be somewhat ambiguous. Eisenberg suggests that this "strategic ambiguity' (1984:230) is useful for examining assumptions, and shaping new praxis.

The journal exercise was meant to disturb students day-to-day practice and make culture visible. An African-american student who was nearing completion of his MDiv wrote the second journal entry that the class members reflected on. In reads in part:

"... I went back to the neighborhood where I was raised. The people that were much older than I are dead, but their abandoned homes and cars are still there. At the community grocery store the seniors are morbidly obese, limbs disfigured from a stroke or some form of paralysis. Those who were old enough to be a big brother or sister to me are doing the same thing they were doing when I was a teenager, sitting under a tree, smoking, drinking and complaining. Guys that I walked to school with in what used to be a neighborhood, but has now become a ghetto, are still walking but unemployed, addicted to drugs, living at home with their mother and their children. Their quality of life is at an all time low. The guys who went to prison are home but they are struggling entrepreneurs operating barbershops and car detail shops.... I am guilty of treating my neighbor's pain and problems as a project or program one can throw money towards.... John Wesley said, "The world is my parish," but if I begin to address some of their surface needs, am I equipped or called to provoke the transformation of the mind in this community?" (Journal Exercise, Student C)

When educators embark on reflective learning, or what the Jesuits call 'contemplation in action,' ambiguity and dis-ease may be important factors in the process. Van Looy et al. trace the way communication can support group dynamics when new ideas are activating a sense of ambiguity and disorientation. Ambiguity, they note, occurs when the learning task extends beyond typical forms of information exchange; "it relates directly to the creation of new knowledge" (2006:187). Educators must be aware of their own tension, and desire for equilibrium during ambiguity. Holding the dynamics of the classroom and the contents of the course in tension with each other requires an active awareness of one's own retreat, or what Sewell calls an attempt to "homogeniz[e] difference and manag[e] divergence" (1999:56).

Just in time teaching requires deep listening and engagement: becoming aware of what is happening internally is just as informative as paying attention to what is happening among the students. In this case, a deep longing to 'make everything okay' and dispel the tension was itself data upon which to reflect. When educators experience tension within – what Heifetz calls "catching the edge of [one's] personality" (Parks 2005:153) – he suggests using it as a learning tool. In participatory environments, learning is an expectation and an outcome for both students and educators.

In any culture there exists the dominant narratives and stories from the margins. Those who live within the dominant narratives often do not have the language or meaning structure to make sense out of the stories of marginalized social groups in the wider culture. The African American storyteller who can no longer make sense of his culture of origin is extremely pertinent because it calls into question the default settings of action and interaction that are normalized in our congregations and contexts: to what degree are we hospitable to the stories of powerlessness?

Interaction creates new knowledge and novel ideas because of the diversity of life experience, assumptions, and perspectives. The language of missional became more exploratory as participants begin to press into existing meaning, and question their frameworks. The tools of the class, which were highly experiential, were geared to cultivate instincts of awareness to the activity of the Spirit of God in the creation. The journaling exercise gave rise to deep tensions of why and how the church is engaged in the communities in which God has placed it. The discussion allowed for vulnerability between diverse groups. It challenged our ability to analyze and develop new narratives and stories.

Identity is shaped and reshaped through stories people tell, share in, hide, and ultimately live within. The task of the educator is to guide the conversation so that diversity is honored within the framework of the course content, paying attention to when the pain is too great, the pain is wasted, or it generates just enough heat to mobilize the students to learn from the presenting situation. Assisting in the transformational process of learning, the educator must allow for the ongoing and novel way people apply what they know to their actions.

Learning Task 3: The Practice of Presence

Though all of the learning tasks were geared toward becoming 'present' to what God is doing, the final learning task in this case study explored the dynamics of active engagement in the classroom. Every student was required to lead a group discussion on one of the required readings from the class. Students were to develop a study guide and keep the conversation moving on the topic. Prior to introducing the book and prior to students gathering in their small groups, they would do an exercise in 'becoming present.' Being fully present to what is happening in the immediate moment is a learned instinct of becoming aware of the patterns of verbal and non-verbal cues that reveal whether the group is ready to do the work (Parks 2005:100).

The students were asked to pay attention to their own cues; whether they were relaxed, nervous, bored, or otherwise occupied by events outside of the classroom. During a period of silence they would be invited to become more present: be attentive to who is in the classroom, what they are doing, and what their body language is telling the rest of the room.. After participating in the exercise of leaving and becoming present several times, students became more aware of when they were truly engaged and when their minds were engaged elsewhere.

The participants in the groups were challenged to be active listeners, responsible for their own learning when their colleague led the exercise. After the book discussion, the class shared their experiences, and explored the connection between being present in the conversation and the interaction over the readings. As the educator, I modeled certain behaviors for the students in the reporting out phase: using silence as a tool, reflect back what was heard and share an insight from the course content, and ask for alternate interpretations and perceptions. The exercise brought a deep learning, not only of the information contained in the reading, but students also reflected on the experience of engagement as a spiritual practice.

There are more stories of engagement and presence and missional purpose that occurred during the quarter. The three exercises explored here were a snippet of the collective learning within the contours of action and reflection. The most profound "ah-ha" moments occurred through these assignments and reflection upon them.

Section 3: Concluding Thoughts for Future Discussion

The Master of Divinity core curriculum at Fuller Seminary requires that students take one missions class, which in my limited experience is frequently addressed in the final year at seminary. Such was also the case when I spoke at the one missions class required at Austin Presbyterian Theological Seminary 10 years ago. Though the contextual and cultural realities are shifting in the academy, the question remains how to use the one opportunity we may have to form Christian leaders who care for the world that God loves, and cultivate new instincts for understanding and recognizing God's missional intent. The following reflections on the practice of participatory environments are limited in scope, but attempt to address some possible challenges to creating this type of experience.

1. *Learning to lead a participatory environment may alter the style and purpose of educational practice.* Each of us may point to a time when learning was transformational. It may have come in a classroom, but it likely wasn't through a Multiple Choice exam. Students retain information, change attitudes, or are motivated to learn more when they have been actively enagaged in the learning process. Bonwell and Eisen (1991) note that while it reduces the amount of available lecture time, the participative atmosphere creates new avenues for creative learning to occur. Manage expectations of the students in the classroom by announcing the different type of learning they will engage in. Large class sizes should not prevent educators from integrating the social and communicative strategies of active learning; the framework expects small group work and shifts the burden of learning from the individual to the system.

2. *How will participatory environments be affected by distributed learning and online courses?* Many internet course tools are geared toward adult education, and are concerned with creating online community (see Bartlett 2008) that can effectively engage in deep learning. However, questions remain regarding how educators create the online experience to capture events as they unfold and use reflection in action dynamics. Creating transformational moments that the community is witness to and participant in will be a point for discovery in online learning.

3. *What adheres? What transforms?* Every educator attempts to make the learning experience interesting enough that the students grasp the necessary information and hopefully will remember its concepts and some content. But one of the delights we have in the classroom is to witness the transformation of the mind in students as they awaken to new knowledge. Throughout the course last fall, the students entered the process of learning how to become more present to the work of the Spirit of God who is intentionally active in our world – both in the 'secular' creation and among the people of God. The final papers were meant to be an active, practical theology reflection developed over the course of the quarter and through some of the learning exercises. The practical aspect of the paper, where students are shaping their own learning environments, is another space for transforming practices. One student, shaping a ministry to African American men at the local barbershop, shared the following goal:

"...as people internalize this way of life, they begin to understand the frame work of transformation. The ordinary men and women of a local church now begin to actively innovate mission-shaped life across the church because they have listened to each other; they have been given the dignity of God's people, and they have discovered that the Spirit of God really is present among them. It is at this point, in the midst of growing experiments, that people realize that they have discovered for themselves a way of being church that isn't dependent on outside programs, gurus, or even ordained clergy. Tangible, measurable, and observable actions occur. This is the point at which a local church tips over to a place from which it can't go back to the old ways of being passive recipients of religious goods and services. Something tells me that in the coming months and years I would do well to remind myself of how important it is to not lose sight of the goal of not turning back. I pray that our first experiment, The Barber Shop Ministry, is the seed that moves us closer to that goal." (D., final paper)

Parker Palmer, writing about his philosophy of teaching, describes it this way: "I [have] learned that my gift as a teacher is the ability to dance with my students, to co-create with them a context in which all of us teach and learn" (1998:72). The steps of participatory environments may be foreign to some; the role of educator, the experience of the students, and the content are woven together as tools for the learning process. It captures the imagination of the student and educator alike, even in the most vulnerable space of ambiguity and engagement. We recognize the future leaders we are equipping today are entering a challenging, adaptive and complex world. Providing them tools to assess honestly, innovate creatively, and engage thoughtfully will require patient leadership and willingness to co-create with our students in the task of learning.

Notes

1   This course primarily addresses the congregation or people of God in the contexts where God has placed them, not cross-cultural missions.

2   Such critiques have been coming from within the academy as well as from practitioners. See McLaren and Campolo (2003), Roxburgh (2006, 2010), Frost and Hirsch (2003) and Van Gelder (2009).

3   Students were introduced to several Practical Theology methods, and were advised to choose a method for their final paper. The cycle above was one of those methods introduced in the class. Branson's model is informed by Groome (1991), Roxburgh (2006), and Anderson (2001). The cycle is not linear; the arrows indicate that there will be movement back and forth as sense is made of action, and reflection may bring groups back to earlier stages of the cycle to study, analyze, and tell stories.

4   The questions were adapted from Branson and Martinez 2011:25.

5   Chris Blantern and Murray Anderson Wallace (2006) explore the boundaries of experience as they noted the conversational patterns during a conflict mediation consultation. They suggest that no learning will take place unless the language and its meaning are disturbed from accepted patterns of interaction.

6   As an example, one triad had a white North American male, a second-generation Latina, and an Egyptian immigrant. During the reflection period, the Egyptian male appeared disturbed. Being attentive to this, he was asked to share a little of his experience. He was astonished by the diverse stories of North America coming from these two people – he had always assumed that the United States was a monolithic culture.

7   The phrase was originally used by William J.J. Gordon to explore the concept of Synetics, but it has been broadly applied in a diverse number of settings. For this course, the real purpose was to encourage students to explore their thinking beyond the taken-for-granted assumptions, where the first thought is "there's nothing new here."

8   Roxburgh and Boren, among others, have made this point as well (see "Introducing the Missional Church" 2009:31).

9   This passage is used frequently in a variety of Missional circles, particularly in Patrick Keifert's Church Innovations Institute (www.churchinnovations.org), and with Alan Roxburgh's Missional Network (www.themissionalnetwork.com). Students had been exposed to "Dwelling in the Word" as part of the regular exercise of the course, which exposed them to dialogic and reflective listening to scripture.

Works Cited

Anderson, Ray Sherman
    2001   *The Shape of Practical Theology: Empowering Ministry with Theological Praxis.* Downers Grove, Ill.: InterVarsity Press.

Bartlett, Clair
    2008   Facilitating online interaction using community building strategies. In *Emerging Technologies Conference.* University of Wollongong. June 18-21.

Blantern, Chris, and Murray Anderson-Wallace
    2006a Patterns of Engagement. In *The Social Construction of Organization*, edited by D. M. Hosking and S. McNamee. Herndon, VA: Copenhagen Business School Press.

Bonwell, Charles C., and James A. Eison
    1991   Active Learning: Creating Excitement in the Classroom. In *ASHE-ERIC Higher Education Report.* Washington, DC: George Washington University.

Branson, Mark Lau, and Juan F. Martinez
    2011   *Churches, Cultures, and Leadership.* Downers Grove, IL: Intervarsity Press.

Campolo, Tony, and Brian McLaren
    2003   *Adventures in Missing the Point.* Grand Rapids, MI: Zondervan.

Cunliffe, Ann L., and John Shotter
    2006   Wittgenstein, Bakhtin, Management and the Dialogical. In *The Social Construction of Organization*, edited by D. M. Hosking and S. McNamee. Herndon, VA: University of Copenhagen Business School Press.

Eisenberg, Eric
    1984   Ambiguity as Strategy in Organizational Communication. *Communication Monographs* 51:227-242.

Fehl, Caroline
    2004   Explaining the International Criminal Court: A 'Practice Test' for Rationalist and Constructivist Approaches. *European Journal of International Relations* 10 (3):357-394.

Fink, L. Dee
    2003   *Creating Significant Learning Experiences.* San Francisco: Jossey Bass.

Freire, Paolo
    2000   *Pedagogy of the Oppressed.* Translated by M. B. Ramos. 30th Anniversary ed. New York: Continuum. Original edition, 1970.

Groome, Thomas H.
    1991   *Sharing Faith: A Comprehensive Approach to Religious Education and Pastoral Ministry: The Way of Shared Praxis.* 1st ed. San Francisco: Harper.

Heifetz, Ronald A.
    1994   *Leadership Without Easy Answers.* Cambridge, MA: Belknap Press of Harvard University Press.

Luhmann, Niklas
    1995   *Social Systems.* Stanford, CA: Stanford University Press. Original edition, 1987.

Mezirow, Jack
    2000   *Learning as Transformation.* San Francisco: Jossey-Bass.

Neville, Mary Grace
    2008   Using Appreciative Inquiry and Dialogical Learning to Explore Dominant Paradigms. *Journal of Management Education* 32 (1):100-117.

Palmer, Parker
    1998   *The Courage to Teach: Exploring the Inner Landscape of a Teacher's Life.* San Francisco: Jossey-Bass.

Parks, Sharon Daloz
    2005   *Leadership Can be Taught.* Cambridge, MA: Harvard University Press.

Pierson, Paul E., Dudley Woodberry, and C. Douglas McConnell
    2012   The End of Missiological Education (As We Know It): the path thus far, at Fuller Theological Seminary.

Roxburgh, Alan, and M. Scott Boren
    2009   *Introducing the Missional Church.* Grand Rapids: Baker Books.

Roxburgh, Alan J., and Fred Romanuk
    2006   *The Missional Leader: Equipping Your Church to Reach a Changing World.* San Francisco: Jossey-Bass.

Sewell, William H. Jr.
    1999   The Concept(s) of Culture. In *Beyond the Cultural Turn,* edited by V. E. Bonnell and L. Hunt. Berkeley, CA: University of California Press.

Swidler, Ann
    2001   *Talk of Love: How Culture Matters.* Chicago: University of Chicago Press.

Van Gelder, Craig
    2007b *The Ministry of the Missional Church: A Community Led by the Spirit.* Grand Rapids, MI: Baker Books.

Van Looy, Bart, Rene Bouwen, and Koenraad Debackere
    2006   The social side of Innovation: a process perspective. In *The Social Construction of Organization,* edited by D. M. Hosking and S. McNamee. Herndon, VA: Copenhagen Business School Press.

Appendix A: Syllabus

TM521: Congregations in the World:
Neighborhood, Workplace, and Society
Mark Lau Branson, Ed.D.

DESCRIPTION: This course focuses on the practices of the local church as it engages in the world as partners in God's mission of restoration to make all things new. Principles from scripture, theology, and social practice will be developed to illustrate the dynamic connections between congregation and context. Building from the praxis-theory-praxis framework of practical theology, students will engage such topics as neighbor hospitality, healthy partnerships, community development and social action, evangelism, and spiritual formation.

SIGNIFICANCE FOR LIFE AND MINISTRY: This course is designed to promote student's authentic, practical engagement with social environments and contexts from a practical theology framework in order to approach and interpret with others their understanding of the church, the culture, and the mission of God.

LEARNING OUTCOMES: Students completing this course will have: (1) developed a conceptual understanding of the missiological purpose and task of Christian ministry in the world through a praxis-theory-praxis perspective; (2) integrated a kingdom perspective into their spiritual and missiological interpretations of culture and congregation; (3) demonstrated the ability to engage a practical theology method for reflection on and evaluation of the congregation's connection to their context and cultures; (4) utilized the concepts, perspectives, experiences and skills from this course for their own spiritual formation and vocational direction; and (5) begun to grasp a vision for and commitment to forming congregations as an incarnational and interpretive presence in the community.

REQUIRED READING:

Arias, Mortimer
    2001   *Announcing the Reign of God.* Lima, OH: Academic Renewal Press. 174 Pages. ISBN 978-1579105631. $21.00

Branson, Mark Lau, and Juan F. Martínez
    2011   *Churches, Cultures, and Leadership.* Downer's Grove, IL: IVP Academic. 275 pages. ISBN 978-0830839261. $15.21**

Escobar, Samuel
    2003   *The New Global Mission.* InterVarsity Press. 192 pages. ISBN 978-0830833016. $10.90.

McKnight, Scot, Kevin Corcoran, Peter Rollins, and Jason Clark
    2011   *Church in the Present Tense.* Grand Rapids: Brazos Press. 156 pages. ISBN 978-1579105631. $14.87.

Roxburgh, Alan and Scott Boren
    2009   *Introducing the Missional Church.* Grand Rapids: Baker Books. 200 pages. ISBN 978-0801072123. $15.54.

Wright, N.T.
    2012   *After You Believe.* New York: HarperOne. 320 pages. ISBN 978-0061730542. $10.87.

Additional articles and chapters in Moodle.

ASSIGNMENTS AND ASSESSMENT:

5% Students will upload Weekly Journal writings (2 per weekend) relating to the content of the lectures, readings, and class interactions, and their impact on student's understanding of vocational ministry and the church in society.

10% Class Discussion and Attendance. It is expected that students will read the required material according to the schedule and be prepared to interact in group discussions and any exercises related to the material. In lieu of attendance, students will turn in a brief summary of their experience of the course, lecture, and events in the classroom after each session.

15% Prepare and lead a small group discussion on one of the required books. Submit a 700-word analytical reading report and proposed interview guide plan (2 pages) for the small group discussion.

30% Create and present a planned missional encounter for a particular ministry area of the church. It may be a men's/women's ministry, youth, children, current missions practice, etc. Anticipate the role this encounter has on the spiritual or communal formation within the people of God, and explain how it can support your congregational activities in the world. (5 - 7pp)

40% Final Paper: utilizing a practical theology method, students will submit a 5,000 word final paper describing current praxis relating to a church's interaction with its context, and prescribing future missional engagement for the people of God. Include the biblical, theological, and socio-cultural reasons for change, expansion, or transformation of current praxis, and suggest possible processes for the church in change.

PREREQUISITES: None.

RELATIONSHIP TO CURRICULUM: Meets MDiv Core requirement in Practical Theology/Spiritual Formation (MIN1) and in Missiology (MIN8).

FINAL EXAMINATION: Final Term Paper.

Utilizing Digital Platforms in Social Justice Education for Students' Transformissional Learning

DUANE BROWN

DOI: 10.7252/Paper.000025

About the Author:
Dr. Duane Brown lives in Wilmore, KY. He is married to Patty and father to three children. Duane served as pastor and church planter in Nova Scotia, Canada for twelve years. He earned the PhD Intercultural Studies in 2009 from Asbury Theological Seminary. Currently, Duane's ministry vocation includes teaching at Asbury Seminary and Asbury University, serving as a national church planter assessor with the Wesleyan Church, and serving as a TransforMissional Coach and Coach Developer for the Wesleyan Coaching Network. Duane has trained church planters and church leaders in Vladimir, Russia and Guyana, South American with Global Partners. Duane also serves as Treasurer and Board Member of the American Society of Missiology (asmweb.org). To find out more go to drduanebrown.com.

Abstract

Educators are beginning to realize that teaching in the digital environment is possible and advantageous for facilitating student learning on issues of social justice. More than absorbing content, learning must involve transformation. The transformissional paradigm is a new, holistic approach to leadership development that holds promise for the field of mission education. Four areas of focus guide instructors toward holistic course designs. Extant approaches for teaching social justice online featured here involve selected readings, service learning experiences, critical reflection and writing, and group discussions.

Introduction

With the recent advent of online learning in the higher education industry, research and writing on curricular approaches to facilitating social justice education online are less than two decades old and remain in the nascent stage of development (Ullman and Rabinowitz, 2004). Some have helped chart the course forward but we have much to learn as we strive toward becoming subject matter experts.[1]

Strait and Sauer (2004) develop the term E-Service to describe a type of experiential service learning within the online learning environment. They feature an e-service model called DLiTE, or Distributed Learning in Teacher Education, for faculty training at Bemidji University in Minnesota. They report a number of benefits and challenges for faculty and students in adopting an e-service model for online education. Strait and Sauer offer five suggestions for faculty seeking e-service learning opportunities: start small, train the students, plan for community partner contact, plan extra time for unexpected outcomes, and include a reflection component.

Guthrie and McCracken's (2010a) qualitative study of social justice facilitation through online delivery systems involves students' perceptions of their involvement with local service-learning projects. Service learning is understood to be a

"...form of experiential education in which students engage in activities that address human and community needs together with structured opportunities intentionally designed to promote student learning and development. Reflection and reciprocity are key concepts of service-learning" (Jacoby and Associates 1996:5)

They write, "Instruction in the virtual classroom, when coupled with on-site service experiences, creates opportunities for a unique combination of learning activities constructed to be individually and collectively relevant to real-world problems (2010:79)." The online course used for this research helped students gain understanding of service learning theory by studying historical models of leadership within social change movements. Students also engaged in ethics and values clarification activities, leadership best practices for social engagement, team-building, and the exploration of specific strategies for social action that foster local and global change.

In another study, Guthrie and McCracken (2010b) feature the benefits and challenges of facilitating social justice learning online at the University of Illinois at Springfield. Using case study methods (Yin, 1994), their findings suggest that, with a robust learning management system in place, students who participate in social justice projects and then critically engage with the experience personally and among peers will usually have a deep and rich learning experience. Likewise, the community and/or receivers of the service-learning projects benefit from the students' commitment to mitigating social problems in the community. Challenges with the format include: ineffectiveness at capturing and managing student learning, large class sizes, difficulties with faculty adapting to new technologies, and socio-economic inequality among students since some students are disadvantaged because they cannot afford the newest and latest technology.

Scholars and practioners in the field of religion recognize the value of facilitating social justice education through service learning experiences for students. They affirm that Judaism and the incipient Church of first century Palestine demonstrated the intentionality by which God designed for society a reigning ethic of justice and compassion for all (Hayes, 2006:90; Deut. 15:4; Acts 2:40-45). The prophet Jeremiah admonished the nation, "Also seek the peace and prosperity of the city to which I have carried you into exile. Pray to the Lord for it, because if it prospers, you too will prosper" (Jer. 29:7). Even Rauschenbusch observed,

> The multiplication of socially enlightened Christians will serve the body of society much as a physical organism would be served if a complete and effective system of ganglia should be distributed where few of them existed. The social body needs moral innervation; and the spread of men who combine religious faith, moral enthusiasm, and economic information, and apply the combined result to public morality, promises to create a moral sensitiveness never yet known (1907:357).

With this in mind, this paper specifically examines the question, "How might professors of mission effectively leverage digital environments to facilitate growth in students' social justice learning with a view to the broader impact on student's transformissional learning? To answer this question, we will explore the following. First, we will consider a new paradigm for leadership learning and development emerging from the field of leadership coaching called the Transformissional paradigm (Ogne and Roehl, 2008), one that has relevance for any Missiologist, professor of mission or student who desires a more holistic and tailored approach to learning and leadership development.

Second, with that in place, the paper will feature curricular approaches currently used in the course I facilitate at Asbury Theological Seminary, CD 501 ExL Vocation of Ministry, where one of the curricular objectives is for students to develop a plan for growth in a life of social holiness.[2] Before we can explore best practices, however, we must address a more fundamental concern.

Online or Sidelined?

For professors of mission, extending impact to students beyond traditional campuses is even more feasible with the advent and growth of Course Management Systems circa 1997 (Ullman and Rabinowitz, 2004). Recent growth in the overall movement toward digital learning is astounding (Allen and Seaman, 2013).

Statistical studies support the conclusion that higher education institutions are adopting digital learning in droves (Allen and Seaman, 2011). A 2005 survey of over 2500 academic leaders, Going the Distance: Online Education in the United States, 2011, reports over 6.7 million consumers linking to online environments for their education needs; an increase of nearly one million students from 2010, or 9.3% (Allen and Seaman, 2011).

However, what of those institutions and faculty trapped on the sidelines, in "analog mode?" Nearly 60% of those offering Baccalaureate degrees stated they remain "undecided" about creating

MOOC's (Allen and Seaman, 2013). Unfortunately, some educators are troubled by the growth of online learning; online education is sub-par, has quality issues, or is the vehicle of last resort for learning.[3]

Case in point: A professor taught regularly about the need for leaders to be culturally relevant. By the clothes the professor wore and the manner in which classes were conducted, however, the message sent was a much different one. While the institution promoted the necessity and value of leveraging the digital environment for the educational process, the professor was unwilling or perhaps unable to adapt to this digital world.

Another significant challenge to embracing the online environment for some professors of mission is the misconception that missiology is practical ministry training only, which is best done in real time, head-on, in a traditional campus environment.

The intent of this paper is not to argue for or against online learning. Rather, it proposed that we take advantage of the opportunities afforded through online learning to inculcate Missiological theory, principles and best practices. In this increasingly competitive environment to secure and/or maintain one's position in higher education and maintain economic viability, those willing to adapt to and embrace online learning will remain viable in the marketplace, reaping the economic and vocational benefits of job security and the personal benefits of knowing that they are able to make a difference from almost any vantage point in the world.

One Online Context – CD 501 Vocation of Ministry

By way of background, the ideas for this paper emerged from my experiences as facilitator for an online course, CD501 Vocation of Ministry, through Asbury Theological Seminary.

The course was originally designed by a team of professors and launched in 2001. A pool of resources, including writings and video lectures, was developed, made available and continuously updated for those facilitating the class. However, facilitators are free to develop resources ad hoc. It is a required course for all students early in their seminary experience, usually within the first two semesters. The course explores key foundational aspects of one's calling in a Matrix of Vocation for Christian ministry (Dinkins 2005).

Figure 1: A Matrix for a Vocation of Ministry

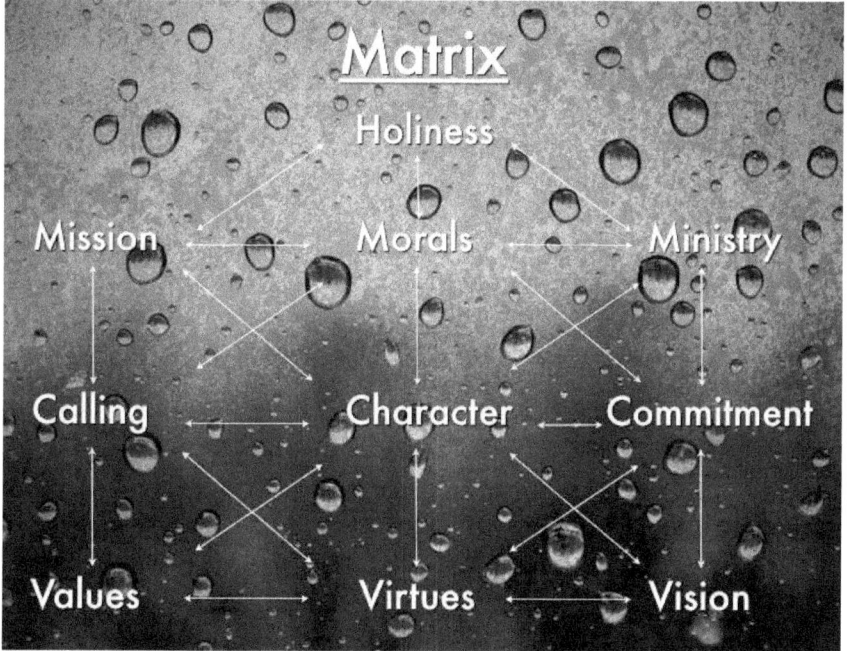

Asbury Theological Seminary uses the Moodle Learning Management System for online delivery of course content. A wide variety of customized facilitation tools exist within the Moodle platform, including technology to convene live, synchronous video learning classrooms with professor and students.

Assignments for the course include readings, weekly forum discussions on assigned topics, leading a spiritual formation group in their geographical context, and the writing of three reflection papers dealing with issues of calling. Students are required to participate in two shorter experiential learning activities as a means to promote curricular objectives, one experience being participation in a cross-cultural worship experience and the other a four-hour social justice experience. A one-page reflection paper is required following each experience. Drawing on these assignments and experiences, the paper features practices and procedures for facilitating student formation and engagement for social justice learning.

The Transformissional Paradigm

Effective educators maximize experiential learning approaches with the end-vision of facilitating life change in students (Taylor 2008). Kolb (1984) suggests adults learn best from a combination of direct experience, or apprehension, and abstract conceptualizations, or "knowing about", in comprehending a matter. Sophocles was famous for saying, "One must learn by doing the thing; though you think you know it, you have no certainty until you try." And Einstein posited, "Knowledge is experience, everything else is just information."

Transformative Learning Theory is instructive in this regard also since it posits that adults cannot learn in new ways until they develop the capacity to reshape pre-existing and perhaps limiting frames of reference (Taylor 2008). Then, through critical self-reflection on various life experiences, transformative learning occurs since adult learners are now thinking autonomously.

For educators who are Christian and thus hold to beliefs such as a stable universe, objective truth revealed by God, a worldview shaped through the lens of scripture, approaches like Experiential Learning Theory and Transformative Learning Theory are certainly valuable. But, it's unlikely that those educators who espouse a Judeo-Christian worldview will be able to fully embrace these perspectives.

In considering additional approaches to learner education and development, Steve Ogne and Tim Roehl (2008) are advancing what they believe is a new paradigm of missional leadership development from the realm of leadership coaching, the Transformissional coaching approach (Ogne and Roehl, 2008). This approach could be situated within Contextual Perspectives for adult learning development (Caffarella and Merriam, 1999). The following explains the development in the shift to this new paradigm for Ogne and Roehl.

Ogne explains that when he began coaching younger, post-modern leaders he decided he had to change his approach; he realized that leaders had to be engaged or measured beyond the level of outward performance since these leaders placed a higher value on relationships, authenticity, and community. For older, more "modern" leaders, it was all about ministry effectiveness or performance for the sake of the growth of the business or organization. Rarely did modern leaders require coaching for personal issues, unless those issues impeded their ability to grow the organization.

The concept of "transformission" backs away from older paradigms of mission. Ogne and Roehl compare Traditional Evangelicals, whose focus is most on overseas missions, and Pragmatic Evangelicals, who support attraction approaches to evangelism and church growth, with Younger Evangelicals, who prefer experiencing God in authentic community, engaging culture in mission without fearing one's culture.

Transformissional Christians have a holistic worldview and broad understanding of the Kingdom of God. They do not support a dualism that separates Christians from non-Christians or the church from the world. Rather, they view the church as God's agent to unleash God's Kingdom into the world. Mission for these followers of Jesus is all about engaging the church with the world, reconciling the Kingdom with world.

This emphasis on reconciliation extends beyond the saving of souls, and includes reconciling communities and nations. Transformissional Christians want to go beyond proclaiming the gospel in word; they desire to serve the culture, provide need-meeting services to the world, and even engage in political agendas. They believe the world is their mission field. Ogne and Roehl suggest, "The church is only truly transformissional when it is able to engage in both the social transformation of the culture and the spiritual transformation of individuals.

With the need arising for a more holistic approach to mission and to reach these Younger Evangelicals, Ogne and Roehl developed Transformissional Coaching, whereby they help "leaders live authentically and incarnationally while leading their churches to connect with the culture and intentionally engage in redemptive relationships" (2008:29).[4] Engaging leaders for transformission involves a distinct process, centering on the question, "Where is God working?" It has four overlapping areas of focus for leaders: (1) to help leaders clarify their call to ministry, (2) to help leaders cultivate personal, godly character so that the leader can be transformed and s/he can help transform their surroundings, (3) to help leader creates and be a member of an authentic community that serves to help its members grow and be accountable to one another, and (4) to help leaders connect with the secular culture for God's Kingdom and redemptive purposes, whatever they may be (See fig. 2 The Transformissional Approach). Being transformissional means that leaders are transformed when they are engaged or "coached" in ways that include all four areas. When leaders are transformed, believe Ogne and Roehl, they become transformissional.

Figure 2: The Transformissional Approach, used with permission

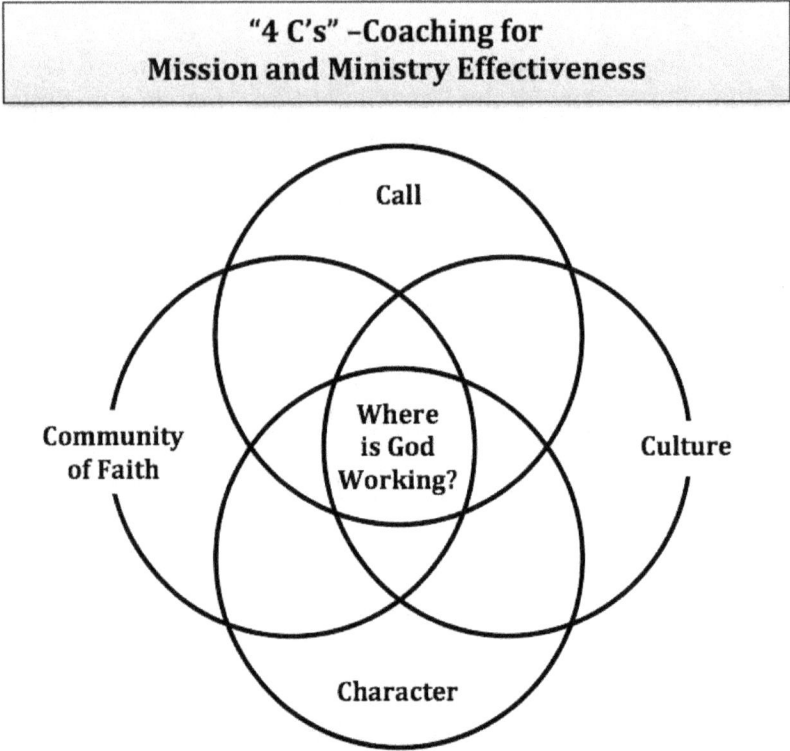

"4 C's" –Coaching for
Mission and Ministry Effectiveness

Call

Community of Faith

Where is God Working?

Culture

Character

The Transformissional Paradigm and Facilitating Social Justice Learning

Ogne and Roehl are not learning theorists in the traditional or academic sense, although Roehl holds a D.Min degree and teaches for the academy part-time. However, both men have spent decades teaching, training, consulting with and developing leaders. Ogne and Roehl possess a unique understanding on how leaders change, grow and develop.

The Transformissional Paradigm has not been officially "tested" in a field research study and to this point has not been featured in any other academic writing. It may have limitations for extension or application beyond religious leadership contexts. Some aspects of the paradigm as under, such as the character component, may be difficult to measure in an online environment.

But, the transformissional paradigm does have value for professors of mission, in particular, who facilitate student learning in a traditional campus setting or a digital setting, and who hopefully teach with the end vision that all students have missional impact for God's Kingdom on earth. The Transformissional paradigm engages believers in mission beyond ministries of word and encourages engaging the culture to alleviate societal ills. Reggie McNeal observes, "The collapse of the church culture means that many spiritual leaders will not serve out their call within the church culture nor be remunerated through payrolls of religious institutions" (200:98). With that in mind, this approach is featured as one more lens to consider in the approach to learner and/or leadership development.

Educators who embrace a transformission paradigm for learning and leadership development will have as their goal the transformission of students within the context of learning. They will embrace holistic designs that include educational content and process that covers the four areas of focus. Facilitating social justice education fits naturally within this paradigm.

Curricular Approaches for Facilitating Social Justice Learning Online

The last section of the paper will feature specific curricular approaches through the online course CD 501 ExL Vocation of Ministry that are used to facilitate social justice education. While the course is not entirely geared to social justice learning, certain aspects of the curriculum address the issue and it is those that will be featured here.

Readings. Students in the course engage a variety of readings that facilitates at least a basic understanding of social justice. The term "social justice," a hackneyism within our religious culture, requires some basic definition for students.[5]

An early reading in the course features Peggy McIntosh's popular but controversial article, White Privilege: Unpacking the Invisible Knapsack. Students are advised that they will likely have to "chew on the meat they find" and "spit out the bones" as needed. In some cases reading the article is very upsetting for students. The article is instructive since it helps expose the "colossal unseen dimensions" within our social system and fosters critical self-reflection for students (1990:36). Another helpful reading is called Test Yourself for Hidden Bias, available at www.tolerance.org. Students read about the development and impact of one's hidden biases and prejudices on one's behavior. Likewise, students are required to participate in a short activity called the "Implicit Association Test." The following is from the website and explains something about the meaning and goal of the test:

> The categorization task you completed is called the Implicit Association Test (IAT). The task assesses associations between concepts by measuring how quickly a person can categorize, for example, GOOD words with White faces compared to GOOD words with Black faces. The test often reveals associations that are different than one's conscious beliefs. (https:// implicit.harvard.edu/implicit/Study?tid=-1

A second and major reading of the course is the book by John Hayes (2006) entitled Sub-merge, Living Deep in a Shallow World: Service, Justice and Contemplation Among the World's Poor. It has been recently added to the curriculum since it seemed that students required something more substantial to read that specifically targeted engagement with issues of social justice and vocation of ministry. The book includes stories, experiences, biblical and theological insights, and reflections - indeed, a manifesto and prophetical call - about the need for Christian believers to become incarnational in ministry to the poor and marginalized around the world. In 1983 Hayes founded InnerCHANGE in Los Angeles, a compassionate order among the poor and marginalized (www.innerchange.org).

The book is most helpful for the course because, first of all, it reminds students that any calling to ministry cannot exclude ministry to the poor and needy. Next, it helps students to address the contradiction that seems to exist within Western Christianity's preoccupation with the pursuit of wealth at the expense of identifying with the poor. Also, it introduces students to the plight of the poor and marginalized around the world and challenges them toward an incarnational model of ministry that will guide them as they "submerge" themselves into alleviating these needs. Students are not required to submit a reflection paper on the book, unfortunately. However, going forward it does seem wise for that to occur so that students can demonstrate in their writing how they have interacted with the material.

In the last week of the module of the course, students focus on issues of gender and the ministry. They read two pieces of literature: a short piece written by the B.T Roberts called Ordaining Women (1891) and an article by M. Robert Mullholland, Jr. Women and Men: Wives and Husband (date unknown). Here students are invited to consider the role of women in leadership and ministry. Surprising, this issue relates much to issues of social justice, especially within the ecclesial culture that has often been dominated by male preachers and leaders. Students are invited to discuss and debate the much bigger issue of women in ministry leadership positions. It does create some healthy tension among course participants, depending on the religious culture of the student and their particular biblio-theological stance on the matter.

Field Experiences. Another curricular approach involves the opportunity for students to participate in two field experiences by visiting the sites and writing one-page reflection papers. The first involves visiting a religious service of a culture and/or ethnicity different than that of the student, where the stated curricular objective is for the student to "Demonstrate a sensitivity to cultural, ethnic, and gender issues with regard to their importance for the vocation of ministry."

Students reflect upon the following questions while attending the service or ceremony: What worship styles are different? What worship styles are the same? How have I been received? At the conclusion of the module, students are required to submit a one-page reflection paper that features the cross-cultural experience and, in part, answers the above questions.

With this experience, students can move outside of their familiar social and religious zones and experience worship in settings where the languages, customs, economic statuses and cultures are different. The experience and reflection helps to expand their worldview, reminding them of the biblical writers vision that someday every "nation, tribe, people and language" will stand before God's throne in worship (Revelation 7:9).

A second visit includes participation in a service-learning project. Students are required to demonstrate a commitment to social justice by investing four hours of service in an organization or club that specifically provides services to the underprivileged or needy. This social justice focus is a significant emphasis within the Wesleyan theological tradition of John Wesley and thus is essential for students seeking ministry within a Wesleyan context or any theological tradition. The assignment is the cornerstone for helping them develop social justice awareness in their future vocation of ministry. It provides a needed and helpful application of the material in Hayes' book Submerge.

At the conclusion of the module, students submit a one-page reflection paper on their four-hour commitment. They describe how they felt and any note-worthy experiences of meeting persons or observing particular needs.

One student shared that the organization he joined with did something very radical and transformissional. The organization works to alleviate the sexual exploitation of women. For this project, they petitioned local florists to donate flowers and then as a group visited girls at the local strip club to deliver the flowers as a gift and pray for the girls. He states that the gesture was very appreciative. And, as a result of the ministry of this organization, one of the girls has left the club in pursuit of other jobs to support her family.

Another student shared a transformissional moment: the ministry she served with offered need-meeting ministries to the homeless. In one instance, a worker was able to build a strong relationship with a client and eventually lead that client to a faith commitment. The worker was able to follow up with the client for ongoing disciple-making, encouragement and ministry.

Finally, one student's transformissional learning involved reflecting critically about social justice and faith sharing. The student shared problem of helping homeless people with housing needs but leaving Jesus and his message of redemption "outside, in the street".

Missing from this assignment is student's reflections on past involvement in ministries of social justice and commitments required going forward to continue working for social justice in society. Students should also be required to identify their passions, giftedness, and the particular areas of concern where they could best serve. Likewise, students must enter into dialogue and critical reflection with course-mates on the experience, as this would increase the depth and richness of the experience.

Online Discussions. The third tool used to facilitate social justice learning in the course Vocation of Ministry is forum discussions. To date, it is the weakest link in the chain for learning about social justice and therefore needs considerable attention going forward. It is a less than effective approach because: (1) discussions are asynchronous, (2) course design requires revamping topics to include at least one week of discussion regarding social justice, (3) students often do not have time to remain engaged with the discussion beyond the required number of postings, thus impacting deep learning, (4) and the largest numbers of posts makes it difficult for the professor to effectively guide all students in the learning process.

That being said, one week is scheduled for students to discuss issues of gender and the ministry. It's helpful that students are exposed to substantive teachings through course readings, for in some instances a student embraces a position without knowing why they do.

One experience of transformissional learning for two participants involved the foci of character and community. The learners vigorously maintained opposing views: one supported women being called into ministry to lead the church and the other did not. However, the question posed had to do with maintaining love and respect for one another as brothers and sisters in Christ despite not being able to agree that a woman could be called by God to full-time ministry. Love and respect for others are ultimately a character issue; maintaining relationship with someone who disagrees with you is an issue of community.

So, as the students discussed the matter it became apparent the disagreements could not be resolved easily. In fact, one student spoke with me on the phone and shared the difficulties of the experience. While it was obvious the relationship between the two was strained, and that the matter wasn't resolved, the students were able to highlight the key question of love and respect in community, realizing that Christians pursuing a vocation in ministry ought always to pursue love and respect and maintain Christian brotherhood and sisterhood in the midst of disagreement. Thus, it's possible to suggest that they continued down the road toward the goal of transformissional learning.

Designing curricular approaches that foster transformissional learning must be an important objective for any facilitator of learning. As has been shown, by use of course readings, experiential learning approaches, critical reflection and writing, group dialogue, and instructor engagement in the learning process, the online environment can be a useful venue for students to be transformed for the sake of mission.

Conclusion

The advent of online learning offers the professor of mission opportunities to engage students from every corner of the world for social justice. Instructors continue ascending a steep learning curve of curricular theory and best practices for guiding online students forward. Thankfully, we are making progress. To foster continued engagement with best practices on the subject, this presentation featured curricular approaches from an extant online course taught

Asbury Theological Seminary, a course that included course objectives to advance student's understanding of and experience with social justice. By featuring a new approach to leadership development applied to learning – the transformissional paradigm – professors now have four areas of focus in which to develop curriculum for social justice and thus move students forward as transformissional agents of change in their culture.

Notes

1   Readers should review docstoc.com for a list of over 90 articles on this subject. Available at http://www.docstoc.com/docs/19878388/ SERVICE-LEARNING-ARTICLE (Accessed 11 May 2013).

2   I'm using the term social holiness interchangeably with the term social justice, although some would argue that we are not being faithful to John Wesley when we use these terms interchangeably. See Thompson A (2011) From Societies to Society: The Shift from Holiness to Justice in the Wesleyan Tradition. Methodist Review 3: 141-172.

3   Please see "The Trouble with Online Education," available at http://www.nytimes.com/2012/07/20/opinion/the-trouble-with-online-education.html?_r=0 (accessed 16 May 2013).

4   Ogne and Roehl do not limit the use of Transformissional coaching to church leaders, obviously, and are regularly involved in coaching leaders who serve in a variety of organizational contexts.

5   During the writing of this paper I've come to realize the need to offer students a basic understanding of this term, something that hasn't been done since I started facilitating the course. It's just assumed that students know what it means. However, when one student wrote me and asked if the service-learning project they participated in was a true social justice project, I realized then that if they have to ask me then it's likely they don't really grasp the meaning of the term.

Works Cited

Allen, I. and Seaman, J.
 2011 *Going the distance: Online education in the United States,* Report, Babson Survey Research Group and Quahog Research Group, LLC, Babson Park, MA, November.
 2013 *Changing course: Ten years of tracking online education in the United States.* Report, Babson Survey Research Group and Quahog Research Group, LLC, Babson Park, MA, January.

Caffarella, R. and Merriam, S.
 1999 *Perspectives on Adult Learning: Framing the Research.* Available at http://www.adulterc.org/Proceedings/1999/99caffarella.htm (accessed 15 May 2013).

Dinkins, B.
 2005 The Matrix of Vocation. In: *Living on Purpose: The Joy of Discovering and Following God's Call.* Dunnam, M. and Moore, S., eds. Franklin: Providence House Publishers, pp. 85-104.

Edmundson, M.
 2012 The trouble with online education. *The New York Times*, 19 July, 12. Available at http://www.nytimes.com/2012/07/20/opinion/the-trouble-with-online-education.html?_r=2& (accessed 12 May 2013).

Guthrie, K. and McCracken, H.
 2010a Making a difference online: Facilitating service learning through distance education. *Internet and Higher Education* 13: 153-157.
 2010b Teaching and learning social justice through online service-learning courses. *International Review of Research in Open and Distance Learning* 11(3): 78-94.

Hayes, J.
 2006 *Submerge - Living Deep in a Shallow World: Service, Justice and Contemplation Among the World's Poor.* Ventura: Regal Books.

Jacoby, B. and Associates
    1996   *Service-Learning in Higher Education: Concepts and Practices.* San Francisco: Jossey-Bass Inc.

Johnson, A.
    2011   From Societies to Society: The Shift from Holiness to Justice in the Wesleyan Tradition. *Methodist Review* 3: 141-172.

Kolb, D.
    1984   *Experiential Learning: Experience as the Source of Learning and Development.* Englewood Cliffs: Prentice-Hall, Inc.

McNeal, R.
    2011   *A Work of Heart: Understanding How God Shapes Spiritual Leaders.* San Francisco: Jossey-Bass.

Mulholland, R.
    ND   *Men and Women: Wives and Husbands.* Available at Asbury Seminary online Moodle Course Management System.

McIntosh, P.
    1990   White Privilege: Unpacking the Invisible Knapsack. *Independent School*, Winter, 1990: 31-36.

Ogne, S. and Roehl, T.
    2008   *Transformissional Coaching: Empowering Leaders in a Changing Ministry World.* Nashville: B&H Publishing Group.

Rauschenbusch, W.
    1907   *Christianity and the Social Crisis.* NY: Macmillan Press.

Roberts, B.
    1891   *Ordaining Women.* Available at http://fmcusa.org/wp-content/blogs.dir/45/files/downloads/2012/05/Ordaining_Women-1.pdf (accessed 23 May 2013).

Strait, J. and Sauer, T.
    2004   Constructing Experiential Learning for Online Courses: The Birth of E-Service. *Educause Quarterly* 1: 62-65.

Taylor, E. W.
    2008   Transformative learning theory. New directions for adult and continuing education. *New Directions for Adult and Continuing Education* Autumn 2008: 5–15. doi: 10.1002/ace.301.

Teaching Tolerance: A Project of the Southern Poverty Law Center
    2013   Test Yourself for Hidden Bias. Available at: http://www.tolerance.org/supplement/test-yourself-hidden-bias (accessed 19 May 2013).

Ullman, C. and Rabinowitz, M.
    2004   Course management systems and the reinvention of instruction. *THE Journal.* Available at http://thejournal.com/articles/2004/10/01/course-management-systems-and-the-reinvention-of-instruction.aspx (accessed 12 May 2013).

A Limited Survey of Theological Rationales Proposed for "Good Works" in Mission

TRAVIS L. MYERS

DOI: 10.7252/Paper.000020

About the Author:
Travis L. Myers (M.A. WCIU, M.Div. SBTS) is a Th. D. candidate (ABD) in missiology at Boston University School of Theology and Gordon-Conwell Theological Seminary. He serves Bethlehem College and Seminary in Minneapolis as Instructor of Missions and Church History and is a former member of faculty at the Cameroon Baptist Theological Seminary.

Abstract

This paper provides a limited though representative survey of some theological bases that have been proposed and/or appealed to for the necessary place of social action in mission. The four categories into which this paper organizes these theological bases, with sub-points, are: 1) The Mission of God, 2) The Kingdom of God, 3) The Commission and Commandments of God, and 4) The Exemplary Model of God. The focus is *not* on arguments for the integration of evangelism and social action in mission or the question of the relationship between them, but on a variety of rationales for the inclusion of social action *per se* in mission(s). Authors surveyed include Orlando Costas, Samuel Escobar, Rene Padilla, Richard Gibb, Andrew Kirk, Andrew Lord, Christopher J.H. Wright, Ron Sider, Tom Sine, Ajith Fernando, and Vinoth Ramachandra. The paper also considers the World Council of Church's 1982 document, "Mission and Evangelism: An Ecumenical Affirmation" since it is commended by evangelicals on occasion and is a document rich in theological justifications for social action in mission. This paper is primarily descriptive, though the author does offer in the conclusion some preliminary thoughts for the proper development of a critical response and his own position.

Introduction and Delimitation of the Topic

This papers provides a limited though representative survey of some theological bases that have been proposed for the necessary place of "social action," "loving deeds," or "mercy ministries" in the church's mission. I have tried to organize in a systematic way the rationale of several theologians, pastors, and Christian activists for the legitimate and obligatory place in mission of ministry to the material (physical) and social needs of individuals and communities as distinct from evangelistic verbal proclamation. My perusal of certain books and documents concerning mission revealed various theological *assumptions* as well as theological and exegetical *arguments* for the inclusion of "good works" in the church's missionary task. The focus of this survey is *not* on arguments for the *integration* of evangelism *and* social action in mission. Nor is this a survey of various positions concerning the relationship between social action(s) and verbal gospel proclamation and the question of "priority." I do include, though, a summary of a few proposals regarding this matter because in some instances a (singular or multifaceted) relationship between evangelism and social action is proposed as part of a larger argument for social action in mission. Finally, I have neither focused on nor critiqued the ideas that 1) social action alone can be an adequate expression of mission, 2) social action is a non-verbal gospel "witness" (i.e. a kind of *evangelism*), or 3) the beneficial outcomes of social action may be deemed a kind of "salvation."[1] The paper aims to be primarily descriptive, though I do venture in the conclusion to offer some preliminary thoughts for the proper development of a critical response and my own position.

Authors surveyed include those from Latin America (Orlando Costas, Samuel Escobar, and Rene Padilla), the United Kingdom (Richard Gibb, Andrew Kirk, Andrew Lord, and Christopher J.H. Wright), North America (Ron Sider, Tom Sine, and John Howard Yoder, e.g.), and Sri Lanka (Ajith Fernando and Vinoth Ramachandra). I have, though not exclusively, focused on evangelical contributors to missiological dialogue and have incorporated the World Council of Church's 1982 document, "Mission and Evangelism: An Ecumenical Affirmation."[2] It is a document dense with justifications for social action and is a source cited by some of the evangelicals surveyed here.[3] The four categories into which I've organized these theological bases are: 1) The Mission of God, 2) The Kingdom of God, 3) The Commission and Commandments of God, and 4) The Exemplary Model of God.

I. The Mission of God (or *missio Dei*)

Contemporary missiological debate "has been dominated" by the framing of mission as *missio Dei*, God's mission, often defined as God's (redemptive) presence and activity in history and the world that reaches beyond the influence of the church.[4] Explaining Christian mission as human participation in the *missio Dei* functions as an argument for social action in mission when *missio Dei* has been defined as including social agendas and implications. The mission of God, in this perspective, begins with the loving nature of a triune God who is both Sender and Sent One for the sake of loving/serving/ saving/blessing others.[5] The Bible's record of God's various actions in history is a revelation of the divine character and divine agenda in which Christians should share and participate with God. Christopher Wright's 500 page theology of mission, *The Mission of God: Unlocking the Bible's Grand Narrative*, is framed within a technical argument for (and exposition of) such a "missional hermeneutic."[6] According to Wright, because God's identity, character, and agenda are revealed in the Old Testament, a range of responses to that revelation by *Christian* readers are thereby rendered appropriate and "indeed imperative."[7]

A. God on Mission and All Creation

God is the loving and personal Creator who has made the world to be a home for persons created for relationship with him. Thus all creation, especially humans created in God's image (*imago Dei*), should be treated with respect.[8] Because sin and the Fall have corrupted all aspects of the created environment, all will likewise be restored via God's mission. Therefore, humans participating in God's mission should act to protect and rehabilitate the earth as God's possession and an appropriate habitat for other people. Mission should include efforts to remove structures and practices that disrespect individuals or societies.

B. God on mission and the Israelites

In the election of Israel as a particular people for God, God had a beneficent *universal* agenda in mind.[9] He would use these "offspring of Abraham" to bless all nations (even "families") of the earth (Gen 12:1-3). Sometimes the Abrahamic covenant functions as a theological basis for social action in mission when the universal blessing promised through Abraham is construed as including material benefit, social justice, or relief from suffering.[10] God's deliverance of the Israelites from slavery in Egypt is a paradigmatic Old Testament event. We see displayed in the Exodus that God is a God of liberation who is opposed to subjugation.[11] Therefore, Christian mission should include activity to liberate captives and relieve the oppressed. J. Andrew Kirk even states in his book, *What is Mission?* that:

> Justice is what God does, for justice is what God is. By definition he acts consistently with his attributes. So we know justice through God's acts of deliverance, through his laws and through the kind of relationships between human beings that he requires...[12]

Kirk then cites Micah 6:8, Isaiah 58:6 and Psalm 72:1-4 as examples of God's requirement of justice in human relationships. The Mosaic covenant's attention to specific matters of justice and the "shape" of Israel's life together[13] as well as the prophets' repeated exhortations concerning community relationships and social justice bear witness to God's character and mission. Wright points out that "the laws God gave and the prophets God sent" addressed social issues more than any other matter besides idolatry.[14] Orlando Costas sums up this perspective thusly:

> We must bear in mind that Christian mission is grounded on the mission of God as revealed in the history of Israel and incarnated in the person and work of Jesus Christ. The Old Testament discloses a God who is opposed to any attempts to subjugate; a God who is on the side of the widow and the orphan, the poor and the stranger; a God who raises the humble and casts down the oppressor; who frees from slavery, demands justice, freedom and peace.[15]

C. God on Mission and the Incarnation of the Christ

Costas succinctly correlates the ministry of Christ with this Old Testament theme of justice and liberation by calling the incarnation of Christ the "incarnation *of this mission*" (my emphasis). Jesus's "identification with the poor" and proclamation of wholeness, liberty, and restoration was the logical consequence of t/his identity, incarnation, and mission.[16] The fifth point of the WCC's "Mission and Evangelism" (1982) says:

> Jesus Christ was himself the complete revelation of God's love, manifested in justice and forgiveness through all aspects of his earthly life...In his obedience to the Father's will, in his love for humanity, he used many ways to reveal God's love to the world: forgiving, healing, casting out demons, teaching, proclaiming, denouncing, testifying in courts, finally surrendering his life.[17]

The document at this point goes on to infer, for the church, a corresponding and consequent "mission of love (Matt 22:37) through all aspects of its life." In a similar way, while not explicitly locating Jesus's ministry in the *missio Dei*, Samuel Escobar seems to assume this motif by joining in the common practice of referring to Jesus's "mission." Because Jesus's mission was "holistic," so, too, should the church's mission be, he reasons in, *The New Global Mission*.[18] He, of course, is also utilizing the theological basis of divine example or *model* that is presented in this paper below.[19] Andrew Lord asserts in his book, *Spirit-Shaped Mission: A Holistic Charismatic Missiology*, that since Jesus came "to destroy the works of the devil" (1 Jn 3:8), Christians should (and can!) engage in "holistic" ministry against evil powers as well.[20]

The gospel of Luke's presentation in chapter 4 (vss. 16-21) of Jesus's self-identification with the fulfillment of Isaiah 61:1-2 and 58:6 is a programmatic[21] text for several advocates of social action in mission. Kirk calls this text "the so-called 'Nazareth Manifesto.'" He affirms that this is Jesus's announcement of the beginning of a Jubilee age of mercy, compassion, and generosity rather than hoarded surplus.[22] Wright deems this a Jubilee age for a mission of "restoration."[23] In their book, *The Message of Mission*, Howard Peskett and Vinoth Ramachandra say the inauguration of this Jubilee "era of the Lord" by the messiah, Jesus, means the church must proclaim Jesus, bring release to others, love her enemies, and work for peace in the world.[24]

Wright enumerates five purposes of God's mission accomplished at/by the cross of Christ (which he calls "the unavoidable cost of God's total mission"): the guilt of human sin dealt with (Is 53:6; 1 Pet 2:24); the powers of evil defeated (Col 2:15); death destroyed (Heb 2:14); the barrier of enmity and alienation between Jew and Gentile removed (Eph 2:14-16); God's whole creation healed and reconciled (Col 1:15-16, 20).[25] Such a "holistic gospel" entails holistic mission by the church. The "Micah Declaration on Integral Mission" is a brief, evangelical document that posits at least a dozen theological bases for missional social involvement. Among them it includes, "On the cross God shows us how seriously he takes justice."[26] Therefore, its authors call upon Christians to "do justice." Ron Sider, in his book, *Good News and Good Works*, proposes a "messianic" model of the atonement that incorporates the three emphases of Jesus's work as teacher, substitute and victor. The human problems of ignorance, guilt, and powerlessness have been dealt with by the death of Christ so that his followers can now battle every manifestation of evil in the world.[27] Sometimes proponents of social action in mission appeal to Titus 2:14, "[Christ] gave himself for us to redeem us from all lawlessness and to purify for himself a people for his own possession who are zealous for good works."[28]

Sider posits the bodily resurrection of Christ, being proof and first-fruit of the future resurrection of Christians (1 Cor 15:35ff; cf. 2 Cor 5:1-4), as an affirmation of physicality as well as of ministry to whole persons. "If the body is so good that the Creator became flesh, rose bodily, and promises to restore the whole created order including our bodies, then any approach to human need that ignores or neglects physical needs is flatly heretical."[29] Besides this theological affirmation and inference, there is an appeal made by some to the resurrection as a divine turning point in the history of redemption. The eighth point of "Mission and Evangelism" asserts:

> The Church proclaims Jesus, risen from the dead. Through the resurrection, God vindicates Jesus, and opens up a new period of missionary obedience until he comes again (Acts 1:11). The power of the risen and crucified Christ is now released. It is the new birth to a new life, because as he took our predicament on the cross, he also took us into a new life in his

resurrection. 'When anyone is united to Christ, there is a new creation, the old has passed away, behold the new has come' (II Cor 5:17).

D. God on Mission via Pentecost and the Apostolic Church

"Mission and Evangelism" continues from this point to a section about conversion and Christian lifestyles. New birth by the Spirit (Jn 3:3) produces a "total transformation of our attitudes and styles of life" characterized by obedience to God's commands. Personal growth in "restoration of the divine image" is experienced.[30] Earlier in the document reference is made to Pentecost (Acts 2:1-39) and the Spirit's coming to the Christian community so that *through them* "the world may be healed and redeemed."[31] The redemptive mission of God in the transformative process of salvation (i.e. *sanctification*) is a theological basis for the one experiencing this change of lifestyle to be at work in a godly, redemptive manner.

Sider, Wright, and Kirk appeal to cosmic redemption (Rom 8:18ff; Col 1:19-20; cf. 2:15) and the new creation (Rev 21:1-22:5), a redemption in response to the Spirit-enabled groaning of the subjected created order, as a basis for social or ecological ministries in mission. Though there is a future, discontinuous aspect to this redemptive action of God (i.e. it will be finally and cataclysmically accomplished at Christ's return), they each assert, for different reasons, that its future certainty entails social action or ecological ethics in mission *now*.[32] Wright says in *The Mission of God*, "Our efforts therefore have a prophetic value in pointing toward the full cosmic realizing of that truth."[33] Elsewhere he writes, "If the planet was created by Christ, sustained by Christ, and belongs to Christ as his inheritance, the least we can do is look after it properly."[34] Kirk seems to echo Wright's assertion of the prophetic value or function of social ministry when he concludes:

[God] is still concerned to service and repair a broken down version of the world, showing what even a partial restoration to life can be like; though eventually a new model will be needed. He is fulfilling his purpose through the consecrated hands and minds of those who know the grace of the Lord Jesus Christ (2 Cor. 8:9).[35]

There is another way that the *missio Dei* motif allegedly provides a theological basis for social action in mission. Sometimes it is simply asserted that beneficiaries of God's broadly redemptive mission should, and/or necessarily (by definition) *do*, become instruments of multidimensional grace. The "Micah Declaration" states, "The grace of God is the heartbeat of integral mission. As recipients of undeserved love we are to show grace, generosity, and inclusiveness."[36] "Mission and Evangelism" states regarding 2 Corinthians 8:9, "To believe in Jesus the King is to accept his undeserved grace and enter with him into the kingdom, taking sides with the poor struggling to overcome poverty."[37]

II. The Kingdom of God

Sider noted in 1993 that use of the word "kingdom" was growing at that time, being employed by social activists, charismatic Christians, and proponents of world evangelization alike.[38] The theological themes of *missio Dei* and the Kingdom of God are closely related and overlapping. Rene Padilla has said the mission of the church is the mission of the reign of God.[39] Various aspects of the kingdom and the church's relationship to it are posited as rationale for social action in mission. The Spirit's role/work in the kingdom is sometimes noted, as is the inspiration to action that the coming kingdom's current (partial, anticipatory) presence provokes.

A. Church and Kingdom

Sider proposes the kingdom motif as the framework comprehensive enough for capturing what the church in mission should be about.[40] What follows is a summary of four relationships between the church and kingdom that are appealed to by various authors as theological rationales for social action by the church in mission.

1. Church as manifestation of the kingdom: Padilla, in *Mission Between the Times: Essays on the Kingdom*, deems the pre-crucifixion mission of Jesus a manifestation of the kingdom in both Jesus's preaching and works.[41] It is the church that, in the post-Pentecost era, "embodies the blessings of the new [kingdom] age."[42] Andrew Lord writes, "Holistic mission flows from the blessings of the eschatological kingdom that has been already inaugurated. It is a kingdom filled with the blessings of liberation, mercy, care, justice, reconciliation and healing."[43] The "Micah Declaration" says that local churches are communities that "embody the values of the kingdom," addressing the causes and results of poverty.[44] In a study of four "holistic" ministries (in London, Mexico City, Colombia, and the Philippines) researcher Thomas McAlpine encountered the following form of this kingdom rationale (quoting one ministry leader in reflection on Matthew 6:10): "As someone has put it, the work of the kingdom is not so much to get people out of earth into heaven, but to get as much of heaven as possible on to the earth and into people."[45]

2. Church as instrument of the kingdom: The church that embodies the kingdom is a church through which the kingdom is coming. Another ministry leader interviewed by McAlpine alluded to Matthew 6:33 and said, "We are trying to set all our church goals in terms of the kingdom of God and recognize that the church is not an end in itself but a means to an end: the end being the establishment of the kingdom rule of God in all areas of the life of our community."[46] Padilla links the Holy Spirit's creation of a new kingdom lifestyle among Christians with the church's continuation and extension of the kingdom.[47] In Richard Gibb's monograph, *Grace and Global Justice: The Socio-Political Mission of the Church in an Age of Globalization*, Gibb infers the church's responsibility "to be engaged in multidimensional liberating activity in the contemporary world" from the universality of God's reign in the world, a reign "that includes not only the personal and spiritual dimensions, but also the social and political realities of human existence." The church serves as embodiment and instrument of the kingdom because the kingdom is both a present and future reality; it is "already" and "not yet."[48]

3. Church as sign of the kingdom: The church as a visible sign for the world of the kingdom's reality and presence is a prominent aspect of the ecclesiological project of Stanley Hauerwas and William Willimon in their book, *Resident Aliens*. The church demonstrates and *explicates* the meaning of the peace and justice that the kingdom brings.[49] Padilla, integrating the concepts of the mission of God and kingdom of God, as well as the doctrines of pneumatology and ecclesiology, says:

God is at work to bring about his purpose for creation. The church in the power of the Spirit proclaims salvation in Christ and plants signs of the Kingdom, always giving itself fully to the work of the Lord, knowing that its labor in the Lord is not in vain (1 Cor. 15:58).[50]

The Micah Declaration says the "signs of the Kingdom" provided by the church attest to the credibility of the church's truth claims and proclamation of the gospel message.[51] A church without these signs can actually "put off" persons otherwise attracted to the person of Christ.[52]

4. *Church as subjects in the kingdom*: Padilla provides another helpful category in his typology of the kingdom's relationship to the church. The church is the community of the messiah; it is *his* church (Mat 16:18). Christians are his subjects in his kingdom. His Spirit empowers their obedience and brings about the "new society" of their life together in the kingdom.[53] As the king's subjects, Christians should obey the commands of Christ, commands to love and good works (see below). Sider appeals to Jesus's warning in Matthew 25 of *false* faith in and/or submission to Christ in order to reinforce the necessity of ministry to the sick, poor, and those in prison.[54]

B. Good Works and Good News in/of the Kingdom

Sider prefers a kingdom framework for thinking about the church's mission because, he claims, it so indisputably holds together in balance both "good news" and "good works." The gospel Jesus proclaimed and delegated to his disciples was not that of individual escape from hell after death but a gospel of God's real and current reign, with real consequences, on earth. The brevity of this paper does not allow for a survey of the proposed relationships between evangelism and social action or the question of which one, if either, has "priority" (and, if so, in what way[s]).[55] However, three aspects of that debate are pertinent to this survey.

First, the idea of social action as a "bridge" to evangelism resonates with the sign concept. Escobar quotes the "Grand Rapids Report on Evangelism and Social Responsibility" to explicate what he means by the bridge idea: "[social activity] can break down prejudice and suspicion, open closed doors and gain a hearing for the gospel."[56] One aspect of this bridging dynamic is the provision by good works of credibility for the good news. Second, the church as manifestation of the kingdom is used as a theological basis by proponents of evangelistic priority as well as (ironically) advocates for social action in mission. The former argue that evangelism must be theologically and temporally prior to good works since good works (of the kingdom) are only done, and always done, by those already converted.[57] Third, Sider bolsters his well-nuanced kingdom framework by citing a helpful caveat made by Orlando Costas: good works have an evangelistic *dimension* whether or not the one doing them consciously *intends* them to be "pre-evangelistic."[58]

III. The Commission and Commandments of God

Rationales for social action in mission include appeals to biblical imperatives, or mandates, and the attendant obligation of Christians to obey them.

A. Great Commission (Making Disciples)

Peskett and Ramachandra include, of course, an exposition of Matthew 28:16-20 in their theology of mission. Being (and making) disciples who obey all that Jesus has commanded (Mat 28:20a) entails living a life of "kingdom-revealing, law-fulfilling, justice-righteousness."[59] Costas asserts that the "missionary mandate" given by Christ to his disciples was given "in [the] perspective" of the Nazareth Manifesto of Luke 4:16-20. "Jesus commands his disciples to continue his work under guidance through the power of the Holy Spirit."[60] Therefore, healing and liberation are missionary activities. Kirk considers John 20:21 to be "the most all-encompassing of the New Testament's texts on mission." For Kirk, being sent out in mission in the same manner that Jesus was sent means doing evangelism, justice, compassion, and non-violence.[61]

B. Greatest Commandment

In Sider's discussion of proper resource allocation in local churches, he considers the parallel texts of Matthew 22:34-40 and Mark 12:28-34. Here Jesus says the "greatest commandment" is to love God and one's neighbor. Sider concludes from this that an approximately equal amount of resources should be devoted to evangelism and social action respectively.[62] In addition, Jesus's commandment to love one's enemies (Mat 5:44, e.g.) is cited by many who advocate social action in mission, especially peacemaking ministries.[63]

C. Epistolary Exhortations

Besides theological constructs derived from the gospels and the commandments of Jesus in the gospels, some advocates of good works in mission appeal to exhortations in the apostolic epistles to early churches. Kirk quotes Paul's instructions to the church in Rome that they "live peaceably with all" and feed hungry enemies (Rom 12:17-21). He takes this as a command to engage in ministries of "overcoming violence and building peace, mission in the way of Christ."[64] One can also find appeals to Galatians 6:10a ("Do good to all people...") in the literature. David Hesselgrave, in his book, *Paradigms in Conflict*, names James 1:27 in a list of seven arguments used by (what he terms) "holists" for their conviction that social action is as vital to mission as is evangelism.[65] While not a direct command, the hortatory import is clear.

D. Stewardship Mandate

The Christian responsibility to steward God's created order receives much attention in Wright's project.[66] He grounds this responsibility fourfold in 1) God's ownership of the good earth, 2) the earth-keeping mandate given to Adam (Gen 2:15), 3) the created realm's redemption by Christ (Col 1:15-16, 20), and 4) "the earth as the field of God's mission and ours." The "Micah Declaration" says:

> There is a need for integral discipleship involving the responsible and sustainable use of the resources of God's creation and the transformation of the

moral, intellectual, economic, cultural and political dimensions of our lives. For many of us this includes recovering a biblical sense of stewardship.[67]

Sider also appeals to a Christian responsibility to steward the earth, citing Genesis 1:27-30, Genesis 2:15, and Matthew 5:45 (noting the precedent of God's care for all created things).[68] Padilla urges affluent nations and individuals to recognize "that economic life has meaning only in the context of human solidarity and stewardship and responsibility."[69]

IV. The Exemplary Model of God

The final theological basis or rationale in this survey is that of God as exemplary model. God the Father and God the incarnate Son are each posited as models for imitation by Christians on mission (or in missions).

A. The Character of the Father

As noted above, Wright's project begins with the seminal idea that the character and identity of God, revealed via his mission in history, entails mission by the people of God. The reasons for this inference include the fact of humans in the *imago Dei* and commandments grounded in the character of God, such as "Be holy because I, the LORD your God, am holy" (Lev 29:2).[70] Holiness, as explicated by Wright, includes social ethics. The "Micah Declaration" says that the cross reveals, "how seriously [God] takes justice" and implies the need to imitate this concern for justice on the part of Christians in integral mission.[71]

Kirk appeals to the concept of God as Father and exhorts those who claim to be God's children to prove their asserted identity and relationship to God by imitating his care for the unrighteous and his mercy upon them, even to those who would be their enemies (and God's enemies).[72] Andrew Lord appeals to the fact that the restored *imago Dei* in redeemed persons is the image of a merciful God. The godly characteristic of mercy ought to motivate ministries of healing and social work.[73] Lord notes the compassionate heart of God is communicated to the Church by way of the Holy Spirit.[74]

Though Sider rejects liberation theology's prioritization of God's alleged "preferential option" for the poor, he does remind readers of God's real concern for the poor and the revealed fact that those who do not seek justice for them do not properly know God (citing Jer 22:13-16; Mat 25). McAlpine notes that while "holistic" mission does not happen exclusively among the poor, faithful ministries will *inevitably* work among *and with* them because of what Psalm 103:6 reveals about God: "The LORD works vindication and justice [or "righteousness"] for all who are oppressed."[75]

B. The Incarnation of the Son

Ajith Fernando deems Jesus to be "the message and model of mission."[76] Escobar unpacks a "Christological paradigm" for mission, an "incarnational pattern" for service in his chapter, "Christ: God's Best Missionary." It is a pattern that should be "taken seriously" and imitated by missionaries today.[77] Sider says that because Jesus taught by word *and* deed, modeling the good news he proclaimed, so should Christians do both in mission.[78] Christology teaches us to do ministry to whole persons, he says.[79]

For Fernando, the incarnation of the Christ means that Christ followers must live lives committed to others to such a degree that Christians share in their sufferings.[80] Like Jesus (and Paul), Christians should choose deprivation for the sake of holistic mission (citing, among other verses, Philippians 2:7-8).[81] Gibb concludes in his study of globalization that Christians should imitate Christ as servant, identifying with the marginalized in a global society for the sake of bringing them tangible benefits.[82] Costas, likewise, sees in the messianic life of Jesus an example of identification with the deprived and marginalized for *and with* whom the contemporary missionary labors.[83] Peskett and Ramachandra, in exposition of Luke 4:16-30, poignantly state:

> Given Jesus's orientation of his ministry towards the 'nobodies' and the 'outsiders' (i.e. 'the poor') of his society, our own relation to 'the poor' of our

contemporary societies, and indeed our global world, becomes not merely a question of 'social ethics' but lies at the heart of our response to the gospel itself. Repentance must include a turning away from complicity in unjust structures of exclusion and repression, and a turning in compassion towards the dispossessed, the rejected and the oppressed.[84]

The "Micah Declaration" says near its conclusion, "We want to see those living in poverty through the eyes of Jesus who, as he looked on the crowds, had compassion on them because they were harassed and helpless like sheep without a shepherd."[85]

Concluding Remarks and Prolegomena to a Proposal

This has been a mere limited sample of arguments and assumptions made by pastors, theologians, and activists in building their respective arguments for the inclusion of social action or "good deeds" in mission(s).[86] Not all of them, in my opinion, are the product of sound exegetical and/or appropriate hermeneutical practice. That said, it should be self-evident that any scholarly attempt to define the "mission of the church" and/or the task of Christian "missions" must be aware of and interact with these several overlapping (even *interlocking*) theological rationales that I have categorized here as having to do with either "The Mission of God," "The Kingdom of God," "The Commission and Commandments of God," and/or "The Exemplary Model of God."

The late missions historian Stephen Neill famously quipped that, "When everything is mission, nothing is mission." Recent books by conservative Reformed evangelicals address their authors' concern that "mission creep" is wrongly marginalizing evangelistic ministry and unduly burdening believers with more obligations than can realistically be met (or than is biblical, anyway).[87] The concern that churches and individual Christians abandon neither verbal articulation of the *evangel* nor attention to making Christian disciples from among *every nation* is a legitimate concern; it is also shared by several (if not all) of those whose views I have surveyed here. Question begging can cloud the debate about the definition of "missions" if the discussion does not pertain as well to the matter of ecclesiology. The resolution to this apparent impasse, I propose, is to always consider Scripture's robust *ontology* of the church (versus mere *marks* of the "true" church) while maintaining some kind of *terminology* that clearly distinguishes pioneer church planting work among all ethno-linguistic people groups on earth from everything else the church *is*, does, and *should be* doing (while promoting *all* of it).

Finally, in a similar way that the kingdom framework holds in balance the place of good news and good works, so does a "discipleship among the nations" motif or framework because it encompasses "all that [the resurrected King Jesus] commanded," whether some particular activity is agreed upon as "mission(s)" or not. The local church is the divinely intended milieu and means for Christian discipleship, including evangelistic activity, cross-cultural mission, and the spiritual formation of converts.[88] Church planting is the work of initiating *and being* a new expression of all that a congregation is supposed to be - as a company of Spirit-empowered (as well as Spirit-acted upon and Spirit-utilized) disciples in covenant relationship - albeit in a new and different place or among a new and different people. It would seem, then, that acts of love, mercy, and even justice amongst themselves (i.e. toward "one another"), toward other Christians, and toward unbelieving neighbors should be part of their experience from the beginning of the new congregation's life together. Love, mercy, and justice should also be experienced as a manifestation and extension of the corporate life and ministries of the sending, birthing, and "mothering" congregation or congregations that temporarily nurture a nascent body.

Notes

1   For biblical-theological arguments against the identification of social justice as an aspect of "salvation," see the appendix in Ronald J. Sider, Good News and Good Works: A Theology for the Whole Gospel (Grand Rapids: Baker Books, 1993), 196-209.

2   World Council of Churches (WCC), "Mission and Evangelism: An Ecumenical Affirmation," in International Bulletin of Missionary Research (April 1983), 65-71.

3   E.g. Howard Peskett and Vinoth Ramachandra, The Message of Mission (Downers Grove: InterVarsity Press, 2003), and Sider, Good News and Good Works.

4   Nigerian diocesan priest and Catholic professor of missiology, Francis Anekwe Oborji, points out this preoccupation with missio Dei and the tendency in its wider definition toward the secularization of mission in his Concepts of Mission: The Evolution of Contemporary Missiology (Maryknoll: Orbis, 2006), 29-30. Charles Van Engen's Mission on the Way: Issues in Mission Theology (Grand Rapids: Baker Books, 1996) is an example of evangelical missiology in which the mission of God idea plays a prominent and pervasive role. Van Engen maintains an ecclesiocentric position. For brief a history of the evolution of the missio Dei concept among ecumenicals, see David J. Bosch, Transforming Mission: Paradigm Shifts in Theology of Mission (Maryknoll: Orbis, 1991; third printing 2007), 389-309; cf. Kirsteen Kim, The Holy Spirit in the World: A Global Conversation (Maryknoll: Orbis, 2007), 28-31. See also John G. Flett, The Witness of God: The Trinity, Missio Dei, Karl Barth, and the Nature of Christian Community (Grand Rapids: Eerdmans, 2010).

5   So Andrew Lord cites Bosch, Transforming Mission, 390, in his Spirit-Shaped Mission: A Holistic Charismatic Missiology (Waynesboro, GA: Paternoster, 2005), 20. See also WCC, "Mission and Evangelism," in IBMR (April 1983), 65-66.

6   Christopher J.H. Wright, The Mission of God: Unlocking the Bible's Grand Narrative (Downers Grove: IVP Academic, 2006), esp. chapters 1 and 2.

7   Wright, The Mission of God, 54.

8   Wright, The Mission of God, chapters 12 and 13; J. Andrew Kirk, What is Mission? Theological Explorations (Minneapolis: Fortress Press, 2000), 103; Peskett and Ramachandra, The Message of Mission, chapter 2; John Howard Yoder, For the Nations: Essays Public & Evangelical (Grand Rapids: Eerdmans, 1997), 182; C. Rene Padilla and Tom Sine, "Micah Declaration on Integral Mission," at the Micah Challenge website, 1. Accessed at micahchallenge.org/article.aspx?menuid=546.

9   Wright, The Mission of God, chapter 6.

10 Ibid.; Yoder, For the Nations, 183; Peskett and Ramachandra, The Message of Mission, chapter 5.

11 Orlando Costas, "Captivity and Liberation in the Modern Mission Movement," in Landmark Essays in Mission and World Christianity, eds. Robert L. Gallagher and Paul Hertig (Maryknoll: Orbis, 2009), 44; Kirk, What is Mission?, 104; Wright, The Mission of God, 265f.

12 Kirk, 104.

13 Yoder, 183.

14 Christopher J.H. Wright, "Whole Gospel, Whole Church, Whole World: We must believe, live, and communicate all that makes the Christian message staggeringly comprehensive good news," in Christianity Today vol 53 no 10 (Oct 2009), 32.

15 Costas, "Captivity and Liberation in the Modern Mission Movement," in Landmark Essays in Mission and World Christianity, 44.

16 Costas, 44.

17 WCC, 66.

18 Samuel Escobar, The New Global Mission: The Gospel from Everywhere to Everyone (Downers Grove: IVP Academic, 2003), 143.

19 See pages 13-15.

20 Andrew Lord in his Spirit-Shaped Mission, 72-73, building upon Walter Wink, Naming the Powers: The Language of Power in the New Testament (Philadelphia: Fortress Press, 1984), 105.

21 Andrew Lord call this text "programmatic" in reference to Luke's portrayal of Jesus's identity and/or Jesus's understanding of his own mission, 63-64.

22 Kirk, 106-107.

23 Wright, The Mission of God, 306-316.

24 Peskett and Ramachandra, 165-171.

25 Wright, The Mission of God, 312-313.

26 Padilla and Sine, "Micah Declaration," 1.

27 Sider, Good News and Good Works, 98-100. Cf. C. Rene Padilla, "Wholistic Mission: Evangelical and Ecumenical," in Constructive Christian Theology in the Worldwide Church, ed. William R. Barr (Grand Rapids: Eerdmans, 1997), 427.

28 The Holy Bible: English Standard Version (Wheaton: Crossway Bibles, 2001).

29 Sider, 142.

30 WCC, 67.

31 Ibid., 66. Cf. Yoder, 183, who appeals to the new lifestyle that was "spread...across the Mediterranean world," by the "apostolic missionary community" (emphasis mine).

32 Sider actually draws the conclusion directly without any mediating reason given. Sider, 95.

33 Wright, The Mission of God, 411.

34 Wright, "Whole Gospel, Whole Church, Whole World," in Christianity Today (Oct 2009), 33.

35 Kirk, 55.

36 Padilla and Sine, 1.

37   WCC, 66. Cf. C. Rene Padilla's call for Christians to "take seriously" (i.e. imitate) Christ's "evangelical poverty" in his Mission Between the Times: Essays on the Kingdom (Grand Rapids: Eerdmans, 1985), 137.

38   Sider, 49. It seems that interest in the kingdom motif is unabated, if perhaps surpassed now by attention to trinitarian and pneumatological models.

39   Padilla, "Wholistic Mission," 428.

40   Sider, 75f. Cf. McAlpine who asserts that the kingdom is the framework in which the church has meaning. Thomas H. McAlpine, By Word, Work and Wonder: Cases in Holistic Mission (Monrovia, CA: MARC, 1995), 112.

41   Padilla, Mission Between the Times: Essays on the Kingdom, 189.

42   Ibid., 68f.

43   Lord, 51.

44   Padilla and Sine, 2.

45   McAlpine, By Word, Work and Wonder: Cases in Holistic Mission, 111.

46   Ibid., 112.

47   Padilla, Mission Between the Times, 191-192.

48   Richard Gibb, Grace and Global Justice: The Socio-Political Mission of the Church in an Age of Globalization (Eugene, OR: Wipf & Stock/ Paternoster, 2006), 207-208. On the mission implications of the kingdom's dual essence (present and future), see also Padillia, Mission Between the Times, 198-199.

49   Stanley Hauerwas and William Willimon, Resident Aliens: Life in the Christian Colony (Nashville: Abingdon, 1989), 38. Quoted by McAlpine, 126.

50   Padilla, Mission Between the Times, 196-197.

51   Padilla and Sine, 2; Sider, 179f.

52   WCC, 67. This is reminiscent of Lesslie Newbigin's designation of the Christian community as "plausibility structure" for the gospel message or claims of Christ.

53   Padilla, Mission Between the Times, 190-191.

54   Sider, 144.

55   For an introduction to this debate, see David J. Hesselgrave, Paradigms in Conflict: 10 Key Questions in Christian Missions (Grand Rapids: Kregel, 2005), chapter 4. Hesselgrave argues for the "primacy" of evangelism. For a more nuanced presentation of the prioritist position, see J. Robertson McQuilken, "An Evangelical Assessment of Mission Theology of the Kingdom of God," in The Good News of the Kingdom: Mission Theology for the Third Millennium, eds. Charles Van Engen, Dean S. Gilliland and Paul Pierson (Maryknoll: Orbis, 1993), 172-178. See also Sider, chapter 10, for a nuanced proposal.

56   Escobar, The New Global Mission, 152, quoting the document as published in Making Christ Known: Historic Mission Documents from the Lausanne Movement 1974-1989, ed. John R. Stott (Grand Rapids: Eerdmans, 1996), 185. Cf. Lord, 48, for his citation of Stott's quotation of the document using the "bridge" metaphor in Stott's introductory essay to Making Christ Known, 20.

57   McQuilken, "An Evangelical Assessment of Mission Theology of the Kingdom of God," 177.

58   Sider, 163-164, citing Orlando Costas, Liberating News: A Theology of Contextual Evangelization (Grand Rapids: Eerdmans, 1989), 136ff.

59   Peskett and Ramachandra, 187.

60   Costas, 44.

61   Kirk, 38-55.

62   Sider, 168-171.

63   E.g. Kirk, 145.

64   Kirk, 146.

65   Hesselgrave, Paradigms in Conflict, 124. Hesselgrave does not cite specific examples, but is an older missiologist who must be familiar with much of the relevant material. Hesselgrave also lists as bases for holism: God's love and compassion for the poor, the exodus deliverance as paradigmatic, the character of the kingdom of God, the Great Commandment (to love), the Great Commission (to make disciples who obey all that Jesus commanded), and the example of the early church.

66   See especially The Mission of God, chapter 12.

67   Padilla and Sine, 2.

68   Sider, 141.

69   Padilla, Mission Between the Times, 140.

70   Wright, The Mission of God, 369-375.

71   Padilla and Sine, 1.

72   Kirk, 145-146. Cf. Sider, 141.

73   Lord, 18.

74   Ibid., 28. Citing Mark Stibbe's summary of John Wimber's charismatic theology of mission in Stibbe's, Revival (Crowborough: Monarch, 1998), 18.

75   McAlpine, 131.

76   Ajith Fernando, "Grounding our reflections in Scripture: biblical trinitarianism and mission," in Global Missiology for the 21st Century: The Iguassu Dialogue, ed. William D. Taylor (Grand Rapids: Baker Academic/World Evangelical Fellowship, 2000), chapter 14.

77   Escobar, 106-111.

78   Sider, 71.

79   Ibid., 143-145.

80   Fernando, "Grounding our reflections in Scripture: biblical trinitarianism and mission," 211.

81   Ibid., 220.

82   Gibb, Grace and Global Justice, 207-208.

83   Costas, 44.

84   Peskett and Ramachandra, 166.

85   Padilla and Sine, 2.

86   E.g. I have omitted the argument from hope or "inspiration" to social action in mission. Gibb finds this inspiration from the atonement, the resurrection (of both Christ and believers), and the future redemption of the cosmos at Christ's return, 208. The "Micah Declaration" posits "treasure in heaven" as a motivation for integrated mission, 2. Padilla finds in expressions of the inaugurated kingdom the promise of its future consummation and inspiration for more social action in "mission between the times," 199. A critical engagement of the issue should include an exegetical consideration of what New Testament authors mean by the Greek term hoi ptōchoi ("the poor"). For contrasting views see Peskett and Ramachandra, 159-161, citing David J. Bosch, Transforming Mission, 99, and Joel Green, The Gospel of Luke, New International Commentary on the New Testament (Grand Rapids: Eerdmans, 1997), 206, on one hand, and Hesselgrave, 128-136, citing Darrell L. Bock, Luke: The NIV Application Commentary (Grand Rapids: Zondervan, 1996), I. Howard Marshall, Luke: Historian and Theologian (Grand Rapids: Zondervan, 1970), William J. Larkin, Jr., "Mission in Luke," in Mission in the New Testament: An Evangelical Approach, ed. W.J. Larkin Jr. and J.F. Williams (Maryknoll: Orbis, 1998) contra Ronald J. Sider, Rich Christians in an Age of Hunger, 2d ed. (Dallas: Word, 1990), 45, on the other.

87   E.g. Michael Horton, The Gospel Commission: Recovering God's Strategy for Making Disciples (Grand Rapids, MI: Baker Books, 2011; also, Kevin DeYoung and Greg Gilbert, What Is the Mission of the Church? Making Sense of Social Justice, Shalom, and the Great Commission (Wheaton, IL: Crossway, 2011). These authors posit a theological and practical distinction between the institutional and the organic church. They argue that a Word- and ordinance-centered great commission to make disciples belongs to the former while the great commandment and stewardship mandate belong to the latter in a way that affords great freedom to individual Christians as to how they apply them.

88   Craig Ott and Stephen J. Strauss, Encountering Theology of Mission: Biblical Foundations, Historical Developments, and Contemporary Issues (Grand Rapids, MI: Baker Academic, 2010), chapter 8; Jedidiah Coppenger, "The Community of Mission: The Church" in Bruce Riley Ashford, ed., Theology and Practice of Mission: God, the Church, and the Nations (Nashville, TN: B&H Academic, 2011), 60-75; and Christopher W. Stenschke, "Paul's Mission as the Mission of the Church" in Robert L. Plummer and John Mark Terry, eds., Paul's Missionary Methods: In His Time and Ours (Downers Grove, IL: IVP Academic, 2012), 74-94.

Works Cited

Adeyemo, Tokunboh
    2000   "Profiling a globalized and Evangelical missiology." In *Global Missiology for the 21st Century: The Iguassu Dialogue.* Ed. William D. Taylor, 259-270. Grand Rapids: Baker Academic/World Evangelical Fellowship.

Ashford, Bruce Riley, ed.
    2011   *Theology and Practice of Mission: God, the Church, and the Nations.* Nashville, TN: B&H Academic.

Bosch, David J.
    2009   "Reflections on Biblical Models of Mission." In *Landmark Essays in Mission and World Christianity.* Eds. Robert L. Gallagher and Paul Hertig, 3-16. Maryknoll, NY: Orbis.
    2007   *Transforming Mission: Paradigm Shifts in Theology of Mission.* Maryknoll, NY: Orbis, 1991. Third printing.

Costas, Orlando
    2009   "Captivity and Liberation in the Modern Missionary Movement." In *Landmark Essays in Mission and World Christianity.* Eds. Robert L. Gallagher and Paul Hertig, 33-45. Maryknoll, NY: Orbis.

DeYoung, Kevin and Greg Gilbert
    2011   *What Is the Mission of the Church? Making Sense of Social Justice, Shalom, and the Great Commission.* Wheaton IL: Crossway.

Escobar, Samuel J.
    2009   "Mission Studies: Past, Present and Future." In *Landmark Essays in Mission and World Christianity.* Eds. Robert L. Gallagher and Paul Hertig, 219-243. Maryknoll, NY: Orbis.
    2003   *The New Global Mission: The Gospel from Everywhere to Everyone.* Downers Grove: IVP Academic.

Fernando, Ajith
>   2000   "Grounding our reflections in Scripture: biblical trinitarianism and mission." In *Global Missiology for the 21ˢᵗ Century: The Iguassu Dialogue*. Ed. William D. Taylor, 189-256. Grand Rapids: Baker Academic/ World Evangelical Fellowship.

Gibb, Richard
>   2006   *Grace and Global Justice: The Socio-Political Mission of the Church in an Age of Globalization*. Eugene, OR: Wipf and Stock/Paternoster.

Hauerwas, Stanley and William Willimon
>   1989   *Resident Aliens: Life in the Christian Colony*. Nashville: Abingdon.

Hesselgrave, David J.
>   2005   *Paradigms in Conflict: 10 Key Questions in Christian Missions Today*. Grand Rapids: Kregel.

Horton, Michael.
>   2011   *The Gospel Commission: Recovering God's Strategy for Making Disciples*. Grand Rapids, MI: Baker Books.

Kirk, J. Andrew
>   2000   *What is Mission? Theological Explorations*. Minneapolis: Fortress Press.

Lord, Andrew
>   2005   *Spirit-Shaped Mission: A Holistic Charismatic Missiology*. Waynesboro, GA: Paternoster.

McAlpine, Thomas H.
>   1995   *By Work, Word, and Wonder*. Monrovia, CA: MARC Publications.

McQuilkin, J. Robertson
>   1993   "An Evangelical Assessment of Mission Theology of the Kingdom of God." In *The Good News of the Kingdom: Mission Theology for the Third Millennium*. Eds. Charles Van Engen, Dean S. Gilliland and Paul Pierson, 172-178. Maryknoll, NY: Orbis.

Oborji, Francis Anekwe
    2006   *Concepts of Mission: The Evolution of Contemporary Missiology.* Maryknoll: Orbis.

Padilla, C. Rene
    1997   "Wholistic Mission: Evangelical and Ecumenical." In *Constructive Christian Theology in the Worldwide Church.* Ed. William R. Barr, 426-428. Grand Rapids: Eerdmans.
    1985   *Mission Between the Times: Essays on the Kingdom.* Grand Rapids: Eerdmans.

Padilla, C. Rene and Tom Sine
    ND   "Micah Declaration on Integral Mission." Micah Challenge. Accessed online at micahchallenge.org/article.aspx?menuid=546.

Peskett, Howard and Vinoth Ramachandra
    2003   *The Message of Mission.* In *The Bible Speaks Today.* Ed. Derek Tidball. Downers Grove: InterVarsity Press.

Plummer, Robert L. and John Mark Terry.
    2012   *Paul's Missionary Methods: In His Time and Ours.* Downers Grove, IL: IVP Academic.

Sider, Ronald J.
    1993   *Good News and Good Works: A Theology for the Whole Gospel.* Grand Rapids: Baker Books.

Stott, John
    2009   *For the Lord We Love: Your study guide to the Lausanne Covenant.* The Lausanne Movement.

Van Engen, Charles.
    1996   *Mission on the Way: Issues in Mission Theology.* Grand Rapids, MI: Baker Books.

World Council of Churches
    1983   "Mission and Evangelism: An Ecumenical Affirmation." In *International Bulletin of Missionary Research* (April 1983): 65-71.

Wright, Christopher J.H.
    2009   "Whole Gospel, Whole Church, Whole World: We must believe, live, and communicate all that makes the Christian message staggeringly comprehensive good news." In *Christianity Today* vol 53 no 10 (Oct 2009): 30-33.
    2006   *The Mission of God: Unlocking the Bible's Grand Narrative.* Downers Grove: InterVarsity Press.

Yoder, John Howard
    1997   *For the Nations: Essays Public & Evangelical.* Grand Rapids: Eerdmans.

APM

Group B: Curriculum Models for Missional Education

Workshop Papers Currently in Press with Other Pubishers:

Teaching for Eschatological Imagination in Missiological Education
by Kathryn Lewis Mowry

Missiology as an Interested Discipline: And Where Is It Happening?
by Dwight P. Baker

Education that is Missional

Toward a Pedagogy for the Missional Church

DOI: 10.7252/Paper.000015

About the Author:
Christopher B. James is a PhD Candidate in Practical Theology at Boston University School of Theology with training from Fuller Theological Seminary, Wheaton College and the Renovaré Institute. His research and teaching center on ecclesiology, mission, and spirituality, and he is currently dissertating on new churches in Seattle. He can be found online at www. jesusdust.com and @chrisbjames.

Abstract

This paper explores the implications of missional theology for Christian religious education in congregations. In particular, it draws on recent notable missional titles to do three things: 1) to clarify the meaning and aims of missional education as Christian education that specifically privileges the goal of helping Christians discover and live into their identity as God's cooperative partners in the *missio dei*, 2) to identify key characteristics of missional education, namely, attention to identity and acuity, life as the classroom, and Scripture as mission narrative, and 3) offer a modest proposal for missional education in the congregational setting through small communities of shared practice.

Introduction

Since the publication of *Missional Church: A Vision for the Sending of the Church in North America* in 1998, which popularized the m-word, authors and publishers have increasingly released titles incorporating it. According to Reggie McNeal, the "rise of the missional church is the single biggest development in Christianity since the Reformation" (xiii). While this may be sensationalizing a bit, there is no question that the missiological ecclesiologies originally proposed by Lesslie Newbigin and David Bosch, which thoroughly informed *Missional Church,* are making a significant impact. Church leaders across North America are increasingly seeking to make theirs a "missional church" as how-to books proliferate. This essay explores the implications of missional theology for Christian religious education. In particular, it attempts—drawing on recent notable missional titles—to do three things: 1) to clarify the meaning and aims of missional education, 2) to identify some of its key characteristics, and 3) offer a modest proposal for Christian education towards the cultivation and ongoing life of the missional church.

I. What is Missional Education?

In order to move toward a tentative definition of missional education, it will be important to discuss the two key terms. The ubiquity of "missional" has made it especially ambiguous. My use of the term regards it as virtually synonymous with "missionary." Thus, a church is missional when its core self-understanding is as a community created by the Spirit to participate in God's mission to redeem the cosmos through Christ (Van Gelder 73). Similarly, an individual may be considered missional when, by nature of their membership in this missionary community, they understand their identity as most fundamentally God's cooperative agent. This corporate and personal sense of identity manifests in "missional living" which is pluriform ministry and service, encompassing a full spectrum from care-full stewardship of creation to active evangelistic work as ambassadors of God's reconciling love.

The second key term, education—referring specifically to Christian education—merits a fuller discussion. The earliest Christians, as Acts makes clear, were known as followers of the Way. According to the *Didache*—the earliest non-canonical source for catechetical instruction—the Christian message is a call to a "way of life" (*The Didache*, 6:3-25). Specifically, Christianity invites all to "a life lived according to the example of Jesus and his teachings" (Groome 51). If Christianity is conceived of as a way of life, then Christian education should be thought of as education *toward* this way of life.[1] This education consists of any and everything that the Christian community intentionally practices, provides, or leverages for the purpose of helping Christians learn this distinct way of life.

While many are aware that Jesus' primary message concerned the Kingdom or Reign of God, not all recognize that his central theme was more precisely the *availability* of this Reign.[2] Thus, they often fail to connect the Reign of God with Jesus' actual manner of life, which manifested and exemplified its accessibility. This is a great omission, for Jesus' way of life was as much a *demonstration* of life lived within the available Reign as his preaching was a *declaration* of it. The meaning of the intimate connection between Jesus' way of life and the availability of the Reign of God for Christian education is that it possesses a singular, rather than dual, aim: Christian education seeks to apprentice followers of Jesus into his way of life, which was precisely life as a citizen in the Commonwealth of God.[3]

Of course, this begs the question of what a way of life within the Reign of God might include. I propose a three-fold answer. Thomas Groome, author of *Christian Religious Education*, asserts that the metapurpose of Christian education is to "lead people out to the Kingdom of God in Jesus Christ" (35) and under this umbrella isolates "twin immediate purposes, namely, Christian faith and human freedom" (82). Reggie McNeal, suggests understanding Christian maturation as "becoming more like Jesus and blessing the world" (100). Both authors highlight my first aim of Christian education, *an outward orientation* such as that which was characteristic of Jesus' way of life; life in the Reign is a life for others. McNeal in speaking of "becoming like Jesus," uniquely draws attention to *spiritual formation* into Christlike virtue as a critical dimension of Kingdom life; the inner life, too, must learn Jesus' way. This is the second element. Groome, speaking of Christian faith as a secondary purpose, points toward the third element: life as a citizen in the Commonwealth of God includes an intimate and trusting *interactivity with God*. These three elements of the way of life toward which Christian education inclines might be labeled as missional (blessing others), formational (spiritual formation in Christlikeness) and relational (relationship with God).

To summarize, *Christian religious education is the pluriform activity of the Christian community that seeks to train Christians in the way of Jesus—life lived in the Kingdom of God. Acquiring this way of life includes: 1) cultivating a personal, interactive relationship with God, characterized by renewed identity, attentiveness and cooperation, 2) undergoing spiritual formation in Christlikeness, such that the inner life bears the fruit of the Spirit, and 3) reorientation of action toward the blessing and liberation of others and the redemption of cosmos.*

Properly conceived, all Christian education is missional. Nonetheless, by missional education, I refer to Christian education that specifically privileges the goal of helping Christians discover and live into their identity as God's cooperative partners in the *missio dei*. Missional education is generally required as a corrective to truncated approaches to Christian education that have omitted the missional dimension, emphasizing only personal relationship with God and/ or spiritual formation in Christlike character. The privileging of the missional dimension of Christian education highlights the proper nature of other two dimensions. In missional education, intimate relationship with the missionary God is seen as beginning point for discovery of one's missional identity. It also stresses that this personal relationship is best cultivated through active attentiveness and willing cooperation. Missional education, moreover, emphasizes how other-oriented the fruit of the spirit is; presenting spiritual formation as more than a means of gaining inner peace and joy, indeed as growing in love of neighbor.

II. What Makes Education Missional?

While missional authors rarely cite Paulo Freire's *Pedagogy of the Oppressed*, its impact is unmistakable to one familiar with his work. Freire, writing in the midst of his experience among the poor of Latin America, conceives of education as *conscientization* —a process in which learners are enabled to "enter the historical process as responsible Subjects" (36). This transformation is most fundamentally one of identity, a change of self-concept from object to subject, from passive observer to empowered agent in the shaping of the world. For Friere, this rising awareness among the poor is what makes possible their liberation, and indeed the liberation of their oppressors (44).

A similar identity shift is a most pivotal missional learning and the key to movement toward missional living. Missional learners discover themselves to be cooperative agents with God in the renewal of all things. This very discovery constitutes, in part, the liberation of their own humanity—for as creatures made in the *imago dei*, humans are intented to manifest and participate in God's earth-tending action—and it opens up the possibility of the liberation of the humanity of others, along with the liberation of the whole earth.

For Friere, conscientization and its concurrent subjectivity result from a developing ability to see the world differently. In particular, it requires learning to see culture as human-made, "not as static reality, but as a reality in process, in transformation" (83). While Friere's vision opens up an uncertain future at the mercy of human agency, missional eyes perceive an agency beyond that of humans alone. Craig Van Gelder, an author with several missional titles, poses two questions as critical for the life of the missional church: What is God doing? and What does God want to do? (118). These questions, which are meant to initiate the process of decision-making and action for the missional church, assume that the church and its individuals have learned to discern God's action and desires.

Thus, renewed vision is a core competency that missional education seeks to cultivate. I have written elsewhere on the nature of missional acuity in an essay titled "Missional Acuity: 20th Century Insights Toward a Redemptive Way of Seeing."[4] In this essay, I offer a description, which I repeat here: Missional acuity is the intimate, experiential knowledge of God that enables one to see God's presence and activity in the world, especially through nature and people which are recognized as bearers of virtue and the presence of Christ. Missional vision arrives as a gift of sheer grace, but the ability to welcome it is cultivated through persistent training, resolute confession of reality as it is revealed through Scripture and Christian tradition, and contemplation of God.

McNeal highlights the centrality of missional acuity in his discussion of practices for what he calls people-development. "The practice of life debriefing will also have the spiritual benefit of helping people see that God is active in their lives every day in every sphere. This is fundamental to helping people live more intentional and more missional lives" (103). As McNeal suggests, the zone in which and for which missional education seeks to train eyes to see God is not limited by the walls of the church. This leads to a critical feature of missional education.

The primary venue for missional education is not the classroom, but the primary places of the learner's lives—their places of work, home, and recreation. David Bosch, one of the earliest and most influential missional authors, states it emphatically: "The context [of disciplemaking] is not in the classroom (where "teaching" normally takes place), or even in the church, but in the world" (Bosch 67). This is because it is in these places that God is already at work but also because it is in these places that God seeks our cooperative partnership. Real life is both the place where the primary missional learning takes place and the place where this learning is enacted.

Thus far, we have identified both the *what* and *where* of missional education, but we have said little about *how* missional education proceeds. To review, *what* missional education seeks is, most pivotally, the critical identity shift toward a missional self-concept as well as the ability to see and discern God's presence and action. *Where* this learning occurs is not the classroom but in whatever places a person spends the majority of their time. We now turn to the *how* question to propose the beginnings of a missional pedagogy.

III. Toward a Missional Curriculum and Method

Missional education seeks to cultivate both missional identity and missional acuity as essential attributes of those who follow Jesus' way of life in the Kingdom of God. As with any educational agenda, knowledge of certain information is indispensible toward this end. Before outlining the pedagogical processes of missional education, I will note some of the pieces of knowledge (and belief) that support development of missional identity and acuity.

The missional curriculum has a unique approach to the classic foci of systematic theology. Preceding any talk of people or churches being missional, is the development of a missional *doctrine of God*. The most basic missional claim, rehearsed tirelessly by authors, is the missionary nature of God. Guder lays the foundation by speaking of witness as theocentric, Christocentric and pneumatological (2000, 62). In so doing, he stresses the intrinsic missional orientation of the triune persons. David Bosch is regularly invoked in this regard:

> Mission [is] understood as being derived from the very nature of God. It [is] thus put in the context of the doctrine of the Trinity, not of ecclesiology or soteriology. The classical doctrine of the *missio Dei* as God the Father sending the Son, and God the Father and the Son sending the Spirit [is] expanded to include yet another "movement": Father, Son, and Holy Spirit sending the church into the world (Bosch 390).[5]

Critical to missional formation is the knowledge that God is, at heart, a missionary and that God has been and is on a mission. This missionary doctrine of God is the foundational first principle for missional education and it sets the curricular trajectory.

Michael Frost and Alan Hirsch are often noted for the directionality in their theology, echoing a similar comment by Bosch above. They speak of beginning with Christology, which determines missiology, which in turn determines ecclesiology (Frost and Hirsch 209). While there may seem to be a discrepancy between Bosch's call to begin with the doctrine of God, and theirs to begin with Christology, missional thinkers reconcile this by taking Christ as the decisive revelation of God. Guder defends his own Christocentricity by invoking Newbigin:

> But a Trinitarian perspective can be only an enlargement and development of a Christocentric one and not an alternative set over against it, for the doctrine of the Trinity is the theological articulation of what it means to say that Jesus is the unique Word of God incarnate in world history (Guder 2000, 48).

This belief in a "missionary God" inevitably gives new texture to the whole catalog of systematic topics. *Eschatology* comes to the fore as the question is raised: Where is God's mission intending to take creation in the end? This question drives toward an understanding of the Reign of God and leads to both a widened *soteriology* and a more robust eschatology that envisions the redemption of the cosmos (not just the soul-salvation of the elect). With this end in mind, questions of *missiology* surface: How has God been about this mission toward that final redemption, historically? How is God working toward it, even now? This second question is where *ecclesiology* takes center stage, and missional thinking has reshaped no doctrinal foci more significantly. A key teaching in missional instruction is the missionary constitution of the church: "definitions of the church should focus on and arise out of the formation of particular communities of God's people, called and sent where they are as witnesses to the gospel" (Guder 1998, 9).

Finally, through the missional paradigm, Scripture's function shifts from being primarily a "devotional aid and an instruction manual" to serving as a narrative which helps the people of God understand God's mission and their role in it" (McNeal 27). The Bible provides the story into which the church has stepped as today's key supporting actor. Moreover, the text inspires and empowers the church to fulfill its role. Guder reads Paul's epistles as a call to practice a missionary lifestyle (2000, 58). Newbigin exemplifies this approach to Scripture, leveraging his own Reformed doctrine of election to trace the missional vocation of God's people through Abraham, Moses, Israel, the disciples and up to today's church (Newbigin 68). More recently, Christopher Wright offers a wonderful reading of the Bible's grand narrative through this missional lens in *The Mission of God*.

Thus far, we have identified some of the key learnings essential to missional curricula as they ripple through the traditional loci of theological reflection. Now we must ask "how is this knowledge gained?" Missional educators heed Groome's warning: "Any form of manipulation or indoctrination is both bad education and blatantly counter productive to the purposes of Christian education. The educational process we use must itself be capable of promoting human emancipation" (98). As a result, while the preceding discussion of theological loci may conjure up images of a (hierarchical) seminary setting, as we have already noted, the role of the classroom is relativized by the primacy of the actual places where people spend the bulk of their lives. How, then, do missional educators equip learners to capitalize on the educative potential of their everyday settings? In truth, these environments do not become fertile for missional formation until the learner has already begun to develop missional identity and acuity. Once these begin to be acquired, even in their nascent form, they can grow to maturity in any setting in which the learner exists. If these firstfruits are born in neither the classroom nor the everyday environs, where does the process of missional education begin?

Perhaps the key pedagogical feature of missional pedagogy is the assertion that participation in mission is not merely an aim of education but its primary vehicle and catalyst. Thus, missional education is not just education *for* mission but education *through* mission. In other words, mission is not just viewed as the outcome of discipleship, discipleship is presumed to be the outcome of mission. Alan Hirsch sources this pedagogical insight in Jesus the educator himself:

> ...this is exactly how Jesus does discipleship: he organizes it around mission. As soon as they are called he takes the disciples on an adventurous journey of mission, ministry, and learning. Straightaway they are involved in proclaiming the kingdom of God, serving the poor, healing, and casting out demons. It is active and direct disciple making in the context of mission (Hirsch 120).

> Reggie McNeal shares a similar sentiment: "The missional church assumes that service to others is the first step, not some later expression of spirituality" (105). Since service is understood to be the "threshold where many of us learn the most about ourselves and come to see God at work in the world," missional churches "deploy people into service as much and as soon as possible" (McNeal 106).

Missional educators embrace a praxis approach. The educational process is therefore imagined as a continuous cycle of action and reflection, rather than linearly as a move from reflection to action. While this praxis learning has a constant circulation from reflection to action and back again, the opening movement, several missional authors assert, is missionary action. According to Hirsch, "mission is the catalyzing principle of discipleship" so wherever the learner may be "the way forward is to put actions into the equation" (120/123). This is the case because, following the Hebrew concept of knowledge "we need to *act* our way into a new way of thinking" rather than the futile Greek attempt to "*think* our way into a new way of acting" (122). This is, no doubt, a simplification of the learning process—for we can only suspect some new thought as prior to this action—but it is one that missional authors repeat.

McNeal insists that expecting people to take away something they learn at church and apply it in their lives is "backwards." Rather, missional educators "help people examine their lives, figure out what's going on, and distill out the issues" and thus prepare the "seedbed where learning and application can occur" (105). Missional educators are interpretive guides rather than didactic lecturers. Here again we see the subtle influence of Paulo Friere. Friere vociferously protested the "banking approach" to education, in which knowledgeable teachers deposit bits of information in passive students, declaring that this model only perpetuates the oppressive regime as it denies learners agency. He proposed radically flattening the hierarchy of these relations with new language, calling the educative partners student-teachers and teacher-students (80). According to the Friere, the educator's primary task was problem-posing; presenting to the student-teachers, depictions of their own reality and calling forth their interpretations and thus agency (79).

Similarly, while missional education launches as direct service, it is paired with reflection facilitated by the educator. This reflection is aided by proper framing of the service at the outset, perhaps by something as a simple a shared a prayer that participants might catch a glimpse of the God who always precedes mission. Because the aims of the missional educator are missional agency and missional acuity, the primary mode of speech for the missional educator is the question. With questions such as What did you see? Where did you sense God's presence or activity? and What invitation to action did you feel?, the missional educator empowers learners to cultivate simultaneously a sensitivity to God-on-the-move and an awareness of their own role and agency within this campaign.

As learners struggle to make sense of their experience, asking questions about the plight of those they serve, the limitations of their own character and strength, and searching for the presence of God in the midst of it all, they become ready to move toward greater understanding of the missionary God who desires intimate relationality and partnership and open to God's means of spiritual formation through Christian practices. At this point in the learning process, bit-by-bit instruction in theology and practices becomes appropriate.

Given this high valuation of missionary action to missional education, it should not be surprising that several author suggest missional educators ought to be practitioners, not pure academics. As practitioners, missional educators are themselves involved in educative action, thus fitting the Frierian designation of the "teacher-student". Hirsch feels so strongly about this that he allows only active missional practitioners to teach at his *Forge Mission Training Network*.

In contrast to those who would make a progression of Henri Nouwen's movements from solitude to community to ministry,[6] missional educators propose just the reverse. Groome, though writing before the missional language arrived on the scene, anticipates the sentiment:

> ...we may well speak of believing and trusting as leading to the overt doing for the "other." But the reverse is equally true and should also be stated. Our life of agape leads to believing and to trusting, with a constant dialectical relationship between what is known and what is done (Groome 64).

What Groome calls the "life of agape" and I have referred to as "missional living," naturally calls for and leads to the development of theological awareness. As both Hirsch and Guder note, quoting Martin Kahler, "Mission is the mother of theology" (Kahler 190).[7]

Just as taking steps forward in mission will drive one toward a deeper understanding of theology, it also leads one toward both intimacy with God and utilization of spiritual disciplines for character formation. Dallas Willard, though not a missional author, suggests a similar pedagogical strategy. When asked what someone should do to grow spiritually, he suggests that they set about to simply do "the next right thing," suggesting that nothing will drive a person into the Kingdom of God like trying to do the next right thing.[8] Pretty soon, he insists, they will find that they can't just do it; they need God's power and this is when spiritual disciplines will begin make sense. Similarly, missional educators believe, participating in redemptive action is bound to spark a journey of theological investigation and renewal of the inner life.

IV. Missional Education in Practice

With the success of *Missional Church*, pastors who resonated with the missional ecclesiology began calling for more practical and actionable resources. One of the earliest and most direct responses to this cry was *Treasure in Clay Jars: Patterns in Missional Faithfulness*, also released by The Gospel and Our Culture Network.[9] As the collaborative project of six authors, including *Missional Church* contributors Darrell Guder, George Hunsberger and Lois Barett, *Treasure in Clay Jars* examines nine congregations on their way toward being missional and identifies eight patterns common to these churches. Our interest in this work will engage only the patterns most relevant to educational practices.

The first pattern in these nascent missional congregations is their commitment to *discerning missional vocation*. This attribute is linked to both missional identity and missional acuity. Missional vocation is missional identity plus a discerned call to participation with God in a particular dimension of mission. Thus, missional vocation is the outcome of missional identity and missional acuity. In this chapter, Hunsberger identifies four questions that missional churches attend to and they are critical for missional learning: *where* are we (geographical, social and cultural context), *when* are we (in the flow of history and change), *who* are we (vis a vis their tradition) and *why* are we (God's general and specific purposes)(39). Practices based on engagement with these questions include use of social science data and analysis (where), congregational and community story-telling (when), theological mining of the tradition and spiritual gifts assessment (who), and reflection on congregational vocation through prayer walks, small group discussion or annual retreats (why).

Pattern two, *biblical formation and discipleship*, bears directly on the processes of missional education. Guder, the author of this chapter, considers discipleship to be "all about" living "in accordance with scripture" and "experiencing the daily renewal of our inner natures" (60). Here we see linkages to the formational end of Christian education. As Guder is quick to point out, "not all Bible study is missional formation" (60). Missional education often takes place in small groups or the "core congregation" which practices a "high level of discipline and commitment (67-68). Importantly, the questions that are brought to scripture are shaped by the missional formation sought. Rather than asking "What can I get out of this?," "the missional approach asks, How does God's Word call, shape, transform, and send me...and us?" (69-70). This question calls for self-analysis and self-criticism which move learners toward what the Bible calls repentance (72).

Practices that demonstrate God's intent for the world is the fourth pattern identified in missional churches. These practices include 1) listening to one another, 2) active helpfulness, 3) bearing with one another, and 4) crossing boundaries, welcoming the "Other". While these are oriented toward those within the church community, they are no less missionally educative, for they enlist individuals in God's other-blessing mission. Additionally, they make the church distinct and visible as "the sign and foretaste of God's reign of justice, freedom and love" (85).

Pattern eight highlights the crucial role of leadership, or *missional authority*, in missional congregations. Interestingly, "missional leaders did not necessarily lead through their "office"" and missional leadership was typically given by a "community of multiple leaders" (140-142). These observations reinforce the flattened hierarchy in which missional educators and learners operate, as suggested earlier. These leaders focus on missional vocation and foster missional practices, publicly living out the implications of missional identity through a distinct lifestyle and challenging others to join them (146-148).

Several other patterns have significance for the educational task. Pattern three indicates that missional churches *take risks as a contrast society*, particularly through practices of generosity (rejecting materialism), practices of commitment to community (against individualism), and reaching those on the edges of society (risking safety and comfort).[10] Pattern five highlights the *missional character of worship*; "concern, involvement, and commitment to persevere in their missional engagement is motivated and sustained in their worship" (113). Pattern six, *dependence on the Holy Spirit*, is manifest largely through the centrality of prayer practices, not merely for devotional purposes, but in pursuit of missional discernment and empowerment.[11] Finally, pattern seven notes that missional churches often resonate with the theme of the *Reign of God*, and understand themselves as an incomplete expression of it.

Beyond this survey of patterns, two explicit references to missional education in this book are worth highlighting. In a parenthetical note, Guder says "The "mission trip" has become a favorite form of missional education in prosperous churches of the West. There is no denying its value, though questions must be raised about the approach" (135). While often yielding questionable benefits for those served, mission trips have the potential of cultivating both missional identity through a week in which participants are self-consciously "here to bless others" and the potential of developing missional acuity if regular times of reflection are led with an eye toward helping participants discern God's presence and activity. In the concluding chapter, editor Lois Barrett asserts that in the missional church "education will be oriented toward proclaiming and being a sign of the reign of God" (151). Indeed, as I have suggested, proclamation and demonstration of the Reign are both ends and means of missional education.

V. A Proposal

While *Treasures in Clay Jars* offers hints regarding the concrete practices of missional education, it intentionally avoids putting forward congregations as models or its descriptions as prescriptive. Jumping into this gap, among others, is Alan Roxburgh, a contributor to *Missional Church* and prolific author, church consultant and head of The Missional Network.[12] Roxburgh offers a straightforward proposal for congregations desiring to "become missional" in *Missional Mapmaking*.[13] I draw largely on what he has put forth in my own proposal for a praxis of missional education toward development of missional agency and acuity.

The beginning of a congregational process of missional education assumes that someone, preferably a leader, already has the seedlings of either missional identity or acuity, if not both. As Roxburgh notes, movement toward missional identity begins with "rediscovering some basic habits and practices of Christian formation critical for discernment and the capacity to name what we are seeing

God do in our time and place" (137). The first steps will be for this individual to begin to develop some practices for cultivating further missional identity and acuity and to draw others into this experience.

The new practices I suggest, while modest, are the beginnings of a change of lifestyle. First, a daily morning prayer of commitment and intercession (ex. "Lord, allow me today to bless those I will meet today as your representative, including, Joe, at work who needs encouragement and Mary, on my bus, who is trapped in a painful relationship") and a daily evening prayer of Examen (ex. Where did I sense God's presence or activity? What invitation to cooperative action did I experience? How did I respond?). Second, a monthly practice of hosting an acquaintance for dinner and exercise of deep attentive listening. Third, cultivation of friendships with non-Christians and the needy, for whom intercession is made daily. Fourth, weekly in-depth engagement with the biblical story through missional questions, preferably in a community context.[14] Of course, it can be exceedingly difficult for an individual to make such a lifestyle change alone, so it will be essential that they invite others to share these commitments.

How can others be drawn into this experience? If the individual is not aware of others that the Spirit is moving in a similar way, they should invite whomever they can to action-reflection events. These events would be service or exposure experiences—such as serving at a soup kitchen or prayer walking through a poor part of town— that include appropriate group prepping and meaningful space for reflection afterward. The prepping might be as simple as a reading of Matthew 25: 31-46 (The Sheep and the Goats) and a prayer for "eyes to see" Jesus in those they encounter. After the experience, the budding missional educator should pose questions such as: What did you see? Where did you sense God's presence or activity? and What invitation to cooperative action did you feel? From these events, the missional educator can invite people to join a small group committed to the practices outlined above, as well as a weekly meal to share their experiences. It would be in the context of these small groups that the most intentional missional reflection would take place.

I am aware that this proposal cultivates *individual* but not— at least initially—*shared* missional vocation. Participants would, I believe, begin to see God at work and begin to see themselves as God's missionary partners, but this would not immediately lead to their congregation as a whole, being in any meaningful sense a missional church. After some months, the small group should be invited to entertain corporate questions such as "What needs are we seeing *together*? What action of God are we seeing *together*? What action are we being called to *together*?" Small group projects may emerge from these conversations. If more than one such small group exists, there should be opportunities to reflect as one large group along these lines, and from this context, larger church-sponsored, projects might begin to take shape.

While projects ought to arise as the result of a maturing of communal missional identity and acuity, it must be remembered that a church is not missional on the basis of any number of mission projects or service activities. Rather, the adjective refers to the *character* of a church. A church only becomes missional as the people (the church!) gain missional acuity and identity, not as the institution takes on mission projects.

VI. Conclusion

In this essay, I have proposed conceiving of the *telos* of Christian religious education as training into the Kingdom way of life that Jesus announced and demonstrated. I identified three dimensions of this way of life: the personal (intimacy with God), the formational (renewal of inner life), and the missional (other-blessing orientation). Missional education seeks particularly to train disciples into the third, missional, dimension of Jesus' way of life, while integrating with both the personal and formational dimensions. The two key competences for missional living, I have suggested, are missional identity or agency (the self-concept that I/we am/are God's cooperative partner(s) in the redemption of the cosmos) and missional acuity (the ability to discern, or see, God's presence, activity and will). Together, these two are the chief aims of missional education.

Toward these ends, missional educators employ a praxis pedagogy, in which mission and reflection exist symbiotically. Emphasis is placed on the priority of active engagement in mission without prerequisite training. Missional educators, themselves learners and practitioners, stress the out-of-classroom environments as the primary context for learning, and facilitate reflection primarily through question-posing intended to cultivate agency and discernment of God's presence, action and invitation. As learners develop a hunger for greater understanding and an inner-life that can sustain missional living, educators introduce key theological concepts and practices.

The missional congregations studied by *Treasure in Clay Jars* enact missional education in diverse ways but share common patterns. They purposefully seek to develop missional vocation through analysis of their geographical, socio-cultural, traditioned and redemptive context. Missional congregations approach the Bible as the key source of missional empowerment and rebuke, often in small group cohorts. Practices of welcoming, listening, helping, and bearing-with one another develop missional identity and make the community a sign of the Kingdom. Leader/educators exist in community and foster missional practices through public exemplification of missional living.

Finally, I proposed a way of initiating missional education in a congregational setting through the purposeful commitment, by individuals and small groups, to practices which cultivate missional identity and acuity: prayers of commitment, intercession and Examen, hosting acquaintances for dinner, cultivating friendships with the lost and needy, and missional engagement with the Scriptural narrative. I conclude with McNeal's charge to those who would undertake missional education:

> We must change our ideas of what it means to develop a disciple, shifting the emphasis from studying Jesus and all things spiritual in an environment protected from the world to following Jesus into the world to join him in his redemptive mission (10).

Notes

1   I have elsewhere explored this theme in greater depth in an essay titled "Conversion as Skill Acquisition" available at http://www.jesusdust. com/2011/02/conversion-as-skill-acquisition.html

2   Dallas Willard made this observation in a public interview with John Ortberg at Catalyst West 2010. The video of this interview is available at: http://www.jesusdust.com/2010/07/john-ortberg-interviews-dallas-willard.html

3   I appropriate the phrase "commonwealth of God" from Brain D. McLaren who proposes it, among others, as contemporary language analogous to the "Kingdom of God." http://bit.ly/dZ05Gl

4   This article is published in Witness: Journal of the Academy for Evangelism in Theological Education, vol. 26 (2012).

5   As noted in Missional Church, Bosch's formulation follows Western tradition, but Orthodox Christians affirm the missionary nature of God while emphasizing that the Father sends both the Son and the Spirit.

6   For example, see Neil Michells' How to Hit the Ground Running: A Quick-Start Guide for Congregations with New Leadership. (2005). Church Publishing, Inc. p. 63.

7   Guder invokes Kahler on page 21 of the Continuing Conversion of the Church. Hirsch does not credit Kahler, but appropriates this quotation on page 125.

8   Heard on several occasions, including Catalyst West 2010 and in services at Menlo Park Presbyterian Church on December 11, 2009. Relevant audio available at http://bit.ly/l85FgZ and http://www. mppc.org/toughquestions under "How do I find God?"

9   The Gospel and Our Culture Network: http://www.gocn.org

10   These practices serve as what Brian McLaren calls "counter-curriculum to teach people the art of living in this new way" against the "covert curriculum" of the dominant societal system. Everything Must Change, 284.

11   Craig Van Gelder explores this Spirit-led characteristic throughout The Ministry of the Missional Church.

12   The Missional Network: http://www.roxburghmissionalnet.com/

13   See my review of Missional Mapmaking in Witness: The Journal for the Academy for Evangelism in Theological Education (2011).

14   These proposed practices have much in common with Roxburgh's on pages 151-162.

Works Cited

Bosch, D. J.
1991   *Transforming Mission: Paradigm Shifts in Theology of Mission.* Orbis Books.

Freire, P.
2000   *Pedagogy of the Oppressed* (30th ed.). Continuum.

Frost, M., & Hirsch, A.
2003   *The Shaping of Things to Come: Innovation and Mission for the 21 Century Church.* Hendrickson Publishers.

Van Gelder, C.
2007   *The Ministry of the Missional Church: A Community Led by the Spirit.* Baker Books.

Groome, T. H.
1999   *Christian Religious Education: Sharing Our Story and Vision.* Jossey-Bass.

Guder, D. L.
1998   *Missional Church: A Vision for the Sending of the Church in North America.* Wm. B. Eerdmans Publishing Company.
2000   *The Continuing Conversion of the Church.* Wm. B. Eerdmans Publishing Company.

Hirsch, A.
2009   *The Forgotten Ways: Reactivating the Missional Church.* Brazos Press.

Kahler, M.
1971   *Schriften zur Christologie und Mission.* Munich: Chr. Kaiser Verlag.

McLaren, B. D.
2009   *Everything Must Change: When the World's Biggest Problems and Jesus' Good News Collide.* Thomas Nelson.

McNeal, R.
    2009   *Missional Renaissance: Changing the Scorecard for the Church.* Jossey-Bass.

Michell, N.
    2005   *How to Hit the Ground Running: A Quick-Start Guide for Congregations with New Leadership.* Church Publishing, Inc.

Newbigin, L.
    1995   *The Open Secret* (Revised.). Wm. B. Eerdmans Publishing Company.

Roxburgh, A.
    2009   *Missional Map-Making: Skills for Leading in Times of Transition* (1st ed.). Jossey-Bass.

Wright, C. J. H.
    2006   *The Mission of God: Unlocking the Bible's Grand Narrative.* IVP Academic.

APM

Group C:
Missiology
in the Social-
Cultural Context

Interpreting the Bible
With the Poor

LARRY W. CALDWELL

DOI: 10.7252/Paper.000017

About the Author

Larry W. Caldwell was Professor of Missions and Hermeneutics at Asian Theological Seminary for 20 years, five of those years serving as Academic Dean, and directed the Doctor of Missiology program at the Asia Graduate School of Theology-Philippines. He also edited the Journal of Asian Mission for many years. He recently returned to the USA to become Director of Training and Strategy for Converge Worldwide and Visiting Professor of Intercultural Studies at Sioux Falls Seminary.

Abstract

Good Bible interpretation is basic to the doing of good theology and missiology. It is foundational to individual and cultural transformation, especially among the poor. Such interpretation involves exegeting both the biblical text and the culturally-specific audience with whom the Bible interpreter is attempting to communicate that text. While the theory of this Two Step approach has dominated western and non-western theology/missiology, in reality the exegesis of the biblical text has far overshadowed the exegesis of the culture of the audience. This paper will attempt to better understand the interplay between textual and cultural exegesis in the context of ministry with the poor by asking: How might this Two Step approach be enhanced in order to help the poor do better Bible interpretation and thus theology/missiology? This question will be answered in three parts. Part 1 will set Bible interpretation in its worldwide context by examining the relationship between colonization and theological/ missiological education, followed by an examination of Bible interpretation and the constituencies it serves. Part 2 will focus on whether or not courses and curricula are truly contextualized for the worldwide church and the need for "lower-based" training programs and "border" pedagogies, including a case study from the Philippines specifically addressing the urban poor. Part 3 examines strategies for professors and institutions as they endeavor to exegete both the biblical text and the culture of the audience. The paper concludes with practical suggestions to help make Bible interpretation with the poor more relevant and engaging within their local contexts.

Introduction

Most of us would readily agree that good Bible interpretation is basic to the doing of good theology and good missiology. But in today's increasingly globalized world how does one determine which hermeneutical methodologies result in good Bible interpretation and thus good theology/missiology? In other words, what hermeneutical methodologies are appropriate for the church in both the western and non-western worlds, especially the church among the rural and urban poor?[1] It is especially this last question that this paper will address. For without Bible interpretation that considers the social dimensions of the people among whom the gospel is bearing fruit, truly holistic individual and cultural transformation will not happen. This is why it is so important to interpret the Bible *with* the poor.

Over the past few decades both the western and non-western (Global South or Majority World) church has been bombarded with a plethora of different hermeneutical methodologies or approaches to the Bible, which has also impacted the doing of theology and missiology. For most professors in most training institutions worldwide the hermeneutical methodology that has dominated the discussion is one that has two simple steps. Step One involves the Bible and is concerned with the question: How is a particular Bible passage to be best interpreted? Through an analysis of the original context of the Scripture passage—often using the tools of the grammatical-historical (or historical-critical) process—the interpreter attempts to ascertain, as best he/she can, what the Bible passage first meant to its original hearers; to understand what the passage meant *then*. Step Two follows on the heels of this first step. Here the interpreter attempts to answer the question: How is that Bible passage to be best interpreted for today? In Step Two the interpreter applies the results of the first step to the particular audience that he/she is ministering with *now*. The interpreter is usually careful to make sure that the second step closely approximates the results of the first step. These two major steps make up what is known as the "Two Step" approach to Bible interpretation.

The methodology of the Two Step approach to biblical hermeneutics has dominated both western and non-western theology and missiology over the past fifty years and continues to dominate even today. Such domination is not a bad thing *if* it is an approach to Bible interpretation that is meeting the needs of the *whole* church.

By the whole church here I am meaning the majority of the whole church—both western and non-western, rich and especially poor—that is predominately made up of pastors, lay leaders and lay people, most of whom will not have the luxury of learning the Two Step approach in training institutions worldwide.

The strengths of this Two Step approach are several: it takes the Bible seriously and allows the biblical text to always take precedence over the world of the interpreter and his/her culture; it deals honestly with the context of the original text and attempts to understand as much as possible the original author's intended meaning; and it takes the best of scholarship and uses it for better understandings of the biblical text and its context. The weaknesses of this Two Step approach are also several: it assumes the universal nature of western hermeneutical methods that may not necessarily be applicable in all non-western contexts; it has grammatical-historical roots with a possible anti-God and anti-Bible bias; it is costly to implement and maintain (requiring books and libraries and/or access to them) and thus is oftentimes limited to more wealthy cultures; and furthermore, it is very complicated to learn, assuming a high educational level and taking years of advanced training to effectively handle the approach.[2] These last two points are particularly relevant to the topic of this paper.

I believe that the weaknesses of the Two Step approach should cause us to re-think its usefulness. Though I do not believe the Two Step approach should be abandoned (and I still use it when I teach Bible interpretation classes), I do believe that some enhancement is necessary. The following question, therefore, is appropriate: How might this dominant Two Step approach be enhanced in order to help the poor do better Bible interpretation and theology/missiology globally? This paper will attempt to answer these questions in three parts. Part 1 will set the scene for Bible interpretation in its worldwide context by first examining the relationship between colonization and theological/missiological education worldwide, followed by a brief examination of Bible interpretation in relationship to the constituencies we serve. Part 2 will then more closely focus on the question of whether or not courses and curricula are truly contextualized for the worldwide church and the need for "lower-based" training programs and "border" pedagogies, including a case study from the Philippines specifically addressing the urban poor. Part 3 follows with some strategies for professors and institutions to understand as they endeavor to exegete *both* the biblical text as well as the culture of the people attempting to interpret that biblical text, especially those who are poor. The paper will conclude with six practical suggestions for professors and institutions to help make Bible interpretation with the poor more relevant and engaging for their local poor contexts.

Part 1: Bible Interpretation in Its Worldwide Context

The topic of theological education—especially Bible interpretation—is vast. I will thus limit the discussion here to two areas: 1) the historical realities of colonization out of which theological educational institutions worldwide—and the Bible interpretation methodologies that they teach—have emerged; and 2) whether theological educational institutions worldwide are meeting the training needs of the various constituencies they serve, especially the poor. These two areas may seem quite unrelated, but in reality they are intimately linked, as I will explain.

Colonization and Theological/Missiological Education

The history of colonization throughout the world is "the elephant in the room," so to speak, that few missiologists, and even fewer theologians, want to acknowledge. A vast number of the non-western nations have a history—for some, fairly recent—which includes colonization. Whether that colonization was British, Dutch, German, French, Spanish, Portuguese or American, it has often created among Christians in these nations a tendency to assume without question that the western theology—and the western hermeneutical methods—that came with the colonizers are still appropriate to use, even though the colonizers might have long gone.

Colonization—and the resulting paternalism that has oftentimes remained—has affected theological and missiological education in many ways, but primarily with regards to curriculum relevance and to dismissing local ways of teaching and learning. Recent ethnographic research has come to label the influence of colonization as "authoritative knowledge." A result of colonization is that those who are colonized eventually take on as authoritative a certain way of thinking or knowing that was at first foreign to that particular culture. Anthropologist Brigitte Jordan describes what happens:

> ...frequently one kind of knowledge gains ascendance and legitimacy. A consequence of the legitimation of one kind of knowing as authoritative is the devaluation, often the dismissal, of all other kinds of knowing.... The constitution of authoritative knowledge is an ongoing social process that both builds and reflects power relationship within a community of practice. It does this in such a way that all participants come to see the current social order as a natural order, that is, the way things (obviously) are.[3]

The kind of theological and hermeneutical knowledge that has gained ascendancy and legitimacy in theological and missiological circles worldwide is predominantly western. And most of us naively assume that this is just the way it is. Such was my own situation when I first began ministry in Asia as a missionary three decades ago:

> I was confronted with the shortcomings of western [...] methods when my wife and I first came to the Philippines in 1980. I was assigned to teach the Bible, theology, as well as the biblical languages, at my denomination's small Bible college located in a rural area on the northern tip of the island of Cebu. The school was isolated in every way: no electricity, no amenities whatsoever; nothing but some classrooms and dormitories located in the middle of a huge sugar cane field. Both the curriculum of this Bible college, as well as the content of most of the courses, were thoroughly western. I soon realized, however, that my Filipino students, obviously enough, were not western. Most were recent high school graduates from predominately poor, rural backgrounds. Though they knew English, many of the first-year students were hearing native English speakers (my wife and I) for the very first time. Nonetheless, in order to adequately understand the content of my courses these students had to think like I thought; in other words, they had to learn to think in western ways. The burden was on *them*, not on me. And everyone at that Bible college, westerner and non-westerner alike, thought nothing of this. It was simply taken for granted.[4]

Back then I did not question the western dominance of both *what* was taught and *how it* was taught. I considered neither the four centuries of Spanish colonization of the Philippines nor the nearly fifty years of its colonization by the USA (up until shortly after World War Two).

What both western and non-western Christians throughout the world must come to see is that the way things currently are—the status quo—should not be accepted uncritically. What must be seen is that the world's colonial history has influenced both the understanding of how to do hermeneutics and theology/missiology as well as how they are taught. Stephen Brookfield's words, although written of critical learning about the natural sciences, apply also to the critical learning techniques assumed in the non-western Bible school and/or seminary classroom:

[Such learning] was developed in a specific context and disseminated through certain already-established networks of communication.... This does not mean ... that we automatically reject these criteria as inherently oppressive or exclusionary because they represent Eurocentric worldviews. But it does mean that we acknowledge that their position of preeminence has not been attained because they exhibit some sort of primal universal force or truth; rather, their acceptance is socially and politically created.[5]

We must, therefore, at least acknowledge the fact that much of the hermeneutics and theology/missiology that is taught in the non-western world—as well as the educational techniques that are used—have come from the way the colonizers did it.[6] This should give us all pause, not least because, as educational anthropologist George D. Spindler notes:

a transcultural perspective on education is essential, for education is a cultural process and occurs in a social context. Without attention to cultural difference and the way education serves those differences, we have no way of achieving perspective on our own culture and the way our educational system serves it or of building a comprehensive picture of education as affected by culture.[7]

The implication of this social context for the doing of hermeneutics with the poor will be further explored in Parts 2 and 3.

Bible Interpretation and the Constituencies We Serve—Are We Truly Socially Engaged?

In 2005 educational expert Manfred Kohl released a devastating study, *The Church in the* Philippines: *A Research Project with Special Emphasis on Theological Education*. This work examined the relationship between the (primarily) evangelical seminaries in the Philippines and the various church constituencies they served. The Kohl Report, as it came to be known, showed that of the 50,000 Protestant churches in the Philippines at that time, about 55% either did not have a pastor (16%) or had a pastor without any formal theological training (39%).[8] And at the current rate that seminaries were graduating pastors, they would never be able to make up the shortfall. Furthermore, the churches of the vast majority of the untrained pastors and leaders were located in poor areas, both rural and urban. Kohl concluded that if these institutions were to meet the theological training needs of their constituencies either a new model of theological education was needed or the existing theological school programs radically revamped.

How does this evidence from the Kohl Report relate to the colonization issue? It relates precisely at the point that the seminaries of the Philippines—and I daresay in most other places throughout the non-western world—have been built primarily on western models of what seminary education is supposed to be like. Such western seminary education is typically for those with advanced levels of education (usually B.A. degrees) and with adequate time and funding resources for several years of full-time training. As this same model of seminary education has become dominant throughout the world, it is increasingly difficult to critique the status quo and analyze whether it is truly meeting the needs of the church worldwide. It thus begs the question: As educators, how well are we really holistic in our social engagement? The Kohl Report shows that this western model is not working in the Philippines in so far that it is not truly supplying sufficient numbers of pastors for the churches of the Philippines, the vast majority of which are among the poor. My travels in the region indicate that this is probably true for much of Asia, if not for most of the non-western world.

Some will argue that the purpose of seminary education is to train those who are indeed at higher educational and social levels so that they can then train the rest. This reasoning is faulty for at least two reasons: First, those at higher educational and social levels often are not able to adequately relate to, and be relevant for, the majority who are at the lower levels. Second, most of those who graduate from seminaries do not even try. More often than not they are recruited by higher-level churches and thus neglect the leadership needs of the poorer churches. This is a natural outgrowth of a colonial mentality that assumes that the education and other benefits at the higher levels will eventually trickle down to the lower levels. Unfortunately, trickle-down theory does not work in economics nor in theological/missiological education. The poor are usually left out of seminary education at many levels; thus the need for other "poor friendly" educational alternatives.

Part 2: Are Courses and Curricula Truly Contextualized for the Worldwide Church?

The Need for "Lower-Based" Training Programs and "Border" Pedagogies

When confronted with the task of making ministry training relevant for the poor, we must ask this question: Are the courses and curricula in our training institutions truly "socially engaged" for rural and urban poor contexts?[9] I maintain that to offer courses and curricula for the rural and urban poor ministry contexts worldwide will mean a radical reconsidering of what the rural and urban poor situations really are and what it is that our pastors and ministry workers really need to learn as they are, or will be, working with the poor.[10]

In considering socially relevant courses and curricula, we can benefit from recent development theory; especially what is known as "participatory rural appraisal" (PRA). Though PRA was begun with the rural poor in mind, its principles apply as well to majority world urban ministry situations, especially among the urban poor. PRA is the new field practice of putting the first last; in other words, recognizing the natural abilities and giftings of poor people.[11] This practice confronts the dominance of those called "uppers" as opposed to the vast majority of the people who are the "lowers." The uppers see grass-roots programs flourish through empowering the lowers to do them.

According to Robert Chambers, one of the early proponents of PRA, top-down systems have "brought bad practice: dominant and superior behavior, rushing, upper-to-upper bias, taking without giving, and arousing expectations which are not met."[12] New lower-based training programs are necessary. Yet such new paradigms

imply and demand changes which are institutional, professional and personal. Institutional change needs a long-term perspective, with patient and painstaking learning and reorientation. Professional change needs new concepts, values, methods and behaviors, and new curricula and approaches to learning. Personal change and commitment have primacy, and can be sought experientially. Learning to change and learning to enjoy change are fundamental.[13]

These new paradigms are a major challenge for "upper" seminaries and faculty whose courses and curricula are based on "top-down" systems.[14] As a result, the poor—and the training that they need—have been neglected. A total rethink is necessary here.[15]

A Case Study from the Majority World: Asian Theological Seminary, Manila, Philippines

This is precisely where I have been most challenged in recent years. When I was the Academic Dean at Asian Theological Seminary (ATS) in Manila, Philippines, one of my priority projects was to help develop a new program in urban poor ministries. But how could we do this in an "upper seminary" with a "top-down" system? The answer eventually turned into the ATS Center for Transformational Urban Leadership that offers courses leading to a Diploma, Graduate Diploma or M.A. in Transformational Urban Leadership (TUL). Built on a foundation of Bible, evangelical theology and applied social sciences, the TUL curriculum includes a majority of courses that are specifically made for Christian practitioners among the urban poor to help them more effectively minister in urban poor contexts. The courses bring together a team of national and international academic and "hands on" experts currently working with the urban poor. All the TUL courses are combined with extensive field internships among the urban poor.[16]

For example, the M.A. in TUL, a 45 semester-unit program of study, includes the following courses:

Core Courses:
Doing Hermeneutics with the Urban Poor
Theology 1
Bible Introduction
Urban Spirituality
Theology and Practice of Community Economics
Urban Poor Church Planting
Leadership in Urban Movements
Theology and Practice of Community Transformation

Specialized Courses:
Services to the Marginalized
Urban Reality and Theology
Educational Center Development
Entrepreneurial and Organizational Leadership
Primary Health Care
Advocacy and the Urban Environment
Language and Culture Acquisition (for non-Filipino students)
Diaspora Missiology

Field and Research Courses:
Research in Church and Ministry
Urban Reality and Theology
Thesis/Project
Field Supervision 1 and 2

Notice that these courses in the M.A. TUL program are not found in the catalogs of typical majority world training institutions (nor of most seminaries in the West).[17] In fact, from a typical seminary's point of view they are indeed quite radical. Where are the classical disciplines?! While we did keep three classical courses in the TUL curriculum (Bible Introduction, Theology 1, and a modified Hermeneutics course) we felt that it was imperative that ATS offer courses that were really needed for effective urban poor ministry and that they be taught by those who were actually "doing the ministry." This caused some headaches for our upper resident faculty, but eventually the TUL program was approved as a separate Center of ATS. The main concerns related to government recognition and accreditation issues. However, eventually the government regulating body for education was highly impressed that a seminary was offering such a practical program.

I was especially challenged by the TUL program when I was asked to teach one of the core courses: "Interpreting the Bible With the Urban Poor." I had taught basic hermeneutics courses for 25 years, but I had little personal experience training the urban poor. I was challenged by the prospect of empowering local leaders of the poor and, as a result, seeing grass-roots Bible interpretation flourish as the poor did it themselves.

This required me to "go back to the drawing board" to develop a "border pedagogy"—the phrase termed by Old Testament scholar D. N. Premnath—that went beyond the traditional approach I had been so fond of:

The term "border" sharply captures the dominant tendency to establish borders or boundaries based on the either-or binaries within Western thought.... The dominant group defines, structures and thereby dominates all constituted as Other. Border pedagogy provides a pedagogical alternative for learners to identify and be critical of these borders that are used to set apart entities and peoples.... [It] seeks to create spaces for ... experiences to be expressed, valued, and thought through by students and teachers alike.[18]

Border pedagogy allowed me to teach my students strategies for exegeting the text of the Bible while at the same time challenging me to help my students develop strategies for exegeting the culture of their urban poor audience. In this way they developed their own strategies for exegeting the text of the Bible with the urban poor.[19] This aspect of border pedagogy involves

the ability to expose the dominant definitions of reality. It enables the learner to recognize cultural codes and social practices that marginalize or even repress alternative ways of perceiving.... The models of the dominant culture need no longer be the sole basis for defining what constitutes proper knowledge.... As learners cross borders, alternative forms of knowledge emerge and the dominant definitions of reality come under closer scrutiny.[20]

As I taught my students, and my students (who, in turn, had been taught by their urban poor communities) taught me, we arrived together at hermeneutical strategies that worked with the urban poor. In almost every class period my students would come back from leading Bible studies with their urban poor groups and report comments that some individuals had made, for example: "I never knew that the Bible was for me," or "I never knew that I could interpret the Bible for myself." It was exciting for me to see that our new approach to Bible interpretation was engaging the urban poor at a much deeper level.

Part 3: Strategies for Exegeting

Both the Text of the Bible and the Culture of the People

It is precisely this kind of interaction between professor, student, and the local church, delineated above, that is so necessary if Christianity is to make an impact among our world today, especially the world of the poor. Such interaction involves the realization, and appropriate use, of new strategies for exegeting the text as well as exegeting the culture of those people we are ministering with. In the past training institutions and curriculums have put great emphasis on exegeting the text (Step One of the Two Step approach), but comparatively very little on exegeting the culture (Step Two). It is in the exegeting of the culture where we increasingly will meet the needs of the church among the poor in the 21st century.

But just how does one practically use the Two Step approach when interpreting the Bible with the poor in order to do better theology and missiology globally? One answer to this question involves examining more closely the details of each step and finding strategies for each step that are appropriate for good Bible interpretation. Here in Part 3 we will examine those appropriate strategies for exegeting the biblical text (Step One) as well as appropriate strategies for exegeting the culture of the rural or urban poor group that is receiving the biblical text from others and/or attempting to understand the biblical text for themselves (Step Two). Exegesis of both the text and the culture will help both the teachers and preachers of Bible interpretation, as well as the target group themselves, to arrive at appropriate interpretive strategies that will help insure good Bible interpretation. Furthermore, such comprehensive exegesis puts equal emphasis upon each of the two steps thereby viewing Bible interpretation as a holistic process.

Reading Strategies for Exegeting the Text of the Bible

When talking about strategies for exegeting the biblical text, what I am really referring to are *reading* strategies to use when interpreting the Bible. Reading strategies are simply the tools that readers need to properly understand the text. Such reading strategies range from minimal to maximal. *Minimal* reading strategies range from reading the specific biblical text alone, to reading it in light of its immediate context, to reading the surrounding chapters or even the entire book where the text is found. More *mid-level* reading strategies range from identifying the literary style (genre) of the text and the possible implications for interpretation, to comparing different uses of a particular word in the text using a concordance, to using a Bible dictionary and/or commentary to better understand the specific text and its context. *Maximal* reading strategies range from doing a word study in the original Hebrew or Greek, to using more advanced exegetical commentaries that refer directly to the original biblical languages, to reading the specific biblical text and context in the original languages of Hebrew or Greek. Figure 1 summarizes the range of reading strategies available when attempting to exegete the biblical text.

Figure 1: Reading Strategies

Minimal reading strategies:
- Reading a specific text
- Reading in light of the text's immediate context
- Reading in light of the context of the chapter and/or book.

Less Training

Mid-Level reading strategies:
- Analyzing the literary genre and possible implications
- Using a concordance for word studies
- Using a Bible dictionary or commentary

Maximal reading strategies:
- Using Hebrew or Greek for word studies
- Using advanced exegetical commentaries
- Reading the text and context in Hebrew or Greek

More Training

Note that there is a direct correlation between how advanced a reading strategy is and the complexity of training—informal and formal—needed to insure the best handling of the particular reading strategy. For example, the strategy of reading a specific text in light of the text's immediate context—or even the entire chapter or book where the text is found—involves little training, can be done informally, and requires no outside resources. However, the strategy of reading a text and its context in the original Hebrew or Greek languages typically requires much formal training, time and a plethora of outside resources (teachers, books, facilities, and the money necessary to support such training).

So what reading strategies are appropriate for Bible interpretation done with the poor?[21] I would suggest that the minimal strategies are the place to begin. While these minimal reading strategies may seem very basic, it is essential that they be mastered in order to insure that the poor will be able to interpret the Bible for themselves both with confidence and with fidelity to the text. Once these initial strategies are mastered then the more advanced mid-level reading strategies may be tackled, in no particular order. These mid-level strategies will all begin to use outside sources;

by "outside" I mean outside of the text of the Bible itself. While the minimal reading strategies are taught by only using the Bible, the more advanced strategies will employ, at minimum, simple reference material on literary genre, a concordance, and an easy to read and understand Bible dictionary or commentary. More time will also need to be spent in training individuals in these mid-level strategies and such individuals will need to have reading skills that are suitable to the strategy, especially when using even a simple Bible dictionary or commentary. Use of such outside texts should be entirely dependent upon the local situation and the appropriateness of such a strategy for both the learner as well as for the hermeneutical community. Learning these mid-level reading strategies will be especially important for the poor pastors and lay leaders.

I believe that it is not necessary to teach most Christians among the poor—including pastors and lay leaders—maximal reading strategies. This statement is in no way intended to be pejorative; I am certainly not speaking against the learning ability or possible educational attainment of individuals who are poor. However, though all individuals in any people group are certainly capable of advanced training in the maximal reading strategies, the following question must always be asked: Is it necessary that they be taught the advanced skills needed for maximal reading before good Bible interpretation can occur? Since individuals found within many of the rural and urban poor of this world have not finished primary school (and many of those who have are still functionally non-readers), maximal reading strategies are probably not appropriate for their hermeneutical context. Furthermore, to train pastors and lay leaders in such strategies will oftentimes bring them to a level of educational attainment that might, in the end, isolate them from their own community. As a result, we may do a disservice to the poor if we fail to take these realities into account.[22]

Relating Strategies for Exegeting the Culture of the People

Exegeting the text of the Bible is one thing. Exegeting the culture of the rural or urban poor group receiving the results of the Bible interpretation in order to best communicate the text of the Bible is another. Once again, exegeting the text is highly stressed in most Bible interpretation programs; exegeting the culture is usually not mentioned much at all. It is a part of the overall exegetical task that has largely been neglected. Instead, any attempts at cultural relevancy are typically left to the very end of the Bible interpretation process, usually referred to as "applying" the text. While application of the biblical text is crucial to any good Bible interpretation, application is but one aspect of exegeting the culture. By using the phrase "exegeting the culture" I mean that the Bible interpreter understands his or her target culture so well that the results of the reading strategies used in the process of exegeting the text will be clearly communicated in culturally appropriate ways. Such application, now in the form of the appropriate communication of the biblical text, helps complete the overall task of Bible interpretation.[23]

When talking about strategies for exegeting the culture, what I am referring to are *relating* strategies to use when interpreting the Bible with a particular people group. Relating strategies are simply the tools that interpreters need to properly communicate the understood text to the people with whom they are ministering. These interpreters include both those who are insiders to the culture as well as those who are outsiders. The insiders need to consider these relating strategies to insure that the Bible is indeed communicated in ways that are appropriate to their own culture. The outsiders need to learn and understand these relating strategies so that they communicate the Bible in ways that the insiders can truly understand.

Such relating strategies, once again, range from minimal to maximal. *Minimal* relating strategies range from learning their mother-tongue language, to understanding their felt needs, life questions and specific history, to discovering their worldview presuppositions. More *mid-level* relating strategies range from understanding how their formal and informal educational systems work, to learning how they react to and interpret different kinds of information, to discovering their methods of perceiving, interpreting and evaluating issues. *Maximal* relating strategies range from telling stories in culturally appropriate ways, to communicating biblical truth in culturally appropriate ways, to dialoging with local oral and written holy material and/or sacred texts. Figure 2 summarizes the range of relating strategies available when attempting to exegete the biblical text.

Figure 2: Relating Strategies

Minimal Relating Strategies:
- Learning their mother-tongue language
- Understanding their felt needs, life questions, and specific history
- Discovering their worldview presuppositions

Less Training

Mid-Level relating strategies:
- Understanding how their formal and informal education systems work
- Learning how they react to and interpret different kinds of information
- Discovering their methods of perceiving, interpreting and evaluating issues

Maximal relating strategies:
- Telling stories in culturally appropriate ways
- communicating biblical truth in culturally appropriate ways
- Dialoguing with local oral and written holy material and/or sacred texts

More Training

Once again, note that there is still a direct correlation between how advanced a relating strategy is and the complexity of training—informal and formal—needed to insure the best handling of the particular relating strategy. For example, while it is acknowledged that learning another language is a difficult task, most outsiders to any people group—including the poor—are able to succeed at this relating strategy, as well as with the two other minimal relating strategies. However, many outsiders fail to adequately advance on to the mid-level and maximal strategies. Why? Because most outsiders, while provided with basic language and culture learning strategies, are usually not provided with the tools to dig more deeply into the culture of the people group. They simply lack the proper training to carry out these necessary mid-level and maximal strategies.[24] This major oversight is not necessarily the fault of the outsiders themselves. In many cases it is the fault of their training institutions that have an inadequate number of "relating" courses in their curriculums. In other cases it is the fault of the agencies that are sending the outsiders who—in the name of expediency, cost, and oftentimes hyper-evangelistic missiological views—consider any more extensive "relating" training unnecessary.

So what relating strategies are appropriate for Bible interpretation done with the poor? Of course the poor are already masters of their own culture and already relate well within it. However, when it comes to their own Christianity, or to their interpretation of God's Word, they have sometimes not been allowed to use those strategies that make up the very essence of who they are. Or they have been afraid to use their own strategies because they feel that somehow their strategies must be inferior to those from the outside. As a result, the poor in many cases have not used their own relating strategies as a part of their Bible interpretation process. They have oftentimes been disenfranchised from their own rich cultural inheritance in regards to both understanding the truths of the Bible and communicating those truths in ways that will be relevant for themselves and for their people. Such a travesty must be addressed both by the poor themselves as well as by those outsiders who work with the poor.

Conclusion: Towards Bible Interpretation *With* the Poor

How well are we, who are mostly non-poor, truly engaged with the poor in regards to Bible interpretation? This paper has suggested that we are on the right track, but there is still some way to go to truly meet the needs of the rural and urban poor of the worldwide church. The challenge for professors teaching at theological and missiological training institutions worldwide is recognizing the authority of God's Word while at the same time being relevant in specific cultural contexts. Though the Bible must always take precedence over any culture, in the final analysis we want our students, upon graduation, to be able to rightly handle the Bible with relevance in the various contexts in which they will be ministering, especially when those contexts will be with the poor.

With this in mind, there are practical steps that professors and training institutions—in both the western and non-western worlds—can take to help make their Bible interpretation and, in turn, their overall theological and missiological education more relevant for their local contexts. These steps include:

Emphasize exegeting the culture. As we have already seen, while most students of Bible interpretation are very familiar with what is necessary to properly exegete a biblical text, they are often not prepared to effectively communicate the results of that exegesis to the people they are ministering with. While their exegetical results of the text are true to God's word, their results often are not very receptor oriented. As a result, it is crucial that training institutions look carefully at their existing curriculums and ask the difficult questions concerning whether or not the training that they offer adequately equips their graduates to properly exegete their own culture, as well as the culture of the people group to which they will be ministering, especially if that group is the poor. This, in my opinion, is the "last frontier" of Bible interpretation that must be addressed in order to insure that truly relevant, applicable, socially engaging and holistic Bible interpretation happens.

Allow for the Holy Spirit and for the community of believers. The advocates of the Two Step approach have oftentimes left out two major elements crucial to good Bible interpretation: interpretation that relies totally on the Holy Spirit and interpretation that is done in community. These two elements—pneumatic and communal—are key, I believe, to any truly relevant Bible interpretation. On the one hand, a pneumatic hermeneutic helps insure that the interpreter is relying on God as he/she interprets a biblical text, and not primarily on humans (whether it is the interpreter him/herself or those resources upon whom the interpreter is relying on to interpret the text for him/her: Bible dictionaries, commentaries, other people's sermons, and the like). A pneumatic hermeneutic also levels the playing field, so to speak, in that all Bible interpreters—regardless of their individual educational levels or academic expertise—have the same Holy Spirit to guide them in the Bible interpretation process throughout the two steps. On the other hand, a communal hermeneutic helps the interpreter make sure that his/her interpretation is truly relevant for the audience that he/she is ministering with. A communal hermeneutic also helps to ensure that all members of the local faith community are being heard as together the community wrestles with how a particular biblical text speaks to them. Both a pneumatic and a communal hermeneutic will also help to insure that a particular Bible interpretation is not false or heretical.

Pay attention to local ministry contexts. Carefully evaluate local ministry contexts and develop courses and programs that truly meet the ministry training needs of the local churches in those contexts, even if this means radically changing an existing curriculum.

Partner with local churches. After paying attention to local ministry contexts this partnering will naturally develop, so that the pastors and lay leaders being trained by the particular institution are appropriately trained for these churches and their leadership needs. Creatively work with the churches to ensure that their training needs are enfolded into new or existing training programs: a "win-win" situation for both training institution and local church.

Enhance the faculty's awareness of local contexts. Develop new faculty, and engage experienced faculty, who are intimately acquainted with the training institution's local context and who ideally have ministered in local churches in that context. Make sure that tenured faculty stay intimately and actively connected with the local church scene.

Offer non-academic tracks and programs. Do not be afraid to offer non-academic tracks and programs to help meet the overwhelming leadership needs of the poor churches throughout both the western and non-western world. Only a very small percentage of pastors—and potential pastors and lay leaders worldwide—have the time, money and qualifications to take M.A. and especially M.Div. programs. Our training institutions must be at the forefront in helping to equip the vast number of these "non-degree pastors" through programs and courses facilitated by existing faculty and masteral graduates.[25]

We have covered much ground in this paper, from colonization and the resulting paternalism that has influenced theological and missiological education and Bible interpretation worldwide, to an examination of the relevance of the courses and curricula that we teach and implement, to strategies for exegeting the biblical text as well as the cultural context, to some practical steps to take in order to make our Bible interpretation more relevant. Certainly there is much for us to ponder as we truly seek to carry out Bible interpretation that truly engages the whole church in the 21st century, especially the church of the poor.

Notes

1   In this paper I use the terms "poor," "rural poor," and "urban poor" interchangeably, though most everything in this paper relates in general terms to all those individuals and groups who are considered economically poor.

2   For a more thorough analysis of the weaknesses of the Two Step approach, especially in non-western cross-cultural situations, see Larry W. Caldwell, "Towards the New Discipline of Ethnohermeneutics: Questioning the Relevancy of Western Hermeneutical Methods in the Asian Context." Journal of Asian Mission 1/1 (1999), 21-43.

3   Brigitte Jordan, "Authoritative Knowledge and Its Construction," in Childbirth and Authoritative Knowledge, eds. Robbie E. Davis-Floyd and Carolyn F. Sargent (Berkeley, CA: University of California Press, 1997), 56.

4   Caldwell, "Towards the New Discipline of Ethnohermeneutics," 25.

5   Stephen D. Brookfield, "Transformative Learning as Ideology Critique," in Learning as Transformation, ed. Jack Mezirow (San Francisco, CA: Jossey-Bass, 2000), 27.

6   See Phil Jenkins, The New Faces of Christianity. Believing the Bible in the Global South (New York, NY: Oxford, 2006), especially Chapter 2. See also the works of R. S. Sugirtharajah, such as Postcolonial Reconfigurations. An Alternative Way of Reading the Bible and Doing Theology (St. Louis, MO: Chalice Press, 2003); The Bible and Empire. Postcolonial Explorations (New York, NY: Cambridge University Press, 2005); and The Postcolonial Biblical Reader, ed. (Malden, MA: Blackwell, 2006).

7   George D. Spindler, Education and Cultural Process. Anthropological Approaches. Third edition (Long Grove, IL: Waveland Press, 1997), 272.

8   Manfred F. Kohl, The Church in the Philippines. A Research Project with Special Emphasis on Theological Education (Manila, RP: OMF Literature, 2005), 19.

9   Of course we must also ask if our faculty are adequately trained for rural and urban poor realities; see Larry W. Caldwell, "Riots in the City: Replacing Nineteenth-century Urban Training Models with Relevant

'Urbanized' Training Models for the Twenty-first Century" in Reaching the City. Reflections on Urban Mission for the Twenty-first Century, eds. Gary Fujino, Timothy R. Sisk and Tereso C. Casiño (Pasadena, CA: William Carey Library), 102-103.

10   Though coming from the standpoint of working towards the contextualization of good theology in Asia, the following articles are helpful starting points for relevant rural and urban poor ministry training: Todd S. LaBute, "Beyond Contextualism: A Plea for Asian First Level Theology," Asia Journal of Theology 20.1 (2006): 36-56; and specifically for the Philippines context see Timoteo D. Gener, "Re-visioning Local Theology: An Integral Dialogue with Practical Theology: A Filipino Evangelical Perspective," Journal of Asian Mission 6.2 (September 2004): 133-166, and Larry W. Caldwell, "Towards an Ethnohermeneutical Model for a Lowland Filipino Context," Journal of Asian Mission 7.2 (September 2005): 169-193. Cf. Jeri Gunderson, "Rethinking Holistic Ministry: Reflections on the Struggle Against Poverty in Asia," Journal of Asian Mission 10.1-2 (March-September): 3-15.

11   See Robert Chambers, Whose Reality Counts? Putting the First Last (London: ITDG Publishing, 1997).

12   Chambers, Whose Reality Counts?, 210.

13   Chambers, Whose Reality Counts?, 210.

14   See Steven J. Friesen, "The Blessings of Hegemony: Poverty, Paul's Assemblies, and the Class Interests of the Professoriate," in The Bible in the Public Square. Reading the Signs of the Times, eds. Cynthia Briggs Kitterdge, Ellen Bradshaw Aitken and Jonathan A. Draper (Minneapolis: Fortress, 2008), 117-128.

15   For a more thorough analysis of the type of rethink that is needed see Larry W. Caldwell, "How Asian is Asian Theological Education?" in Tending the Seedbeds. Educational Perspectives on Theological Education in Asia, ed. Allan Harkness (Quezon City, RP: Asia Theological Association, 2010), 23-45.

16   For more information see the Asian Theological Seminary's Center for Transformational Urban Leadership website at https://sites.google.com/site/atscourseofferings/center-for-transformational-urban-leadership-ctul.

17   Exceptions to this include those institutions connected with the Encarnacio Alliance of urban poor movement leaders, under the direction of founder Viv Grigg. Three currently affiliated institutions are: Asian Theological Seminary in Manila, Philippines; Hindustan Bible Institute in Chennai, India; and Azusa Pacific University in Los Angeles, USA. For more information on how a North American university is creatively meeting the need for relevant urban ministry workers see Azusa's website at www.apu.edu/clas/globalstudies/urbanleadership/courses.

18   D. N. Premnath, Border Crossings. Cross-Cultural Hermeneutics (Maryknoll, NY: Orbis, 2007), 6.

19   Cf. Larry W. Caldwell, "Interpreting the Bible With the Poor," in The Church and Poverty in Asia, ed. Lee Wanak (Manila, RP: OMF Literature, 2008), 171-180. See also Hans de Wit, et. al, eds., Through the Eyes of Another. Intercultural Reading of the Bible (Elkhart, IN: Institute of Mennonite Studies, 2004) and Caldwell, "Towards an Ethnohermeneutical Model for a Lowland Filipino Context."

20   Premnath, Border Crossings, 7.

21   In this paper I am specifically limiting myself to those rural and urban poor groups that are at least marginally literate and who have the Bible, or portions of it, translated into their own language. Oral poor groups demand entirely different strategies in terms of Step One of the Two Step approach, although the initial minimal reading strategies listed above can also be done in listening to the text.

22   Elsewhere I have argued at length concerning the pros and cons of some of the maximal reading strategies for Bible interpretation done today in non-Western cultures, especially those cultures that oftentimes do not have a history of such maximal reading strategies. I will not reiterate my points here except to say that I am increasingly of the opinion that such maximal reading strategies are sometimes highly overrated—except for academics—and come directly from the dominance of the West in Bible interpretation and theological education worldwide. See my "Towards the New Discipline of Ethnohermeneutics" and my "A Response to the Responses of Tappeiner and Whelchel to Ethnohermeneutics." Journal of Asian Mission 2/1 (2000), 135-145. Of course a small number of individuals within any people group, including the poor, should be taught and be able to competently handle the maximal reading strategies for two reasons: first, to help their hermeneutical community (i.e. local

church) avoid possible heretical interpretations; and second, to be able to effectively dialogue with advanced readers from other groups who also have these maximal reading skills.

23   I am well aware that there is much debate among scholars as to whether interpretation (exegesis) is limited to Step One, and that it is application that we are really referring to in Step Two. However, I believe that we need to increasingly see that interpretation (exegesis) is also needed for Step Two. If we only look for application in Step Two we may be limiting the relevancy of the entire interpretation process.

24   For more information on how to dig more deeply into a culture see Caldwell, "Towards an Ethnohermeneutical Model for a Lowland Filipino Context." Cf. Tom A. Steffen, Reconnecting God's Story to Ministry. Cross-Cultural Storytelling at Home and Abroad (Waynesboro, GA: Authentic Media, 2005) and Leonora Tubbs Tisdale, Preaching as Local Theology and Folk Art (Minneapolis, MN: Fortress, 1997).

25   For example, Sioux Falls Seminary, where I teach, is currently working on a non-academic training track that will help equip recent refugee arrivals in Sioux Falls and the dozens of small ethnic churches that have recently sprung up in the area. The majority of these urban poor refugee pastors and lay leaders have limited formal academic training but nevertheless have a calling to serve the church and need the opportunity to be equipped for such service.

Eugène Casalis and the French Mission to Basutoland (1833-1856)

A Case Study of Lamin Sanneh's Mission-by-Translation Paradigm in Nineteenth Century Southern Africa

W. Benjamin Beckner

DOI: 10.7252/Paper.000016

About the Author:

Benjamin Beckner (D.Min, Gordon-Conwell Theological Seminary; M.Div. Trinity Evangelical Divinity School; D.E.U.G., Faculté Libre de Théologie Évangélique, Vaux-sur-Seine, France; B.A., Asbury College) is adjunct instructor of Missiology at the Institut Biblique de Genève in Switzerland and at the Institut de Théologie de Jérusalem in Israel. Missionary to francophone Europe since 1984, and following several church planting projects in Belgium, Benjamin is invested in training and mobilization for cross-cultural and global mission in French- speaking Europe. He recently presented a paper on the theme of Missions and Colonialism at the Eugène Casalis Symposium in Morija, Lesotho, held on the occasion of the bicentennial of Casalis' birth and cosponsored by the National University of Lesotho and the University of Paris VII Diderot. Member of REMEEF, a network of francophone evangelical missiologists, as well as ASM, he has published articles on missiological themes in numerous French publications.

Abstract

In his work, *Translating the Message: The Missionary Impact on Culture*, Lamin Sanneh claims that, from its beginnings at Pentecost, Christian mission, through its practice of vernacular language transcription and Bible translation, characteristically makes "the recipient culture the true and final locus of the proclamation, so that the religion arrives without the presumption of cultural rejection" (p. 29). In this paper we evaluate the Paris Evangelical Missionary Society's mission to Basutoland (1833-1856), spearheaded by Eugène Casalis and Thomas Arbousset, in light of Lamin Sanneh's theses with regard to the Christian gospel and its missionary propagation. We will pay particular attention to the missionaries' attitudes towards the Basotho people, language and culture; their ambiguous relationship to European colonialism; and their contribution to the founding of modern Lesotho. What were the primary factors of the French mission's success in establishing an indigenous church, a self-propagating movement, and ultimately in laying the groundwork for a nation?

"The Word became flesh, and dwelt among us" - John 1:14

Introduction

In his groundbreaking monograph, *Translating the Message: The Missionary Impact on Culture* (Sanneh 1989), African scholar Lamin Sanneh,[1] claims that the historical coincidence of European imperialistic colonialism and the heyday of modern missions has oftentimes allowed for fanciful conjectures with regard to the relationship of the two phenomena:

> At its most self-conscious stage, mission coincided with Western colonialism, and with that juncture students of the subject have gone on to make all kinds of judgments about the intrinsic bond between the two forces. Historians who are instinctively critical of received tradition in other spheres are more credulous in perpetuating the notion of mission as "imperialism at prayer" . . . Mission came to acquire the unsavory odor of collusion with the colonial powers. . . . The forces pitted against a fair understanding of mission in the late twentieth century are formidable . . . many people are committed to the ideological position that mission is oppressive, and anachronistic to boot (1989: 88).

Sanneh, himself a convert from Islam in his home country of Gambia, takes to task this well-worn caricature of nineteenth century European missions as essentially a tool of Western cultural imperialism. Sanneh asserts: "Modern historiography has established a tradition that mission was the surrogate of Western colonialism, and that . . . together these two movements combined to destroy indigenous cultures. . . . I wish in this book to present another point of view (1989: 4)."

Eugène Casalis and Thomas Arbousset, French Protestant missionaries sent to southern Africa by the newly formed Paris Evangelical Missionary Society (PEMS), arrived in Basutoland (today's Kingdom of Lesotho) in June of 1833, responding to an invitation from King Moshoeshoe. From their base station in Morija, they would transcribe Sesotho (the language of the Basotho people) and begin the translation and diffusion of the Scriptures; instigate literacy, social and commercial projects; and ultimately contextualize the gospel among the Basotho. Their labors gave birth not only to the Lesotho Evangelical Church,[2] but also to the nation of Lesotho.[3] Their experience illustrates a mid nineteenth century case study of the impact of Bible translation on both culture and nation in southern Africa.

The French mission to the Basotho is a clear counter-example of the largely imaginary and revisionist caricature of nineteenth century missions as the puppet and pawn of imperialist powers. PEMS pioneer missionaries Casalis and Arbousset, whose work issued in an authentic, autonomous and indigenous African church and, ultimately, in a nation, demonstrated exemplary anthropological methodology, linguistic skill, and cross-cultural aptitude.

Thesis and Argument of This Paper

In this article we will attempt to establish that the Paris Evangelical Missionary Society's adherence to the premises of the mission-by-translation paradigm, as described by Lamin Sanneh, was the primary human factor in the founding of the indigenous Church of Basutoland (which would become the Lesotho Evangelical Church in 1963). After taking a closer look at Sanneh's contradistinctive paradigms of mission-by-translation and we will then examine and evaluate the initial efforts of the PEMS mission among the Basotho, paying particular attention to the missionary intuitions, attitudes and praxis of Eugène Casalis and Thomas Arbousset with regard to the Basotho people, language and culture mission-by-diffusion. Additionally, we will observe how Casalis and Arbousset, through their contextualizing activities, acted as vernacular agents, inspiring indigenous sentiment and thereby laying the groundwork for the founding of a nation.

Lamin Sanneh's Mission-by-Translation Paradigm

Sanneh states his thesis concisely:

Christianity, from its origins, identified itself with the need to translate out of Aramaic and Hebrew, and from that position came to exert a dual force in its historical development. One was the resolve to relativize its Judaic roots. . . . The other was to destigmatize Gentile culture and adopt that culture as a natural extension of the life of the new religion (1989: 1).

For Sanneh, the gospels are "a translated version of the message of Jesus, and that means that Christianity is a translated religion without a revealed language" (2003: 97). He muses: "Christianity seems unique in being the only world religion that is transmitted without the language or originating culture of its founder" (2003: 98). Consequently,

Christians found themselves propelled toward a popular mode for translation and for communicating the message. . . . Christians became pioneers of linguistic development. ... The resulting literacy . . . produced social and cultural transformation. A culture that for the first time possessed a dictionary and a grammar was a culture endowed for renewal and empowerment (2003: 98-99).

Vernacular transcription and Bible translation by missionaries "is more than just a tactical concession to win converts. It is, rather, an acknowledgment that languages have intrinsic merit for communicating the divine message. They are worthy of God's attention" (2003: 100).

Christianity's cross-cultural expansion in history, beginning with the experiences of the early church recounted in the Acts of the Apostles, was accomplished through the practice of what Sanneh calls "mission by *translation*," which is ideologically opposed to and ultimately incompatible with what he refers to as "mission by *diffusion*" or "mission as *cultural imperialism*." To support his case, he alludes to historian Arnold Toynbee, who, in Sanneh's words, affirmed that, continuing the legacy of the early church, modern missions". . . followed the logic of the translatability of Christianity and submitted the religion in the most intimate way to the terms of local culture. By so doing, such missionaries had become indigenizers in the best sense of the term, rather than cultural imperialists (1989: 90)."

New Testament Precedents

Sanneh's starting point is the nascent church in the Acts of the Apostles, with the query: "How might the church, Gentile or other, rise to its missionary obligation unless it believed that its experience, which is necessarily culturally defined, was in some fashion normative of the divine truth?" (1989: 28-29). He then outlines two ways to proceed, two paradigms:

> One is to make the missionary culture the inseparable carrier of the message. This we might call mission by *diffusion*. By it religion expands from its initial cultural base and is implanted in other societies primarily as a matter of cultural identity. . . . Conversion that takes place in mission by diffusion is not primarily a theological inquiry. It is, rather, assimilation into a predetermined positivist environment. The other way is to make the recipient culture the true and final locus of the proclamation, so that the religion arrives without the presumption of cultural rejection.[4] This we might call mission by *translation*. It carries with it a deep theological vocation, which arises as an inevitable stage in the process of reception and adaptation. . . . Conversion that takes place in mission as translation rests on the conviction that might be produced in people after conscious critical reflection. What is distinctive about this critical reflection is that it assumes . . . a relativized status for the culture of the message-bearer (1989: 29).

Despite the early attempts on the part of the Jerusalem apostles to assimilate non-Jews through the postexilic practice of cultural proselytization—the predecessor of mission-by-diffusion—the combination of a series of cross-cultural missionizing experiences along with strategic interventions on the part of the Holy Spirit allowed the early church to radically redirect its missional theology and praxis in harmony with the entirely new paradigm of mission-by-translation, which is on the supposition of individual spiritual conversion. This reorientation had several unforeseeable and beneficial consequences with regard to apostolic mission:

In Paul's mind mission was the solvent of cultural xenophobia, essentially his own. . . . No one is the exclusive or normative pattern for anyone else, and no one culture can be God's favorite. . . . The result is pluralism on a radical scale. . . . Mission helps to burst the old wineskins with the pressure of cross-cultural interpretation dissolving the barriers of cultural exclusiveness (1989: 29-30).

The conversion of Paul the Jew *cum* Apostle to the Gentiles—which debuted with his life-transforming encounter with the resurrected Christ on the road to Damascus—was only complete when, through his multiple encounters and sustained collaboration with Gentiles whose lives had been transformed by the same resurrected Jesus, Paul surrendered his cultural imperialism and self-sufficiency, exhorting other believing Jews to do likewise. Sanneh writes:

The emergence of the Gentile church produced profound theological repercussions, which it fell to Paul to try to enunciate and systematize. . . . He came to be in radical tension with his own cultural roots, not because those roots were unsound but because the Gentile breakthrough had cast a shadow over any claims for cultural absolutism, Jewish or other. . . . Paul's ambiguous and often very critical relationship to Judaism cannot be isolated from his participation in the Gentile mission, and with good reason. As missionaries of the modern era were to find, encountering the reality of God beyond the inherited terms of one's culture reduces reliance on that culture as a universal normative pattern. A fresh standard of discernment is introduced by which the essence of the gospel is unscrambled from one cultural yoke in order to take firm hold in a different culture. . . . The center of Christianity, Paul perceived, was in the heart and life of the believer without the presumption of conformity to one cultural ideal[5] (1989: 24-25).

At the very heart of Sanneh's thesis is the concept of translation, and at the heart of translation, writes Andrew Walls, is the Christian doctrine of the Incarnation:

Christian faith rests on a divine act of translation: "the Word became flesh, and dwelt among us" (John 1:14). Any confidence that we have in the translatability of the Bible rests on that prior act of translation. There is a history of translation of the Bible because there was a translation of the Word into flesh. . . . In prophetic faiths God speaks to humanity: in Christian faith, God becomes human. . . . Incarnation is translation. When God became man, Divinity was translated into humanity, as though humanity were a receptor language. . . . Bible translation as a process is thus both a reflection of the central act on which the Christian faith depends and a concretization of the commission which Christ gave his disciples. Perhaps no other activity more clearly represents the mission of the Church (Walls 1996: 26-28).

At the dawn of Christianity, then, "the spiritual and theological issues raised by the demands of the cross-cultural translation of the Gospel involved an immense struggle, evidence of which is found throughout the New Testament" (Smith 2003: 69). Only multiple and often spectacular interventions by the Holy Spirit allowed the early church and its apostolic founders to break out of their captivity to Hebrew religion, culture and language, overcoming their ethnic and linguistic chauvinism in order to move forward with their worldwide mission to the nations. Without the momentous decision taken by the Jerusalem Council recorded in Acts chapter 15 to admit cultural pluralism within the church, it is not an exaggeration to affirm that the spread of Christianity beyond the otherwise watertight frontiers of Jewish ethnocentrism would have permanently aborted.

Although there are some notable exceptions,[6] Christian missionaries throughout the history of the expansion of the church have considered languages in all their diversity as adequate vehicles for communicating the gospel to humanity in all of its linguistic and ethnic varieties. Consequently missionaries have gone to great pains and vast resources have been garnered in order to translate Christianity's foundational document, the Bible, into the vernaculars.

Historical Evidence of Dual Paradigms

By way of contrast, Sanneh identifies Islam as the major proponent of mission-by-diffusion: "Islam . . . exemplifies this mode of mission. It carries with it certain inalienable cultural assumptions, such as the indispensability of its Arabic heritage in Scripture, law, and religion" (1989: 29). Islam's theological attachment to Arabic as its sacred language of revelation and consequently to Arab culture as its carrier explains why mission-as-diffusion has prevailed as its preferred paradigm of expansion. In summary:

> There are striking differences between Islam and Christianity in spite of their common missionary ambition, yet nothing is more fundamental than their contrasting attitudes to the translatability of their respective Scriptures. Scriptural translation . . . is the vintage mark of Christianity, whereas for Islam universal adherence to a nontranslatable Arabic Qur'an remains its characteristic feature" (1989: 211).

Sanneh bolsters his case from Christian history with references to the missionizing works of Cyril and Methodius among the Slavs; Roman Catholic missions in America, Japan, and India; and, later, Protestant missions in India and Africa, concluding with David Livingstone, for whom the vernacular Bible had become the "real engine of mission" (1989: 114). If Roman Catholic missions in the early modern era recognized and accommodated the vernacular in the liturgy and the discipline of the church, Protestant missions "in their translation work made mother tongues the centerpiece of mission. . . . Thus were sown the seeds of vernacular renewal . . . encouraging popular movements in areas of missionary outreach" (1989: 124).

Sanneh goes further in his analysis: "Missionary adoption of the vernacular . . . was tantamount to adopting indigenous cultural criteria for the message, a piece of radical indigenization" (1989: 3). Meticulous, dynamic, and culturally-sensitive translation of the Scriptures into the vernaculars, followed by the forming and nurturing of indigenous churches to which it invariably gives rise, has probably been the single most strategic missionary activity in the history of the Church. Kwame Bediako corroborates this analysis:

It is to the undying credit of the modern missionary enterprise from the West, and to the lasting benefit of the newer churches which have resulted, that the value of the vernacular Bible for converts was generally recognized quite early. There is probably no more important single explanation for the massive presence of Christianity on the African continent than the availability of the Scriptures in many African languages (Bediako 1997: 62).

Sanneh does not gloss over the obvious humanity, neither of the first century apostles nor of Western missionaries in the nineteenth and twentieth centuries: all were subject to some degree of cognitive dissonance, of incoherence and inconsistencies, and of errors committed against the recipients of mission. Sanneh does not claim that Christian mission has never employed the methods of mission-by-diffusion. In this regard, he cites the Jerusalem apostles who at first attempted to fulfill their universal mission according to the Jewish paradigm of cultural inclusion and diffusion, but which they quickly abandoned in favor of the new paradigm, which Jesus had exemplified in his own teaching and practice of mission. Neither does Sanneh contend that mission-by-diffusion, as historically practiced by Islam, for example, has never or could never employ practices normally associated with mission-by-translation. He concludes, however, that mission-by-diffusion is "unquestionably the stronger strand in Islam whereas mission as translation is the vintage mark of Christianity" (1989: 29).

Although on occasion Sanneh may get close to eulogizing certain missionaries for their perspicacity and competence, he generally describes them as deeply sincere servants who—largely in spite of themselves, their mission agencies, priorities and strategies—managed to accomplish at the very least the one right thing, that is, translating the Bible into vernacular languages and then contextualizing the gospel into local cultures.

For Sanneh, the act of transcription and translation functions as a catalyst that may very likely bear unexpected fruit:

When one translates, it is like pulling the trigger of a loaded gun: the translator cannot recall the hurtling bullet. Translation thus activates a process that might supersede the original intention of the translator. Mainly for this reason we distinguish between the motive of mission and the consequences, between the "trigger," so to speak, and the "bullet" (1989: 53).

Sanneh continues: "Missionary translation was instrumental in the emergence of indigenous resistance to colonialism" (1989: 123). In the case of the emerging African church, "vernacular translation often converged with steps to encourage indigenous ascendancy.... In their vernacular work, Christian missions helped nurse the sentiments for the national cause, which mother tongues crystallized and incited (1989: 125)."

The practice of mission by translation tends then to issue not only in the founding of indigenous churches, but may also, through its affirmation of local language and culture, lead to different forms of indigenous and even nationalist sentiments and causes. Sanneh goes as far as to claim that the "seeds of the divergence between mission and colonialism were sown with the translation enterprise" (1989: 112-113).

For Sanneh, the contention by critics that Christian mission necessarily interferes with indigenous cultures—a sensitive charge and deserving of careful consideration—is probably overdrawn, simplistic, and in most instances, unwarranted. Such criticism

... denies the possibility of genuine cultural exchange and, beyond that, it seals culture from the possibility of change. . . . Enough has been said to suggest that even when it was blatant cultural interference, mission excited sufficient vernacular initiative to commence a critical appropriation process.... It is one of the interesting ironies of the Western missionary enterprise that the evangelical motive actually helped to shield indigenous populations from the unmitigated assault of the West and that, through the elevation of the vernacular in translation, missions furnished the critical language for evaluating the West in its secular and religious impact (1989: 202-203).

Rather than being the puppets of Western colonialism and the rapists and destroyers of cultures, missionaries of the nineteenth and twentieth centuries were, more often than not, the bane of colonial powers and the defenders, preservers and revitalizers of ancient cultures. Sanneh wrote:

> Men and women who were never distinguished as explicit champions of their own culture found the attractions of another irresistible, and as a consequence became promoters of the lore and wisdom of other people. Whatever their motive, such missionaries were laying the foundations of indigenous revitalization to which the Christian cause would be tied (1989: 25).

Bediako generalizes: "The phenomenon of African Christianity in the twentieth century, therefore, far from signifying an acute Westernisation of African life, may rather be the evidence of how much African peoples feel at home in the Gospel of Jesus Christ" (2003: 62). Sanneh concludes:

> Thoughtful missionaries understood that God had preceded them in Africa, ... that translation involved esteem for the vernacular culture, . . . and that, finally, linguistic investigations and the systematic inventory of indigenous resources were likely to touch off wider and longer-lasting repercussions in the culture (1989: 166-167).

Mission-by-Translation In the Work of Eugène Casalis and Thomas Arbousset

It has been well documented that Casalis and Arbousset rejected key ideological, attitudinal and behavioral tendencies often associated with mission-by-diffusion, namely: racial supremacism, European ethnocentrism, and the cultural imperialism characteristic of the European colonization of Africa.

But did Casalis and Arbousset, and the PEMS after them, in fact wholly embrace the premises of mission-by-translation? Did PEMS missionaries consider Sesotho language and Basotho culture as adequate mediums for the translation of the Scriptures and as adequate carriers of the Christian gospel?

As we have seen, at the heart of the mission-by-translation paradigm is ... *translation*, the act of transmitting meaning from one linguistic medium to another, with all the inherent structural and cultural challenges and risks. With their acquisition of Sesotho, Casalis and Arbousset would begin their own process of missionary translation and incarnation of the gospel into Basotho culture, which would not only alter the course of Basotho history, but also set the direction and the standard for future PEMS work.[7]

After their arrival in Basutoland, Casalis and Arbousset learned Sesotho in an amazingly short time, a feat that, according to biographer Marie-Claude Mosimann-Barbier, may be explained in part by the prior linguistic work in Bechuana (a language closely related to Sesotho) completed by Scotsman Robert Moffat, aided by Casalis' fellow PEMS missionaries Samuel Rolland and Prosper Lemue.[8] Casalis' natural flair for language and his interest and training in linguistics would aid not only in capitalizing on Moffat's work but also in simultaneously unlocking the secrets of the Sesotho language and Basotho culture.

In order to discover or construct dynamic equivalents for translation purposes, and following the example of Moffat, Casalis and Arbousset actively engaged native elders in the work. South African anthropologist David B. Coplan comments: "If anthropology is most fundamentally an exercise in translation, then the recruitment of elders as collective, dialogic critics of the missionaries' efforts to translate the gospels into Sesotho stands out as exemplary ethnographic method (2003: 4)."

Mosimann-Barbier brings to light a significant contrast between the work of Casalis and Arbousset and that of the future colonizers:

> The French missionaries never at any moment attempted to impose their language on the Basotho, contrary to the later practice of the colonizers who considered the indigenous languages to be inferior. Casalis justifies this choice and, ahead of his time,

emphasizes the importance of preserving the mother tongue: "As concerning awakening the conscience, touching the heart, producing life-transforming convictions, the instrument *par excellence* is the mother tongue. As poor and ill-conceived as it may be, it possesses accents whose significance cannot be measured by philosophers" (Mosimann-Barbier 2012: 260-261).[9]

Casalis' study of Sesotho led him to the conclusion that « the Basotho idiom has furnished all that is necessary for reproducing divine thought with clarity and without abusive long-windedness" (Mosimann-Barbier 2012: 251). In another place he summarizes: "The language which the Basotho speak, and which is understood by thousands of other natives, has been mastered, rendered more supple and even enriched, to the point of being sufficient for all religious and social purposes" (Casalis 2011: 338).[10] Casalis and Arbousset discovered in Sesotho what they had to some degree expected: vocabulary and concepts sufficient to translate and contextualize the gospel and with which to communicate the whole counsel of God contained in the Scriptures.

In short, Casalis unambiguously espoused the central premise of Sanneh's mission-by-translation paradigm, namely, the prioritizing of the transcription of the language and translation of the gospel, which, far from being bound to a divinely appointed language and culture of revelation, is destined for vernacular transmission and eventual inculturation. The analysis of Sesotho and the translation of the Bible into this previously unwritten language would open windows of insight into the culture of the Basotho—its belief system and values, history, hopes, and fears—which Casalis and Arbousset believed would then provide keys for the missionizing of the Basotho people.

Casalis and his missionary colleagues held in high regard the Basotho people, their language and culture, which, to the degree that it was possible for Europeans, they adopted as their own. George McCall Theale, in his Basutoland Records, concluded:

The French missionaries sent to our country for life pondered problems from the vantage point of the natives . . . . They did not seek to turn the Basotho into simple reproductions of the white man but rather encouraged them to progress in the furrow of their own conduct, adopting their way of thinking. This is the secret of their success as civilizers and of the great influence to which they attained in Lesotho (Mosimann-Barbier 2012: 226).[11]

Coplan suspects that Casalis' interest in Basotho culture went beyond the mere search for keys to aid in communicating the gospel message: "One cannot avoid the impression that Casalis found the study of the 'natural history' of Basotho culture and the practice of comparative ethnology... rewarding for their own sake: evangelization as a pretext for ethnology" (2003: 4). French africanist Alain Ricard concurs with this analysis: "I believe Moshoeshoe . . . had sensed in Arbousset this curious and fertile respect which gives birth to great works and nourishes great friendships" (2012: 17).

Both Coplan and Mosimann-Barbier identify several apparent inconsistencies and paradoxes in the attitudes and behavior of PEMS missionaries. For example, Coplan evokes Casalis' aversion to some Basotho customs, such as:

. . . bridewealth, polygyny, rites of initiation, and magical procedures in healing (which) blinded him to the integral value of these practices in the overall moral economy and social system that he so brilliantly documented, analyzed, and otherwise respected and admired. The Calvinism of the PEMS was unfortunately not only in prejudice but also in substance directly opposed to core elements of Sesotho, including those that underpinned the existing political and social order. (2003: 6).

Mosimann-Barbier elicits the lack of tolerance on the part of Casalis vis-à-vis certain Basotho superstitions, witchcraft, water witching, ancestor veneration, circumcision and initiation rites, and especially polygamy.[12]

Coplan admits, however that "despite his disapproval of Basotho custom as obstacle to Christianity, Casalis could not 'help feeling a certain respect for these traditions'" (2003: 6). Mosimann-Barbier underscores the role of missionary negotiation with Moshoshoe in the disappearance of several of the above practices: ≪ Depending on the moment, the king opted either for tradition or for the new religion. . . . The king thus was able to obtain, most often by persuasion and example, that his people gradually renounce a certain number of Basotho customs" (2012: 220, 222).

We may conclude that PEMS missionaries did not impose their cultural views on Basotho society, but attempted to use persuasion and negotiation, allowing Moshoeshoe and his elders, through their system of *pitso* (national assembly), to propose and initiate change and promote gradual transformation.

For Casalis and Arbousset, Basotho language and culture became, in Sanneh's words, the "true and final locus of the proclamation" and "a piece of radical indigenization." Coplan summarizes the indigenizing posture and nature of PEMS work in respect to Basotho culture in general:

> The PEMS became the commoners' church, transforming itself into the Lesotho Evangelical Church, the champion of independence and indigenousness, making Sesotho tradition and history respectable and maintaining its reputation for intellectualism, local literature, and pride in Basotho heritage (2003: 10).

Despite weaknesses and flaws in missionary transmission, the fruit of the PEMS mission in Lesotho was indeed an indigenous church. Possessing the Scriptures in the vernacular, the Basotho church theoretically and potentially possessed the instrument by which she might measure not only her own work and culture, but also that of her founding missionaries.

Awakening Indigenous Sentiment Among the Basotho

Did gospel translation into the vernacular by PEMS missionaries in Lesotho, like the "trigger of a loaded gun," activate a process whose consequences might "supersede the original intention of the translators?" (Sanneh 1989: 53).

With all the imperfections of its human agents, the practice of mission-by-translation should naturally give birth to indigenous sentiment, which may then express itself in the form of local and, in certain contexts, even national causes. As we have seen, Sanneh claims that, in the case of the emerging African church, "Christian missions helped nurse the sentiments for the national cause, which mother tongues crystallized and incited" (1989: 125). This was certainly the case in Lesotho, where admittedly, even before the arrival of missionaries, the dream of a Basotho nation had already been born in Moshoeshoe. PEMS missionaries arrived on the field with their own dreams of Christian nationhood, as exemplified by Samuel Rolland who had "dreamed for them (these nations) nationhood, their own language, a firmly established political independence" (Mosimann-Barbier 2012: 2).[13]

The economic contribution missionaries made to the growth of the national cause is well documented. However, without the transcription of Sesotho—a supra-tribal *lingua franca*—it is difficult to imagine that Basotho efforts alone would have culminated in nationhood. The transcription of Sesotho is probably the single most important factor in unifying the Basotho in their march to nationhood. Claude-Hélène Perrot affirms; "By reducing Sesotho to a written language, the missionaries contribute to national unification" (1963: 105).

Other crucial factors for the growth of the national cause were the diplomatic, logistical and moral support of the missionaries, the introduction of Christianity and the establishment of a national church under indigenous leadership. Coplan remarks that the description and analysis of Basotho political and legal systems not only "reflected French missionary interest in the development of the Basotho towards nationhood," but also "served the strategy of converting the Basotho aristocracy 'from the top down' in the building of a 'national church'" (2003: 5). Perrot concurs with this connection between organized religion and national sentiment:

> The imported religion may consolidate national unity as it does not recognize traditional tribal and clannish distinctions. ... The major Christian holidays to which a station invites its neighboring stations and which assemble thousands of participants coming often from distant places reinforces this nationalizing tendency (1963: 105).

Despite the imperfections of its human agents, the practice of mission-by-translation among the Basotho by Casalis and Arbousset gave birth to an indigenous church, to indigenous sentiment, and finally to nationhood.

Conclusions

Eugène Casalis and Thomas Arbousset, from the beginning and throughout their mission to the Basotho, practiced mission-by-translation as evidenced by their commitment to mother tongue translation as the centerpiece and the motor of their work. Their attitudes and approach to the Basotho people and their culture were consistent with the esteem in which they held their language. Having provided the Basotho with their vernacular Scriptures, errors committed in the process of missionizing could conceivably be corrected with time by the indigenous and indigenizing Church of Basutoland in its outworking and incarnating of the gospel in its own context and in neighboring lands.

The vernacular renewal of Basotho culture was the fruit of the combined actions of the transcription of Sesotho, the translation and diffusion of the Bible in Sesotho, and the introduction of Christianity into Basotho society. Given their considerable investment in Bible translation, literacy and the founding of schools and churches, it is abundantly clear that PEMS missionaries possessed a full sense of their theological vocation vis-à-vis the Basotho, a hallmark of mission-by-translation.

It is difficult to assess to what degree conversions were the result of "conscious critical reflection" and "theological inquiry," the hallmark of mission-by-translation, rather than the mere "adoption of a new cultural identity and assimilation into a predetermined positivist environment" (Sanneh 1989: 29), the hallmark of mission-by-diffusion. However, the PEMS missionaries' insistence on personal conversion, along with the practice of public baptism of new converts, was a safeguard that, at the very least, ensured a minimum of individual theological understanding and engagement on the part of many, if not most converts.

Casalis and his colleagues approached the Basotho culture, in Sanneh's words as, the "true and final locus of the proclamation," demonstrating their commitment to Basotho language and culture as a new home, a new heartland for the gospel. Their close association and at times complicated collaboration with Moshoeshoe throughout the Basotho mission as it unfolded are evidences of their long-term commitment to an indigenous church firmly anchored in Basotho soil. In order to achieve this, they made serious efforts to relativize their own European and French culture of origin.

Lamin Sanneh has perhaps written prophetically with regard to Christianity's pluralist heritage and its ongoing practice of mission-by-translation in our day:

> We stand today at the threshold of a new phenomenon in the history of the church when peoples and cultures are flocking to the cause, conscious as never before of the particular, unique contribution they can make. Christianity has become a pluralist dispensation of enormous complexity, and religious statesmanship requires the flexible approach of translatability to foster this pluralism rather than opposing it as a threat. How well Christians manage their great pluralist heritage in these twilight years of the twentieth century will have enormous implications for the kind of society people live in (Sanneh 1989:6).

Notes

1   Professor of history and of Missions and World Christianity at Yale Divinity School.

2   Formerly, the Church of Basutoland. Today, 180 years after the arrival of Casalis and Arbousset in Basutoland, 90% of the population of the Kingdom of Lesotho considers itself Christian, of which 48% is Roman Catholic and the rest Protestant or Independent of one sort or another. The Lesotho Evangelical Church, the direct descendant of PEMS work which numbers over 270,000 adherents, represents the largest non-Catholic group in Lesotho at 15.3% of the Christian population, or 13% of the total population. (See Jason Mandryk, Operation World, Seventh edition, Biblica Publishing, Colorado Springs, 2010, p. 531.)

3   Basutoland became a protectorate of the United Kingdom in 1868, gaining its independence as the Kingdom of Lesotho in 1966.

4   That is, rejection by the agents of mission of the host culture as an adequate medium for communicating the gospel message.

5   That is, the cultural ideal of the missionary.

6   During numerous periods of Christian history the progress of mission slowed or came to a grinding halt due in large part to reversion to the attitudes and practices of mission-by-diffusion and its imposition of a Christianized sacramental language (such as Latin and Old Church Slavonic) and culture on unevangelized peoples.

7   Anthropologist David B. Coplan writes: "The Lesotho mission was the main spiritual colony of French Protestantism, indeed the model for all the others, and it fathered the development of the modern French Calvinist Church and its humanistic orientation in both France and Switzerland." David B. Coplan, "Imperial Culture in Countries Without Colonies: Africa and Switzerland," paper presented to the Conference, Nineteenth Century PEMS Missionaries and the Foundations of Anthropology in Southern Africa, University of the Witwatersrand, October 25-28, 2003, p. 10. Internet (accessed 17 October 2012): http://pages.unibas.ch/afrika/nocolonies/coplan.paper.rtf

8   See Marie-Claude Mosimann-Barbier, Un Béarnais en Afrique australe ou L'extraordinaire destin d'Eugène Casalis, L'Harmattan, Paris, 2012, p. 246.

9   Original quote from Eugène Casalis, Les missions et les langues nationales, Amsterdam, 1867, p. 11.

10   Originally published by Librairie Fischbacher, Paris, 1886.

11   Original quotation, George McCall Theal, Basutoland Records: Copies of Official Documents of Various Kinds, from 1833 to 1868, Capetown, 1883, Basutoland Records, vol 11, p. XXIV.

12   See Mosimann-Barbier, op. cit, p. 103.

13   Original quote: Timothy Holmes, in Daniel C. Bach, La France et l'Afrique du Sud: histoire, myths et enjeux contemporains, Khartala/ CREDU, Paris/Nairobi, 1990, p. 87.

Works Cited

Bediako, Kwame
    1997   *Christianity in Africa: The Renewal of a Non-Western Religion.* Maryknoll, NY: Orbis Press.

Casalis, Eugène
    1867   *Les Missions et les langues nationales,* Amsterdam.
    2011   *Mes souvenirs. Du Béarn à l'Afrique du Sud, l'histoire d'un missionnaire explorateur au XIXe siècle.* Mornant, France : Éditions Lirice. Originally published in Paris by Librairie Fischbacher, 1886.

Coplan, David B.
    2003   "Imperial Culture in Countries Without Colonies: Africa and Switzerland." Paper presented to the Conference, *Nineteenth Century PEMS Missionaries and the Foundations of Anthropology in Southern Africa.* University of the Witwatersrand, October 25-28. Internet (accessed 20 October 2012): http://pages. unibas.ch/afrika/nocolonies/coplan.paper.rtf

Mosimann-Barbier, Marie-Claude
    2012   *Un Béarnais en Afrique australe* ou *L'extraordinaire destin d'Eugène Casalis.* Paris, L'Harmattan.

Perrot, Claude-Hélène
    1963   "Premières années de l'implantation du christianisme au Lesotho." (1833-1847), in *Cahiers d'études africaines,* Vol. 4 N°13, pp. 97-124.
    1990   "Les missionnaires français et la construction d'un état." In Daniel C. Bach, *La France et l'Afrique du Sud : histoire, mythes et enjeux contemporains,* Paris/ Nairobi: Khartala/ CREDU.

Ricard, Alain
    2012   "Une cordée créatrice." In *Mission,* n° 224, October, p. 17.

Sanneh, Lamin
    1989   *Translating the Message: The Missionary Impact on Culture.* Maryknoll, NY: Orbis Books.
    2003   "The Bible and Its Mother Tongue Variations." In *Whose Religion is Christianity? The Gospel beyond the West,* Grand Rapids: Wm. B. Eerdmans Publishing Company.

Smith, David
    2003   *Mission After Christendom.* London: Darton, Longman and Todd Ltd.

Theal, George McCall
    1883   *Basutoland Records: Copies of Official Documents of Various Kinds, from 1833 to 1868.* Capetown, vol 11, p. XXIV.

Walls, Andrew
    1996   "The Translation Principle in Christian History." In *The Missionary Movement in Christian History: Studies in the Transmission of Faith.* Maryknoll, NY: Orbis Books.

The Transformational, Intersectional and Transcendental Agenda of Mission

Quest for a Spirituality of the Road

THIAS KGATLA

DOI: 10.7252/Paper.000024

About the Author:

Associate Professor, Science of Religion and Missiology at the University of Pretoria. He joined the staff of the Faculty of Theology at the University of Pretoria in 2010 after serving as a Professor of Missiology and Religious Studies at the University of Limpopo for eighteen years. At the University of Pretoria, Thias Kgatla teaches African Traditional Religions, Theology of African Independent Churches, Church and Cultural Communication, Theology of Mission, and Emerging Contextual Theologies. His major research spans the societal conflicts in the areas of witchcraft, politics and economic related violence in South Africa and the role the church should play.

Kgatla has lived and worked in South Africa and he has published articles in accredited journals in Missiology and religious Studies. He has served in executive committees of several ecumenical bodies and moderator of his Uniting Reformed Church in Southern Africa. He received his MTh, DTh (Missiology) and DLitt et Phil (Religious Studies) at the University of South Africa.

Abstract

Even the inspiring assumptions of a Rainbow Nation, the work of the Truth and Reconciliation Commission, and the miracle of a peaceful transition from apartheid to a democratic order in South Africa could not create the new society that the world had hoped for. Since 1994, the social problems and conflict that had evolved in South African communities for decades before the demise of apartheid have acquired new faces. This paper suggests new ways of analysis and the introduction of a spirituality for life and affirmation guided by Ubuntu, an 'I-Thou' spirituality that seeks new ways of healing broken relationships, through authentic transformation, intersectionality and transcendence. A transformational, intersectional approach with internal recognition of socially interwoven relatedness and the complexity of oppression and exclusion can set the stage for coexistence in a society with a history of conflict and bitterness and open up exclusive and oppressive relations for a new spirituality in South Africa.

Introduction

In South Africa, we envisaged forging the social bonds required to help a racially divided society and heal the victims of the previous oppressive system of apartheid to find meaning in coexistence as a Rainbow Nation, uniting individuals into civic communities beyond closed families and groups; but this has remained an empty dream. Racial inequality, intolerance and abject poverty continue to be evident in various institutions where different groups compete for high stakes. The level of social unrest, accompanied by violence between those who previously fought as 'comrades' in the Struggle against apartheid, is on the increase. The ills of the apartheid era have mutated and continue to haunt the very fabric of society. Even the church, endowed with the responsibility of bringing good news to the communities is divided by human greed, inequality, poverty and ideology has become dumbfounded if not totally ineffective.

A recent study by scholars at the University of the Witwatersrand, entitled *The Smoke that Calls: Insurgent citizenship, collective violence and the struggle for a place in the new South Africa: Eight case studies of community protest and xenophobic violence,* led by Karl von Holdt and Adèle Kirsten, reveals the social crisis that society has with regard to social cohesion (Kirsten and Von Holdt 2011:2). The centre cannot hold. The violent responses to the failure of elected officials to fulfil their promises are, in part fuelled by high levels of unemployment, poverty and asymmetrical power relations. There is a high level of anger in communities against the apparent self-enrichment of those in power and the neglect of the marginalised and the poor. The perception of the poor is that they will never get out of the vicious circle in which they exist and attain the virtuous one envisaged by the National Development Plan Commission[1] (Terreblanche 2012:121). The present government policies on development and transformation seem as unproductive as the apartheid measures. It has also become common practice for those who seek public office to exploit communities' vulnerability and discontent and unseat those in leadership to take their positions[2] (Langa 2011:62).

South Africa is economically better off than many other African states, and it is theoretically capable of feeding its entire people, but every night, many still go to bed on an empty stomach. South Africa has one of the most unequal distributions of income in the world. The inequality gap between the very rich and the very poor is so large that there is no sign that it could ever be reversed. According to Terreblanche (2012:80) in 2008 the income distribution of the total population in South Africa the top 20 per cent (10million individuals) received 74,7 per cent of total income, while 50 per cent (25 million individuals) received only 7,8 per cent. According to Terreblanche 83 per cent of this 20 per cent were whites (3,7 million individuals) and 11 per cent (4.4 million individuals) were Africans while Coloureds and Indians formed 25 percent and 60 per cent respectively. There is certainly something seriously wrong that politicians cannot get it right to lead the country out of the morass of apartheid.

According to Terreblance (2012:124) the old immoral and inhumane system of apartheid has been replaced with another immoral and inhumane system adopted by the African National Congress leadership in early1990s. The country's wealth is still in the hands of a minority, which now includes the few members of the black community who have become members of a black elite and who are now co-owners of the country's wealth with their white counterparts. Not enough has changed from the apartheid era (prior to 1994) to the present dispensation – in fact, many people in the country perceive the situation as worse than it was in the apartheid past[3].

Terreblanche (2012:124-129) lists eight fundamental wrongs that the ANC government could not put right. These include failure to address the apartheid legacy of abject poverty; a white elite have been allowed to transfer their wealth from the apartheid time into the new South Africa while the black elite was created with lucrative opportunities (undeservedly accumulated) at the expense of the black majority; the new black elite with an extravagant get-rich-quick mentality who are prepared to use devious methods of getting rich ushered in with revolutionary implications. The country did not succeed in creating Mandela's 'people-centred-society' and Bishop Tutu's "Rainbow Nation". There has been an elite compromise and conspiracy that leaves the country as divided as it was during the apartheid time with new kinds of cleavages within and between different racial population groups, according to Terreblanche (2012:126).

Given the situation above, one would expect that the majority poor black would use their vote to get a caring political party. But because of abject poverty and a high level of illiteracy the only choice they have is to stay alive (Terreblanche 2012:83). By being poor and desperate, with apartheid experiences still harbouring in their memories, and with no political party that seems capable of addressing their plight, the only tangible exercise they can engage in is to participate actively in service delivery protests.

The situation calls for a radical process of transformation which will challenge all the assumptions of a Rainbow Nation and Madiba's miracle complacency. There is a risk that, without a meaningful transformative agenda that could usher in an ethos of openness, coexistence, relatedness, justice and shared values as a nation with a common destiny, the current culture of violence[4] will become entrenched. Collective violence, which will ultimately undermine all government efforts to uplift the poor and marginalised, can be avoided only if the deep anguish of those who are oppressed is alleviated and if those who are living in a ghetto are brought to the centre and can participate in a common agenda (Mogapi 2011:123).

The assumptions that underpin the construct of the Rainbow Nation and "people-centred-society" are predicated on a stable environment, certainty, justice and rationality. Such assumptions are invalid and fail to address the crisis of frustration caused by self-serving political agendas and shrewd capital ownership. The increasing anarchy caused by the failure to transform South African society from an apartheid paradigm to one with an authentic spirituality of life is gradually engendering a culture of 'invade and grab' or 'loot and set on fire'. This paper calls for a new meaning and understanding based on an authentic spirituality of life that can bring fresh hope of empowerment and peace to a divided nation. This call is based on a transformational epistemology and is influenced by the need for ongoing spirituality that stretches beyond the limits imposed by past poverty, unemployment and inequality. The paper employs intersectionality as an analytical tool.

Defining Transformation

Daszko and Sheinberg (2011:1) and Ravindran (2012:1) warn that transformation has become a buzzword that is both overused and misunderstood in today's world. Thousands of people hear the slogans of transformation in their communities, but they see no change in their lives. Political, religious, and other community leaders 'talk the language' and may even try to take action in pursuit of what they understand to be transformation, but can often show no tangible benefits in what they are aspiring to (Daszko and Sheinberg 2011:2). In some circles, 'transformation talk' has become a catchphrase used to lull the general public and especially the impoverished majority, into contentment while the powerful extract the economic benefits to themselves (Terreblanche 2012:122). On the other hand the phrase may be used to replace those in power. An accusation that a leader is 'untransformed' can become the basis and grounds for replacing such a leader without due process to prove his or her incompetence (Dlamini, Langa and Von Holdt 2011:46-47). Transformation should also not be turned into a talk-show by the leaders to remain intransigent. Authentic transformation should be about giving people on the margin of power more space, confidence, competence, freedom, and resources to act on their own judgement (Ciulla 2005:59).

Transformation is a missional agenda of the church. At the 9th WCC General Assembly held in Port Alegro, Brazil, the assembly gathered around the theme: "God, in your grace transform the world". The theme of the assembly epitomised the prophetic mission of the church based on the Lord's Prayer in Mat. 6. The mission of the church to the world involves transformation that brings new hope, life and prosperity for all. In South Africa a spirituality of transformation is urgently needed lest the whole of society disintegrates into civil war (Mail & Guardian 6/10/2012). The violence presently engulfing society will eventually undermine the democratic order and the gains of the last two decades if left unattended.

Transformation should not be confused with just any kind of change – it should involve 'moving from one state or position to another' for the benefit of all (Daszko and Sheinberg 2011:1). According to Daszko and Sheinberg (2011:2), transformation requires the creation or change of a whole form or structure for the benefit of the whole. It implies a change that brings an incremental benefit. Kgatla (1988:177) relates transformation to the Greek word *metanoia*, a change of people's mind-set, a radical and profound revision, a stretching beyond the limits. As Einstein put it, 'No problem can be solved from the same level of consciousness that created it' (cited in Parameshwar 2005:1). Transformation occurs when a new vision is continually created to interrogate existing assumptions, beliefs, patterns, and habits to bring about incremental change which will benefit the whole of society. Transformation happens when people 'manage a system focus' to create a new inclusive future that is empowering to all (Daszko and Sheinberg 2011:2).

Williams (2000:168), referring to the legacy of apartheid in South Africa, defines transformation as making a direct impact on the extent to which there is a structural shift from dominant, exclusive relations of power and privileges to a more equitable, inclusive dispensation within a new order. He cautions that the term transformation can be variously interpreted because of its myriad contexts (Williams 2000:169). In the South African context, with regard to past imbalances, transformation often concerns itself with reconfiguring and reconstituting existing bodies of perceptions, deconstructing dominant Western-centred perceptions and low self-esteem among Africans (Williams 2000:169) or even a culture of entitlement. The goal of transformation is not necessarily to replace one notion of social change with another, but, rather, to attempt to emphasise the good values that can be taken from any group and to form inclusive, empowering values (Williams 2000:169). Its objective is to reconstitute and empower life-giving relations of co-existence.

As Williams (2000:169) suggests, the term transformation in the South African context has a political and social content. For Bosch (1991:3) transformation has to do with giving account of the hope Christians have. It requires an intentional agenda of de-racialisation and a reconstruction of 'damaged' self-esteem that has deteriorated into black self-hatred and self-destruction. Transformation has to do with relationships that, when improved, can strengthen the bonds of spirituality and togetherness. In this context, spirituality refers to the quality of a person's sensitivity to the things that matter most to community coexistence and relationship-bonding (Whitfield 1987:127). A spirituality of life has a direct bearing on love, justice, peace and the well-being of the other. According to Whitfield (1987:127), spirituality is a healing and growth-inducing process that is ultimately fulfilling. Spirituality involves a journey of discovery and restoration that transcends previous levels of consciousness, awareness and a unity of being, as it meets new challenges in a life of community (Whitfield 1987:128).

For many black South Africans, the government's failure to transform society from one which was differentiated and structured to benefit a few, which leaves the majority perceiving themselves as being left to their own devices, calls for collective social revolt. If people feel that the peaceful means they can use to call on their government to resolve their problems do not work, they will resort to violence (Mogapi 2011:123). The society harbouring such perceptions is a society which is heading for total collapse; hence many people are calling government for service delivery because they think the only effective way of getting the attention of the government to their plight is through barricading streets, setting tyres on fire, looting and burning property. The 'smoke' that comes out will draw the attention of the government to their plight.

Social inequalities, poverty, high levels of unemployment and a lack of radical government programmes to address the plight of the poor remain key issues, reminiscent of apartheid, to many black people. According to Mogapi (2011:123), the South African government is trapped in self-defencive tactics of denial when it diverts money to security agents instead of using funds to address social inequalities that give rise to security concerns. Even the promises of the National Development Plan that promise to break the vicious cycle of poverty and enter a more virtuous one of rising confidence, investment, employment and incomes, and falling levels of inequality in 2013 remains a tantalising mirage if the ANC policy of black elite formation is combined with an unwillingness to address the plight of the poor black majority.

Statements such as one made by President Jacob Zuma, quoted in the *Sowetan* on 1 November 2012 (speaking at the official opening of the National House of Traditional Leaders in Parliament), who made the claim that the gap between the rich and the poor in South Africa is widening a 'farce', are out of touch with reality. On that occasion the President argued that people are getting grants that they did not get during the apartheid era and on that score the gap between rich and poor was closing. Such an argument is in effect an admission that the government is unable to solve many of the problems facing the country. Given the high reported level of corruption, bribery, and incidents where young girls who are beneficiaries of child grants misuse such social grants to pay for hairdressing appointments and buy beauty products, it is clearly unjustifiable to say that the gap between the rich and the poor is narrowing on the basis of social grants (*Sowetan* I November 2012). According to the survey done by Pondering Panda, Consumer Insight Company, news release of 11 December 2012 45 per cent of teenagers fall pregnant to get government grants. The government support grant is seen as an incentive for teens from low-income families to have children. It is thus important that the government takes heed of how its hand-outs are viewed by the youth but not as a means of narrowing the gap between rich and poor in South Africa.

Transformation is hard to achieve even if political and community leaders do know what it implies, and what it requires to empower people. If they lack the will to take radical decisions to change the country to be a household where everybody has enough to live on their utterances remain empty rhetoric. Furthermore, if public institutions that should serve as vehicles of transformation do not adjust and comply with the directives of transformative policies, transformation will remain hard to achieve. Institutions such as institutions of higher learning, the judiciary, businesses in the private and public sectors, and the other public services should serve as custodians of an ethos of transformative social relations (Williams 2000:170). In reality, in South Africa, some of these institutions are deliberately sabotaging government measures that would bring about the desired change in our society by ignoring or delaying the effective implementation of such measures, for example, by arguing that people of colour are incompetent (2000:170) and therefore resist policies such as Black Economic Empowerment. In this context, incompetency is 'measured' in terms of colour.

Intersectionality and Change

Transformation should be undergirded by programmes and projects that address the historically created unequal relations of power, accessibility and participation, and it requires a methodological framework to facilitate it. To re-arrange a previous human-designed order into one that actualises participation by all, accountability and empowering symmetrical relations, and that embraces the notion of 'one nation, one destiny', one needs analytical tools that can guide the process. In order to re-engineer, reconstruct and realign the social order in a previously racialised space and in militarised communities, one needs a kind of social analysis capable of detecting shifting societal reconfigurations and reinstitutions. Towards this end, the concept of intersectionality is employed in this paper.

Intersectionality challenges a simplistic categorisation of people based on their race, the colour of their skin, gender and group (Flera 2010:153). It is true that people may be oppressed using categories such as race, sex, gender, ethnicity and class, and within those categories there are further divisions that can make people the targets of specific oppression. Disability, for example, may become a category used for oppression within an oppressed group. Any transformative agenda that fails to recognise this category will liberate only some people, who will in turn oppress others in their midst. An intersectional analysis takes into account the historical, social, political and economic context and recognises the unique experiences of individuals based on the intersection of the identifying grounds for discrimination (Ontario Human Rights Commission 1995:1).

The intersectionality approach allows a particular experience based on the confluence of the identifying grounds involved to be acknowledged and attended to. In a similar vein, the Ontario Human Rights Commission concludes that human rights claims in Canada should recognise that individuals have multiple identities which shape the experiences of those who are marginalised. Understanding these identities and their intersection can help human rights practitioners to assist those who come before the courts for a remedy (Ontario Human Rights Commission 1995:2). This paper attempts to address the question of the constellation of rich whites and rich blacks in South Africa forming a common identity and how this new order indiscriminately deprives many people across the colour line.

Based on the theoretical lens provided above, this paper argues that there has been vast confluence and reconfiguration of discrimination/exclusion identities in South Africa, even after 1994. A de-racialisation of South African society by repealing suppressive and oppressive Acts has allowed many black people to rise to positions they could not access in the past. Some have moved from rural areas into urban areas, while others have come from a situation of abject poverty to untold of richness. Some sectors of the previous establishment have converged and reconfigured themselves to become even more exclusive of others who do not share their identity. Prof Terreblanche, an economist, describes them as the middle-class who have become 'gated-in behind high walls' from impoverished poor South Africans.

Feminist scholar Yuval-Davis (2011:200) affirms that intersectionality analysis is easier when one investigates specific case studies. An example here is a study of how foreigners are treated and further oppressed in South Africa. As previously disadvantaged black people, they fall into the category of the poor, and suffer additional oppression based on their foreignness. Xenophobic attacks are often carried out on foreign nationals on the basis of their not being citizens of the country, and yet they suffer the same inequalities as citizens of South Africa. People living with disabilities become victims of similar prejudices because they are different, even when they are members of another marginalised group. The reality of discrimination and oppression is fractured, messy and complex, as Ravelli and Webber (2010:215) argue.

Being different within the same homogeneous oppressed group may perpetuate exclusion and discrimination. Marginalisation within communities is a slippery, shifting and multi-layered concept (Kagan 2002:1). Individuals or groups might enjoy high social status at some point in time, but, as social change occurs, they lose their status and become marginalised. The risk of marginalisation, according to Kagan (2002:2), increases or decreases as life cycles continue. A group or individual dominant today may become marginalised in future. This marginalisation occurs as society is reconfigured to effect new changes in groups which were previously defined differently. Leonard (1984:180) defines such social marginality as 'being outside the mainstream of productive activity or power'. Leonard (1984:181) defines these new groups of people who remain outside the dominant arena as experiencing involuntary social marginality. Their experience of marginality can arise in a number of ways, such as disability, ethnicity, class, race, sex, economic and political status. Leonard (1984:181) argues that marginalisation constitutes exclusion, preventing people from fulfilling individual and group aspirations. Those who are marginalised have very little control over their lives and resources, and they are at the receiving end of negative public attitudes. Unless they are radically liberated and empowered, marginalised people are likely to remain dislocated and alienated from the mainstream of economic resources.

In South Africa, as already indicated in this paper, many people still believe that the demise of apartheid signalled the end of marginalisation and exclusion. However, it is becoming increasingly clear that the introduction of a new political order in South Africa did not go far enough to empower previously marginalised people so that they have control over their lives. In addition to the racial category resulting in exclusion and marginalisation that existed before, new forms of discrimination, inequality, deprivation and oppression have been introduced and are being maintained. To many people affected by the scourge of the new culture of exclusion and marginalisation their survival rests in waging a struggle against their own government. Hence, new ways to struggle for survival have been devised by those who are excluded and oppressed.

Towards a Transcendent Spirituality of Life and Inclusion

Human beings are often seen as selfish beings that build 'protective walls' around themselves to keep others from entering their space (Schmitt 1995:35). They create a space to ensure their self-preservation and exclusivity (1995:35). It was for this reason that Jesus announced that he had come in order that all might have life – life in all its fullness (John 10:10). Paul is also alluding to this fact when he says Christ has broken down the wall that separated people and kept them enemies (Ephesians 2:14). To view oneself as separate and autonomous for the sake of one's own survival is self-centred and exclusionary to others. It is sin that Christ annulled on the cross. It is clear that those who wield power in any society tend to resist any change that threatens their position of security, those who challenge the establishment. They will always want to influence and shape others' thoughts in order to maintain control over them, as their decisions are always decisive sources of choice and action (Schmitt 1995:38). The decisions made by a person in authority are invariably self-regarding wherever his or her own good is the primary guide (Schmitt 1995:38).

Schmitt (1995:80) argues that any real social transformation starts when the notion of autonomy and private space is invaded and turned around to look at being in relation with others. Only when people are 'opened-up' to others to engage in a dynamic relationship can one hope for lasting peace. An empowering turn-around strategy involves a reconstruction of feeling with the other in such a way that the two parties start to hear one another with more clarity, which in turn leads to new relationships (Schmitt 1995:112). The strategy includes empathy, which involves sharing feelings in the most intimate way.

Schmitt (1995:84) identifies two different senses of being in 'empathy'. There is empathy between people who act separately from each other, and there is also empathy in relation, which leads to equality in relationships (Schmitt 1995:86). It opens one's security to the other with a view of empowering the other. Empathy that is in relation to and open to the other with a view to empowering the other can prevail between people of different status, races, genders and ages. It is not stereotyped by these categories but transcends them in order to reach out to people on the margins of the groups concerned. Such spirituality goes beyond the boundaries created by prejudices to empower all parties to reciprocate in embracing one another (Schmitt 1995:87).

In South Africa, as in many nations of the world with a history of inequality, there are people in privileged positions who consider themselves as having an innocent relationship with the poor and marginalised. They have a covertly oppressive attitude in relation with others (Schmitt 1995:112). For example, many middle-class white people still think of themselves as leading unprejudiced, open-minded and fair-minded lives that are helpful to black employees. This is also true of a black middle-class which has ascended the ladder of the privileged. In the main, their actions show that they are much less transformed in their relations with those over whom they have more power than they think. Mogapi (2011:123) found that the South African government, for example, no longer perceives social protests as genuine attempts to gain improved service delivery, but sees them as exaggerated complaining and lawlessness. The government's covert denial of the plight of the downtrodden in the country is a betrayal of its own declared policy that South Africa belongs to all the people that live in it. A denial of the reality of the causes of violence in the country could easily provide a covert path to evading responsibility for transformation.

The biggest injury inflicted on the oppressed people by the government and those in positions of control is ignoring or dismissing their complaints as being frivolous (Schmitt 1995:163). When complaints of being systematically ignored, excluded and even belittled go unheeded, this can eventually lead to alienation and even self-hatred, which can result in indiscriminate destruction of property and life. Alienation, in the sense used by Karl Marx (Kunin 2003:6), refers to the exclusion of people from that which is rightfully theirs. When people are alienated, they have a sense that they are less than human, or have failed to express themselves fully. Karl Marx described another form of alienation, when people are not powerless in the economy and political sphere, but find themselves in a world that they did not create, in which they are constantly reminded that they do not belong (McLellan 1973:10). Such alienation is typical of the perception that many poor communities in South Africa have and leads to a sense that the only 'language' the government hears is violence hence the adage of 'smoke that calls'. Such a path can lead to genocide.

Spirituality of life is the opposite of such a catastrophe. It seeks to empower those who are compelled to live in a reality that has been assigned to them by a dominant society. It resists any 'quarantine' imposed on them by the elite for their protection.

Spirituality of Ubuntu

Another way of explaining transformative transcendent spirituality of life is to compare it with the African-Biblical concept of Ubuntu. Ubuntu as a concept is derived from a transforming intimate relationship between God and his creatures. When God realised that Adam did what God had forbidden him to do and Adam was going to die, God called: 'Where are you?' God showed his humanness and restored the first couple to their original state by allowing his Son to die for them on the cross. Ubuntu thus belongs and resides in the essence of God. Because God is a person with personal attributes such as unconditional love and creative relationship with his creatures, he is able to transcend the boundaries of sin and reaches out to human beings on the basis of Ubuntu. Ubuntu does not impose conditions before it can be demonstrated. His goodness, humanness and Ubuntu were engraved in his creatures at creation, and even the damaging nature of sin did not obliterate it. Thus, Ubuntu emphasises relations and relationality, and can reach beyond limits in order for us to make empowering contact with the other.

The Jewish philosopher Martin Buber's (1958:26) 'I-Thou' philosophy of personal dialogue displays a striking congruence with Ubuntu. He argues that in order for a person to be truly in relationship with another, the person must open him or herself up to the other. One's boundaries or 'guard' should be removed in order to allow the other to enter into one's private space. According to Buber (1958:28), human beings become aware of each other as having a unity of being when they are in an 'I-Thou' (subject-to-subject) relation. This is precisely what Ubuntu is about. It elevates individuals from an 'I-Stranger' relationship to a Human-God relationship of mutuality and reciprocity. It is opposed to separateness and detachment. In the present South Africa, I-Thou relationship is no longer confined to I(black)-Thou (white) but it has been conceived as I(rich)-Thou (poor).

Ubuntu owes its origin to the nature of God. Buber (1958:26) argues in this regard that an 'I' which has no 'Thou' has a reality that is incomplete – a relationship without God – and is disjointed, because it lacks reciprocity. An Ubuntu relationship presupposes the involvement of the liberating presence of God. Such a relationship knows no barriers or selfish relations.

The Ubuntu adage 'a person is a person through other persons' stresses the 'betweenness' that relates people to one another in a mutuality that Buber (1958:14-15) calls love. True love does not cling to the constructs of 'I' or "Thou', but includes an exchange between God and his creatures. This transcendent relationality was espoused by Jesus when he said: 'Unless you turn and become as children, you shall not enter the Kingdom of heaven' (Matt.18:3). Ubuntu breaks out of the circumscribing boundaries erected by a selfish 'I' that establishes a self that is separate from other selves (Buber 1958:27). Ubuntu implies an act of humility, an act that presupposes a self-emptying in order to create primary and foundational relationships. Isolationism, insulationism, separateness and exclusionism need to be overcome before empowerment can occur (Horner 2011:73-76), before an Ubuntu relationship is established.

Empowerment Annihilates Alienation and Marginalisation

Transcendent transformative spirituality takes the annihilation of the alienation and marginalisation of people as its point of departure. It is characterised by the notion of levelling the playing field between those who have power over others and those who are without power. In a situation where one has power over others, there can be no spirituality of transformation. In such a relationship, one dominates others to make them dependent. By contrast, in transcendent empowering relations, one enters a disempowered space in order to empower others to ensure their freedom and self-determination (Myers 1999:116). A transcendent transformative spirituality embraces values such as altruistic love, and adopts a positive attitude to intrinsically motivate the downtrodden, thus increasing their sense of spiritual survival to call them to a life with meaning, one that makes a difference (Liu 2007:4). A transcendent transformative spirituality has no desire to manipulate others, but targets the forces that are designed to rob others of a full sense of wholeness, harmony, well-being, and it is intrinsically related to God. It strives to help the powerless feel enabled to make their own decisions, lead their own life in freedom and accomplish that which they want to accomplish (Liu 2007:4).

Transcendent transformative spirituality is empowering – it aims to give people the confidence, competence, freedom, and resources to act on their own judgments (Ciulla 2005:59). It is different from a bogus spirituality that creates false expectations about change, and then fails to deliver on its promises. An authentic transformative spirituality aims at restorative social harmony by accommodating those who have been excluded, while re-adjusting and restoring them to authentic relations (Liu 2007:10). It aims at changing people's status from one of bondage in which previous relations are defined in terms of power, to one where empowering relationships are defined in terms of shared values and a common destiny (Myers 1999:115).

This paper has attempted to argue that the violence occasioned by the economic, political and social exclusion in South Africa can be addressed and stopped. It does not need military might to bring it to a halt but rather empowering relationships. Authentic transformation has to take root which will reverse all that hinders empathetic relations, deep coexistence and sharing. The concept of Ubuntu should be a guiding principle for the new order where people humanity and rights are entrenched.

Notes

1   The National Development Plan (NDP) is a government commission that offers a long-term perspective. It defines a desired destination and identifies the role different sectors of society need to play in reaching that goal. The NDP aims to eliminate poverty and reduce inequality by 2030. According to the plan, South Africa can realise these goals by drawing on the energies of its people, growing an inclusive economy, building capabilities, enhancing the capacity of the state, and promoting leadership and partnerships throughout society.

2   This is in itself a sign that there is no trust or hope in those who are in power that they would ever turn things around for the benefit of the whole country.

3   This is just a perception held. The present situation cannot be compared with that of apartheid.

4   Comblin (1998:194) identifies today's violence as the violence of city: the violence of young people with no future, the violence of organised crime, and of drug traffickers. In South Africa, there is another form of violence: the violence of factionalism where 'comrades' fight for power.

Works Cited

Buber, M.
:   1958   *I and thou*, translated by R.G. Smith. [Online] Available from: http://www.angelfire.com/md2/timewarp/ buber.html [Accessed: 25 February 2013].

Ciulla, J.B.
:   2005   Ethics: The heart of leadership. In *Leadership and the problem of bogus empowerment.* Oxford: Blackwell.

Comblin, J.
:   1998   *Called for freedom: The changing context of Liberation Theology.* Maryknoll, NY: Orbis.

Crenshaw, K.W.
:   1994   *Mapping the margins: Intersectionality, identity politics, and violence against women of colour.* New York, NY: Routledge.

Daszko, M. and Sheinberg, S.
:   2011   Survival is optimal: Only leaders with new knowledge can lead the transformation. [Online] Available from: http://www.mdaszko.com/theoryoftransformation [Accessed: 25 February 2013.]

Dlamini, J., Langa, M. and Von Holdt, K.
:   2011   Kungcatsha: Sending a message to the top, in *The Smoke that Calls: Insurgent citizenship, collective violence and the struggle for a place in the new South Africa. Eight case studies of community protest and xenophobic violence,* K von Holdt et al. Johannesburg: University of the Witwatersrand, Centre for the Study of Violence and Reconciliation, 45-56.

Fleras, A.
:   2010   *Unequal relations.* Toronto: Pearson Canada.

Horner, D.
:   2011   *When missions shapes the mission: You and your church can reach the world.* Nashville, TN: Band H.

Kagan, C M.
    2002   Working with people who are marginalized by social system: Challenges for community psychological work. Manchester: Manchester Metropolitan University.

Kirsten, A. and Von Holdt, K.
    2011   Introduction, in *The Smoke that Calls: Insurgent citizenship, collective violence and the struggle for a place in the new South Africa. Eight case studies of community protest and xenophobic violence,* K von Holdt et al. Johannesburg: University of the Witwatersrand, Centre for the Study of Violence and Reconciliation, 2-4.

Langa, M.
    2011   Azania: Violence is the only language that this government knows, in *The Smoke that Calls: Insurgent citizenship, collective violence and the struggle for a place in the new South Africa. Eight case studies of community protest and xenophobic violence,* K von Holdt et al. Johannesburg: University of the Witwatersrand, Centre for the Study of Violence and Reconciliation, 57-69.

Leonard, P.
    1984   Personality and ideology: Towards a materalist understanding of the individual. [Online] Available from: http://www.fineprint.com [Accessed: 22 February 2013].

Mogapi, N.
    2011   Collective violence and collective trauma, The traumatic past of Apartheid and the paradox of the new democracy, in *The Smoke that Calls: Insurgent citizenship, collective violence and the struggle for a place in the new South Africa. Eight case studies of community protest and xenophobic violence,* K von Holdt et al. Johannesburg: University of the Witwatersrand, Centre for the Study of Violence and Reconciliation, 119-129.

Myers, B.L.
1999   *Walking with the poor: Principles and practices of transformational development.* Maryknoll, NY: Orbis.

Nash, J.C.
2008   Re-thinking intersectionality. *Feminist Review*, 89: 1-2

Ontario Human Rights Commission
2001   *An international approach to discrimination.* Toronto: Ontario Human Rights Commission.

Schmitt, R.
1995   *Beyond separateness: The social nature of human beings – their autonomy, knowledge, and power.* Oxford: Westview.

Sowetan
2012   Take back your dignity. Misuse of social grants is rife, 25 May.

Von Holdt, K., Langa, M., Molapo, S., Mogapi, N.. Ngubeni, K., Dlamini, J. and Kirsten, A.
2011   *The Smoke that Calls: Insurgent citizenship, collective violence and the struggle for a place in the new South Africa. Eight case studies of community protest and xenophobic violence.* Johannesburg: University of the Witwatersrand, Centre for the Study of Violence and Reconciliation.

West, C.C.
1999   *Christian mission and modern culture: Power, truth, and community in modern culture.* Harrisburg, PN: Trinity.

Whitfield, C.L.
1987   *Healing the child within: Discovery and recovery for adult children of dysfunctional families.* Deerfield Beach, FL: Health Communications.

Williams, J.J.
2000   *South Africa: Urban transformation.* Cape Town: School of Government, University of the Western Cape, 2000, Vols. 17, No 3. 167-183.

Yuval-Davis, N.
    2011   *The politics of belonging: Intersectional contestations.*
            London:Sage.

APM

Group D: Issues in Social Engagement

Workshop Papers Currently in Press with Other Pubishers:

A Wolf in Sheep's Clothing? A Missiological Examination of the United States Evangelical Adoption and Orphan Care Movement
By Sheryl J. Ryan

"Save the Mothers"

A Maternal Health Missiology

Daniel D. Scott

DOI: 10.7252/Paper.000019

About the Author:
Daniel D. Scott is Associate Professor of Christian Ministries at Tyndale University College and Seminary in Toronto, Canada and the Managing Director of Save the Mothers—a maternal health organization.

Abstract

Some 287,000 women die yearly from something that is preventable; they die because of complications during pregnancy and childbirth. The risk of maternal death is particularly high in sub-Saharan Africa. Women in this region don't have access to the care they need. The right of such access must first be embraced by the wider society so that women will seek maternity services and so that when they do, they are met by an effective maternity care system.

Reducing the number of mothers that die in childbirth is one of the United Nations' Millennium Development Goals (MDG # 5). Yet the target set for 2015 is unlikely to be met. Indeed, the global picture of maternal mortality and morbidity has changed very little over the past twenty years despite isolated (and often medically-based) efforts to improve the situation.

A Canadian obstetrician, who is also an SIM missionary (named Dr. Jean Chamberlain Froese) has developed a multidisciplinary approach to this very complicated social and cultural problem; working with Ugandan colleagues, Dr. Froese founded the Save the Mothers' program at Uganda Christian University. It offers a Master in Public Health Leadership with a focus on training national, primarily non-medical advocates to bring about political and cultural change. Using this program as a case study, suggestions will be given for developing a Maternal Health Missiology.

Maternal mortality and maternal morbidity are among the greatest tragedies in our day. In the 20th century, pregnancy and childbirth killed more than tuberculosis, suicide, traffic accidents and AIDS combined. During the same century, more women died in childbirth than were soldiers killed in both world wars. Today, for every woman who dies in childbirth, about twenty women suffer injury, infection or disease—almost six million women each year. Some develop a fistula, a tear in the bladder, rectum or birth canal that leaves them incontinent: these women will be thrown out of their families and villages, like lepers. Save the Mothers, a small Canadian NGO, is training cross-disciplinary professionals to bring about the systemic change needed to ensure that women are safe. This paper will provide a maternal health missiology, using Save the Mothers as a case study, by looking at the lives of three biblical women (Eve, Rachel and Mary) and one man (Boaz).

Dr. Eve Nakabembi is a Ugandan obstetrician. Recently married, and expecting her first child, she knows first-hand the tragedy of women and their children dying in Uganda from pregnancy and pregnancy-related complications. After carrying the child for a number of weeks, she experienced difficulty. Fortunately, Dr. Eve survived. Her child did not. But the danger of giving birth is something she also encounters daily in her professional work. One recent night, while on rounds at her hospital, eight mothers died in childbirth. Another time, while performing a Caesarean section, the power went out in the hospital. Left in darkness, she had to do the incision by the light of her cell phone—holding her phone in one hand and the scalpel in the other. In frustration, Dr. Eve said that something has to be done. She is a highly competent physician, but there are factors affecting the lives of women that are beyond her control.

The mothers who die in her operating theatre point to a larger, more horrifying reality. Eight hundred women die every day in childbirth--fourteen a day in her country of Uganda alone. If two jumbo jets crashed in one day, it would be the lead item in the news that day. If two jumbo jets filled with pregnant women crashed in one day, it would be the lead item in the news for weeks! Maternal death of that magnitude happens everyday and yet not enough is being done to change this tragedy. Reducing the percentage of mothers dying is a United Nations' Millennium Development Goal (Number Five) and it is unlikely the goal set for 2015, "reducing the maternal mortality ratio by three quarters between the years 1990 and 2015," (UNICEF 2005)[1] will be reached. In fact, high-level consultations are taking place to determine maternal health priorities, post 2015.

The statistics reflect the injustice wrought by acute poverty, that is, over ninety-nine percent of maternal deaths occur in developing countries (WHO 2012). Health care is simply unavailable, inaccessible, unaffordable, and frequently of poor quality to women in the developing world. Bleeding, infections, unsafe abortion and obstructed labour, are some of the preventable and treatable complications that lead to death (WHO 2005).[2] There are three major delays that lead to mothers dying from pregnancy complications: the delay in the decision to seek care; the delay in the arrival at a health facility; and the delay in the provision of adequate care (Thaddeus and Maine 1994:1091-1110).

To stem the tide of maternal death, and to help address the first two delays, Dr. Eve Nakabembi became the Academic Director of a unique Master in Public Health Leadership (MPHL) program operated by Save the Mothers[3] at Uganda Christian University (UCU).[4] Courses are taught by local experts (in such fields as public health, obstetrics, gender issues, sociology, etc.) who have the necessary academic credentials to teach at the graduate level. Courses in the MPHL include: Foundations of Public Health and Safe Motherhood, Epidemiology, Biostatistics, Research Methods and Monitoring and Evaluation. As working professionals, students study on a part-time basis over two years. The program is designed so participants can continue to work while studying, and involves nine weeks of in-class training with two or three modules per year. Between modules, students are assigned supplementary readings and are expected to create, implement and evaluate a major project, or to carry out a research project that challenges them to prove that their new skills will make a difference in and through their own professional sphere of influence.

The program consists of small and large group sessions with an emphasis on problem-based learning and group activity. Included in the course work are field visits, participation in a mentorship program, written assignments and an oral class presentation.

Save the Mothers recently launched an international cohort of students in the MPHL program at UCU. It sought out students from other East African nations (including Tanzania, Rwanda, Southern Sudan, Kenya, Democratic Republic of Congo, etc.) to study in the MPHL program at the Save the Mothers' training centre in Mukono, Uganda. The MPHL program now has two different groups of students--a Ugandan cohort and an East African cohort.

The graduates of this program, founded by Canadian obstetrician, Dr. Jean Chamberlain Froese,[5] are advocating for systemic change across a variety of fields—health care, social work, business, media, government, and the faith community to name a few. To date, some two hundred and fifty East African professionals have studied in the MPHL program.[6] Graduates are working towards needed societal change to reduce maternal deaths.[7] Child educators are writing books and implementing programs (such as after school maternal health clubs and theatre groups that perform plays about maternal health) designed to inform children about the importance of good maternal health and to communicate these messages to family members at home. Journalists are raising public awareness of the factors that lead to maternal death and of the need to resolve maternal mortality's causative issues. Policy makers are introducing legislation aimed at supporting maternal health initiatives. Lessons learned[8] in the training of multidisciplinary leaders for health promotion in developing countries involve the choosing of the right champions (or students) and the flexibility of the program (Chamberlain and Watt, 2012:344-348).

The Mother Friendly Hospital Initiative (MFHI), developed by Save the Mothers (with support from Uganda's Ministry of Health and the WHO office) is directly addressing the third delay—at the hospital.[9] A team of Ugandan and Canadian experts in obstetric and health administration has developed a curriculum to train STM MPHL graduates at Uganda Christian University as Mother Friendly Hospital resource teams. Save the Mothers supports the teams, providing them with the skills to work with hospital administrators and staff in assessing, recommending and implementing changes, and monitoring the maternal and newborn services in their hospitals. These teams strive to provide needed life-saving equipment and to ensure safe environments for mothers to deliver their babies thus facilitating the institutions becoming "Mother Friendly Hospitals." The program also seeks to improve the knowledge and clinical skills of the hospital staff who care for mothers and their babies.

The problem is not just that more doctors, more medicine or more money are needed. A radical change in the way women and mothers are treated by societies in the developing world—Sub Saharan Africa, Afghanistan, Haiti, India, as examples—needs to occur. The solution requires ordinary people who want to make connections that create extraordinary outcomes (Westley, Zimmerman, Patton, 2006). It involves the recognition that much variation exists between cultures and that flexible, locally meaningful systems need to be established (Miller, McDaniel, Crabtree, Strange, 2001). "Successful practices...make good sense of what is happening, and effectively improvise to make good practice jazz."[10] Furthermore, given that there is a large and growing Christian population in Sub-Saharan Africa, and there are Western Christian missionaries involved in stemming the tide of maternal mortality and morbidity, a biblical and theological basis for maternal health needs to be articulated. Such a missiological framework can be derived by considering the stories of three biblical women (Eve, Rachel, and Mary) and one man (Boaz, the husband of Ruth). The following attempts to articulate such a biblical and theological foundation for maternal health as mission.

In some cases, asserting this theological framework must go up against patriarchal prejudices about the role of women. Indeed, asserting this biblical and theological foundation is vital in much of East Africa (and arguably worldwide) to correct anti-feminist interpretations of Scripture. There is a clear and important role for women in society, and this fact can be found in the biblical story. Too often, devaluing women—especially as the expendable property of a father/husband who can be discarded should they die or be maimed in childbirth—is justified on biblical misinterpretation. What is worse, many Christian organizations fail to correct this misogyny because of a fixation on other issues.

The biblical story is clear about the importance of women, including to the messianic mission itself (and not simply as child-bearers). Eve, the first woman created, wife of Adam and mother of Cain, Abel and Seth (Genesis 4:1-2, 25)[11] is condemned to bear children in pain for eating the forbidden fruit. She and her husband are banished from the Garden of Eden and desperately wish to return. And yet, in the first messianic prophecy—"and I will put enmity between you and the woman, and between your offspring and hers; he will crush your head, and you will strike his heel" (Genesis 3:15)—there is a sense that she and all humanity will be "saved through childbearing" (1 Timothy 2:15) as the Messiah crushes the serpent's head. One commentator makes a compelling case that Eve (and Adam) thought that through their childbearing the Messiah would be born. This writer makes his case by considering the meaning of the names: Eve "life-giver;" Cain "acquired;" and Abel "breath." That is, according to this commentator, Eve the mother of humanity announces at the birth of Cain "I have brought forth or acquired a man, even the deliverer" (Genesis 4:1). She, of course, is mistaken in thinking that her firstborn son, Cain, is the Messiah of all humanity and the means by which they might return to the Garden. Cain kills Abel and his short life is like a breath. Later, at the time of Seth's birth, Eve makes the statement: "God has granted me another child in place of Abel, since Cain killed him" (Genesis 4:25). This time Eve acknowledges that God is the source of providing the son. "What she had to learn, and what God taught her through Cain's ensuing sad history, is that the deliverer could never come by her or her husband's own doing but would be God's gift. So the second time around she says, "*God* has granted me another child in place of Abel."" (Boice, 1982).

Although Adam and Eve do not directly bear the Messiah as they hope or think, through their offspring, Jesus the Messiah is eventually born. The Pauline phrase "woman will be saved through childbirth" often reads with great difficulty for interpreters, but the inevitable sense is that the salvation of woman—and indeed of humanity—comes from a woman, God in Christ.[12] "One relatively common attempt to resolve the difficulties is to assume that the singular subject of "will be saved" is Eve and the "childbearing" is the birth of the Messiah Jesus, implying that Eve's sin is reversed with the coming of the work of Christ" (Mickelson, 1986: 296).

The biblical character Eve suggests that the salvation of humanity is directly related to child bearing. If the stakes are so high, then maternal health ought to be a high priority. If the coming of the Messiah is to be through one woman, should not all women be equally valued?

Scripture repeatedly makes mention of the need to care for the fatherless and the orphan (for example, Exodus 22:22-24). Interestingly, it rarely, if ever, comments on those children who lose their mother. The exception is Rachel. She is an Aramaean woman and the second wife of Jacob, who, like many biblical women, has difficulty conceiving. She eventually does conceive and gives birth to Joseph, Jacob's favourite son. The birth of Rachel's second son Benjamin brings about her death through childbirth (Genesis 25:18-19). Jacob loves Rachel dearly, partly because of her great beauty and the many years he has to serve his father-in-law before they are married. When she dies he is filled with grief and erects a memorial pillar over her grave. The location of this pillar is known in Saul's day, when it is described as being on the border of Benjamin and Zelzah (1 Sam 10:2). Ramah is thought to be the location of this grave marker and the place from which the voice of Rachel is heard weeping for her motherless children: "A voice is heard in Ramah, lamentation and bitter weeping. Rachel is weeping for her children; she refuses to be comforted..." (Jeremiah 31:15).

The reference to Rachel's weeping occurs in Jeremiah's Book of Consolation and in the midst of a beautiful, but difficult, poem (Jeremiah 31:15-22). The crucial verb in this initial part of Jeremiah's poem is "heard." In Jeremiah's prophecy, God hears the weeping of Rachel. He is not completely detached from his people. God is able to hear the mourning from Ramah. Rachel's children are his as well and thus God is also concerned about their plight. This concern is evidenced by God's response to Rachel's weeping. Furthermore, God hears the moaning of Rachel's children, personified as "Ephraim." The emphatic repetition of the verb "to hear" serves to enforce the fact that God has heard the grieving: "I have surely heard the moaning of Ephraim" (Jeremiah 31:16). The soliloquy in Jeremiah 31:20 reveals the heartfelt response of God not only to the moaning of Ephraim but also to the weeping of Rachel. God's pathos ridden words to Ephraim are:

> Is not Ephraim my dear son,
> The child in whom I delight?
> Though I often speak against him,
> I still remember him.
> Therefore my heart yearns for him;
> I have great compassion for him.

Particularly poignant is the line "my heart yearns for him." The response of God to the remembrance of God's people (and hearing Rachel weep) is that God is filled with distress, agitation and grief. The best understanding of the phrase, it could be argued, would be "my heart grieves for him."[13] This is the sense that the Japanese theologian Kazoh Kitmori takes and uses as the basis for his *Theology of the Pain of God*.[14]

Is it too much to suggest that in light of the pain God experiences at the death of the mother Rachel and the effects of her death upon her children, the heart of God must be distressed and agitated by the deaths of mothers in our day? World Health Organization statistics reveal that every other minute a woman dies from preventable complications from pregnancy or childbirth (WHO 2012). The unfortunate consequence is that this high rate of maternal mortality leaves over one million orphans behind. Without a mother to care for their needs, these little ones are ten times more likely to die within two years of their mother's death (UNICEF 2005). Sarah Brown, wife of the former British Prime Minister Gordon Brown, made the following statement in a speech given to the African First Ladies Summit in Los Angeles, organized by USDFA and African Synergy:

> I don't believe that we will make the progress on HIV/ AIDS without addressing   maternal   mortality. We will not make the progress we want on malaria without addressing maternal mortality. We will not make progress on getting more children to school without reducing maternal mortality.
>
> But we will make progress on all these things and on nutrition, on empowerment and education, on health care, on immunization, even—I believe—on the environment, if we make progress to reduce the number of mothers dying needlessly in childbirth. When one mother survives, a lot survives with her.[15]

The efforts of most relief and development organizations, Christian ones included, focus on care of the orphan. While the care of orphans is vital and necessary, greater attention must be given to the roots of the problem, that is, saving the lives of mothers. Cutting down the weed without dealing with the root will not bring about the desired result. If God grieves at the death of Rachel, then surely attention to mothers should be a high priority.

The final lines of Jeremiah's poem in the midst of the Book of Consolation portraying the grief God experiences have been a topic of considerable debate.[16] Here at the end of the poem (Jeremiah 31:22), the statement is made that Yahweh will create a new thing on the earth—a woman will encompass a man. The Septuagint provides no clue, it simply translates "men will go about in safety." The oldest interpretation is that of Jerome's in his translation based on the Hebrew text and his commentary. He postulates that the phrase was a prophecy about the Virgin Mary's protecting embrace of the Christ in her womb.[17] In his commentary, Jerome states "The Lord has created a new thing on earth; without seed of man without carnal union and conception, 'a woman will encompass a man' within her womb—One who, though He will later appear to advance through the stages of infancy and childhood, yet, while confined for the usual months in his mother's womb, will already be perfect man."[18]

The information about the mother of Jesus and the one who 'encompasses a man' is largely confined to the infancy narratives in Matthew and Luke. Herein we learn that when the angelic announcement of the birth of Jesus occurs, Mary is living in Nazareth, in Galilee, and is engaged to a carpenter named Joseph. The conception of Jesus is described as 'of the Holy Spirit' (Matthew 1:18; Luke 1:35), and his birth as taking place in Bethlehem (Matthew 2:1; Luke 1:5; 2:4). It is recorded that after the birth the holy family lived at Nazareth. Matthew alone records the flight into Egypt, where Joseph and Mary and the child Jesus take refuge from the jealous anger of Herod. At the end of Jesus' life, Mary is at the foot of the cross (John 19:25), when she, and the beloved disciple, are entrusted by Jesus to each other's care (vv. 26-27). Even in his death Jesus keeps the commandment to "honour your father and mother." Following the example of our Lord, there ought to be care for mothers, our own, and by synecdoche, all mothers. It is interesting to note that while tradition tells us that Joseph likely died early in Jesus' life (the last time Scripture mentions him is in the anecdote about Jesus as a boy with the teachers in the temple) God in His providence saw fit to ensure that his son had a mother throughout the duration of his life.

When Christians stand to confess their faith in the words of the creed—"I believe...in Jesus Christ...our Lord, born of the Virgin Mary"—they acknowledge that God has created something new. Mary, the Mother of God, has a special place in the minds of Christians because she gave birth to Jesus Christ, the promised and longed-for Messiah. Through a difficult labour, encountering the same delays that cause mothers to die in childbirth today, her womb surrounded and protected the baby Jesus. Indeed, the salvation of the world was entrusted to her. Using Paul's language from Galatians, "when the fullness of time had come, God sent forth his Son, born of a woman, born under the law, to redeem those who were under the law, so that we might receive adoption..."

So far, the biblical and theological basis for maternal health has focused on women—Eve, Rachel and Mary. Now, we turn to a man. Boaz, a man of standing, saves the lives of two mothers—Ruth and her mother-in-law Naomi. When their husbands die, they are destitute. Naomi returns to her people and Ruth, an outsider, a foreigner, follows her.

Fortunately, Naomi has a relative on her husband's side— Boaz. The systems are in place to help him help them. The family system works. Naomi cares for Ruth. Ruth cares for Naomi. Naomi uses her family connections on her husband's side to receive support. The social welfare system works. Widows are allowed to glean in the fields during harvest time to obtain the food they need for survival. The legal and financial systems work. Boaz goes to the city gate (where business is conducted) and finds a quorum of ten men required for a legal transaction. He negotiates with another relative of Ruth for some property and, with the purchase of the property, the opportunity comes to marry Ruth. He seals the deal with an ancient custom of taking off his sandal and giving it to the other. As a result, he marries Ruth and promises to take care of her.

In Ruth's situation the systems functioned as they were meant to, to protect the weak and vulnerable. But systems break down. And in many places in our world today, when they break down, mothers die in staggering numbers. Their deaths are entirely preventable. Something has to be done. The cry of the psalmist, "Hear, O Lord, my righteous plea; listen to my cry. Give ear to my prayer...keep me as the apple of your eye; hide me in the shadow of your wings," is the cry of many women in our day. They could easily be saying the same things the psalmist said, "Rise up, O Lord...rescue me...O Lord, by your hand save me."

Boaz is the means God uses to answer this prayer from the lips of Ruth. And by saving her from destitution, others are also saved. Later in the book of Ruth we read that Ruth and Boaz have a child named Obed. The women of the city say to Naomi (in what was to be a positive prophecy), "Bless the Lord who has given you this grandson. May he be famous in Israel. May he restore your youth and take care of you in your old age, for he is the son of your daughter-in-law who loves you so much, who has been kinder to you than seven sons." Boaz and Ruth's son Obed has a son named Jesse who has a son named David, the King of Israel. Through David's line comes Jesus of Nazareth.

In the gospel of John, Jesus the distant descendant of Ruth, the mother saved by Boaz, has upset the religious establishment in Jerusalem. There is a plot to kill him. The High Priest suggests "it is better for you that one man die for the people than the whole nation perish." John, the gospel writer interprets "He, the High Priest, did not say this on his own, but as high priest he prophesied that Jesus would die for the Jewish nation, and not only for that nation but also for the scattered children of God."

And so, you see the effects of saving one mother. Boaz saves Ruth. Ruth becomes the great, great, great, great, great, grandmother of Jesus. Jesus becomes the Saviour of the world. Save the mother and you save others. To illustrate this further, permit a personal example. I booked a hair appointment not so long ago. I called the barber using the Save the Mothers' cell phone. While sitting in the chair, the woman cutting my hair asked about the name that came up on the call display. Was it, "Save the Mothers' or was it 'Save Them Others?: she asked. You see the letters are the same and without spaces on her call display it is easy to see how she could mistake 'Save the Mothers' with 'Save them Others.' Yet, that is the point, isn't it? If you save the mothers, you save them others. When a child looses his mother in the developing world, he receives the inheritance of poverty and disease.

Dr. Eve Nakabembi, the first academic director of the Save the Mothers' Master in Public Health Leadership program and Dr. Jean Chamberlain Froese, the founder of Save the Mothers, know all about this. They know if you save the mothers, you save the child. If you save the mother and child, the society is better off. Save the mothers and you really do save them others. Boaz was a mother saver. The Twenty First Century needs more men (and women) like Boaz who bring about systemic change so that mothers like Eve, Rachel and Mary survive childbirth. The Canadian NGO Save the Mothers is attempting to do its part to train cross-disciplinary professionals to provide the climate and conditions for mothers to live.

Notes

1   Indeed, even at the outset of the MDGs, there was concern at the overly ambitious nature of the goal. See a piece from September 2006, A. Rosenfield, D. Maine, L. Freedman, "Meeting MDG-5: an impossible dream?" The Lancet Volume 368, Issue 9542:1133-1135.

2   The maternal health issue that receives the most attention within the Christian community is usually abortion, perhaps followed closely by issues related to family planning. As a result, Save the Mothers has adopted a value statement that allows them to maintain their convictions and yet function in a pluralistic society. The statement reads: "The lives of mothers, their babies, (both born and preborn) are worth saving. We promote their well-being through strategies that support healthy pregnancies. Abortion should be avoided through family planning and abstinence (as appropriate). Save the Mothers does not provide termination of pregnancy, but encourages women who have suffered complications of abortion (whether spontaneous or induced) to seek medical care."

3   The purpose of Save the Mothers is to promote the education of professionals and societal leaders on the causes of high maternal and infant morbidity and mortality within their communities, including the development and delivery of local post-secondary education programs to support the growth of indigenous expertise in addressing these problems.

4   See "The Enhancement of East African Universities' Contribution towards the Attainment of Millennium Development Goal 5—Improving Maternal Health," sponsored by Mobilizing Regional Capacity Initiative (MRCI) of the Association of African Universities (AAU), a DFID Sponsored Initiative. Also, Dr. Archna Gupta a MD who is completing her Master in Public Health at the University of Toronto carried out an evaluation of the "continuum of change" that is generated by the STM program—whether the program is training local leaders with a multidisciplinary approach. Outcomes assessed as part of her Master's thesis fall into two categories: 1. The impact of the program on the individual learner; 2. And the impact of the program on the broader community.

5   Jean Chamberlain Froese, Where have all the mothers gone? Bellville, ON: Epic Press, 2004.

6   See Nicholas Wolterstorff's helpful essay "Teaching for Justice: On Shaping How Students are Disposed to Act" in Clarence W. Joldersma and Gloria Goris Stronks Educating for Shalom: Essays on Christian Higher Education, Grand Rapids, MI: William B. Eerdmans Publishing Co, 1994: 135-154. Another helpful piece is the chapter "Shalom and Social Transformation," in Harvie M. Conn and Manuel Ortiz, Urban Ministry: The Kingdom, the City and the People of God Downers Grove, IL: InterVarsity Academic, 2001: 340-357.

7   See Deborah J. Cohen and Benjamin F. Crabtree, "Implementing Health Behavior Change in Primary Care: Lessons from Prescription for Health," The Annals of Family Medicine 2005: 512-519.

8   A. Kleinman, L. Eisenberg, B. Good, "Culture, illness, and care: clinical lessons from anthropologic and cross cultural research," Ann Intern Med 1978 February 88(2):251-8.

9   A ten-step approach has been articulated by the Save the Mothers team to measure the standard of care: 1. Respectful and dignified maternity care; 2. Complies and maintains the MFHI Emergency neonatal and obstetrical care checklist; 3. Effective communication to community about availability of quality maternal and newborn care; 4.   Ensure appropriate documentation of levels of care; 5. Protocol establishment and reinforcement; 6. Nurture friendly and well motivated health care professionals; 7. Mother centred care with feedback system; 8. Functional referral network (inter-hospital/health unit communication); 9. Adheres to Baby Friendly hospital initiative; and, 10. Commitment to on-going certification by the Mother Friendly Hospital Initiative.

10   William L, Miller; Rueben R. McDaniel; Benjamin F. Crabtree; and Kurt C. Strange, "Practice Jazz: Understanding Variation in Family Practices Using Complexity Science," The Journal of Family Practice, October 2001 Vol. 50, No. 10:1-11.

11   Most Biblical quotations are from the New International Version.

12   See two very helpful essays: David M Scholer, "1 Timothy 2:9-15 and the Place of Women in the Church's Ministry" and Catherine Clark Kroeger, "1 Timothy 2:12—A Classicist's View" in Alvera Mickelsen, Editor, Women, Authority and the Bible, Downers Grove, IL: InterVarsity Press, 1986: 193-248.

13   The verb hamah is used figuratively of the soul and is often translated "murmur." It can describe a soul in distressful prayer (Psalm 55:17 (18); 77:3 (4)) or in deep discouragement (Psalm 42:5 (6)). As the subject of the noun meyeh, hamah refers to the thrill of deep-felt compassion or sympathy. The thrill of loving concern is seen in the excited exclamation of the beloved, "My feelings (literally, bowels) were aroused for him." The phrase in Jeremiah 31:20 is the most definitive statement of the concept of the suffering of God in the book of Jeremiah. God is so intensely involved with Rachel and Ephraim that he grieves.

14   Kazoh Kitamori, The Theology of the Pain of God. Richmond: John Knox Press, 1965. Although Kitamori does provide a fairly extensive exposition of his exegetical findings in Jeremiah 31:20, these are only an appendix to his writing. The majority of his work revolves around a philosophical and theological explanation of what Kitamori refers to as "the heart of the gospel"—"the pain of God." Using Hegelian logic, the love of God and the wrath of God which oppose each other, in Kitamori's view, are encompassed in the pain of God.

15   Sarah Brown's speech "Build for Mothers and You Build for Everyone" as it appeared in the Huffington Post accessed at http://huffingtonpost. com/sarah-brown/build-for-mothers-and-you_b_189527.html. Accessed May 15, 2013.

16   See, for example, Phyllis Trible, "The Gift of a Poem: A Rhetorical Study of Jeremiah 31:15-22" Andover Newton Quarterley 17 (1977):271-80; William L. Holladay, "Jeremiah 31:22b Reconsidered: 'The Woman Encompasses the Man,'" VT 16 (1966):236-9; "Jeremiah and Woman's Liberation," Andover Newton Quarterly 12 (1972):213-23; and Bernard W. Anderson, "'The Lord has created something new': A Stylistic Study of Jeremiah 31:15-22," CBQ 40 (1978):463-78.

17   The Jewish wedding ceremony is thought to bear witness to this interpretation. The last part of the wedding processional at a traditional Jewish wedding involves the bride's encirclement of the groom. When the bride reaches the marriage canopy, she walks around the groom seven times, with her mother and mother-in-law following her. By drawing a circle with her own body she creates an invisible wall and then steps inside. This signifies togetherness and distinctiveness from the rest of society. The tradition is thought to be based on the messianic understanding of Jeremiah 31:22. Blu Greenberg, "Marriage in the Jewish Tradition," Journal of Ecumenical Studies 22:(1985) 3-20.

18   As quoted in The Catholic Bible: New American Bible, Personal Study Edition, Indexed edited by Jean Marie Hiersberger, p. 1098.

Works Cited

Boice, James Montgomery
>1982 *Genesis: An Expositional Commentary Volume 1 Genesis 1:1-11:32.* Grand Rapids, MI: Zondervan Publishing Corporation.

Brown, Sarah
>2009 "Build for Mothers and You Build for Everyone" as it appeared in the *Huffington Post* accessed at http://huffingtonpost.com/sarah-brown/build-for-mothers-and-you_b_189527.html. Accessed May 15, 2013.

Chamberlain Froese, Jean
>2004 *Where have all the mothers gone?* Bellville, ON: Epic Press.

Chamberlain, Jean, and Watt, Susan
>2012 "Training Multidisciplinary Leaders for Health Promotion in Developing Countries: Lessons Learned." In *Health Promotion Practice.* Pp. 344-348. Vol. 13.

Cohen, Deborah J., et al
>2005 "Implementing Health Behavior Change in Primary Care: Lessons from Prescription for Health." In *The Annals of Family Medicine* Pp. 512-519 3 (2).

Conn, Harvie M. and Ortiz, Manuel
>2001 "Shalom and Social Transformation." In *Urban Ministry: The Kingdom, the City and the People of God.* Pp. 340-357 Downers Grove, IL: InterVarsity, Academic Press, 2001.

Hiersberger, Jean Marie, ed.
>ND *The Catholic Bible: New American Bible, Personal Study Edition, Indexed.* P. 1098.

Kleinman, A., Eisenberg, L, and Good, B.
>1978 "Culture, illness, and care: clinical lessons from anthropologic and cross-cultural research." Pp. 251-258. *Ann Intern Med* 88(2).

Kroeger, Catherine Clark
1986   "1 Timothy 2:12—A Classicist's View." In *Women, Authority and the Bible.* Alvera Mickelsen, ed. Pp. 225-243. Downers Grove, IL: InterVarsity Press.

Miller, William L., et al.
2001   "Practice Jazz: Understanding Variation in Family Practices Using Complexity Science." *The Journal of Family Practice* 50(10):1-11.

Rosenfield, Allan, Maine, Deborah, and Freedman, Lynn
2006   "Meeting MDG-5: and impossible dream?" In *The Lancet.* Pp. 1133-1135. Volume 368, Issue 9542.

Scholar, David M.
1986   "1 Timothy 2:19-15 and the Place of Women in the Church's Ministry." In *Women, Authority and the Bible.* Alvera Mickelsen, ed. Pp. 193-224. Downers Grove, IL: InterVarsity Press.

Scott, Daniel D.
2012   "The Enhancement of East African Universities' Contribution towards the Attainment of Millennium Development Goal 5—Improving Maternal Health," supported by Mobilizing Regional Capacity Initiative (MRCI) of the Association of African Universities (AAU), a DFID Sponsored Initiative.

Thaddeus, S. and Maine, D.
1994   "Too far to walk: maternal mortality in context." In *Soc Sci Med* Pp. 1091-1110 38(8).

UNICEF
2005   "Millennium Development Goals." Accessed on May 15, 2013.   http://www.unicef.org/mdg/

Westley, Frances, Zimmerman, Brenda, and Patton, Michael Quinn
2007   *Getting to Maybe: How the World is Changed.* Toronto: Vintage Canada.

Wolterstorff, Nicholas
    2004   "Teaching for Justice: On Shaping How Students are Disposed to Act." In *Educating for Shalom: Essays on Christian Education.* Clarence W. Joldersma and Gloria Goris Stronks, editors. Pp. 135-154. Grand Rapids, MI: William B. Eerdmans Publishing Company.

World Health Organization
    2005   "Why do so many women still die in pregnancy or childbirth." Accessed on May 15, 2013. http://www.who.int/features/qa/12/en/
    2012   "Maternal Mortality" Accessed on May 15, 2013 http://www.who.int/mediacentre/factsheets/fs348/en/

Beyond Western
Approaches to Missions

Postindustrial Missions & the
Missiology within Hip Hop Culture

DANIEL WHITE HODGE

DOI: 10.7252/Paper.000023

About the Author:
Contact at dwhodge@northpark.edu   Director of the Center for Youth
Ministry Studies & Assistant Professor of Youth Ministry at North Park
University. Daniel White Hodge has been engaged with urban youth work and
ministry for 20 years and is the author of The Soul of Hip Hop: Rimbs, Timbs,
& A Cultural Theology (IVP 2010), Heaven Has a Ghetto: The Missiological
Gospel & Theology of Upac Amaru Shakur (VDM Academic 2009), and of the
forthcomig publication The Hostile Gospel: Seeking God in Post Soul Urban
American Hip Hop (Brill Academic 2013).

Abstract

There is no argument that the past 50 years have brought societal, economic, religious, and missiological change. Moreover, within the past decade we have witnessed a rise in those categorized as 'nones' (those without religious affiliation and/ or atheist gnostic) which represent a growing demographic of young adults (18-30). The changing context of urban as a more cultural term rather than geographical location has also brought with it cultural groups such as Hip Hop into once all White affluent suburban contexts. Also, what once "worked" in missions now needs to be reevaluated and deconstructed to continue a fresh and new approach to the Missio Dei within postindustrial contexts. Thus, the once Western ideal of a White, male, evangelical missionary is quickly fading. In this paper, I will argue that Hip Hop culture, in its spiritual and missional stance, creates a strong missiology for the nones, postindustrial people groups, and young adults. I will briefly historicize the societal change within the last 40 years and how Hip Hop exudes a missiological message, and finally, I will argue that the Missio Dei is fulfilled within Hip Hop's ethos by looking at artists Tupac, Lauryn Hill, and Lupe Fiasco for and to missions among the nones and young adult populations.

Introduction

For nearly the last four decades, the urban sub-culture of Hip Hop has provided an outlet and a voice for many people in the inner city. Hip Hop culture has become much larger than its initial sight of simply being a musical genre. In fact, Hip Hop is much more complex than just its music, it engrosses the issues of race, gender, politics, class, sexuality/ sexual orientation, and spirituality head on and encourages strong personal consciousness, self-development, and a connection to helping the surrounding community (Dyson 1996; Hodge 2009, 2010b; Kitwana 2003; Pinn 1995). Using rap music as one of its vehicles of communication to send and fund its message (Hodge 2010b; Smith and Jackson 2005), Hip Hop is a voice which speaks for the marginalized, the poor, the downtrodden, and the oppressed (Chang 2005; Dyson 2001; Hodge 2010b; Kitwana 2003; One 2003). It is a voice which rejects dominant culture, and seeks to increase social consciousness along with racial/ ethnic pride. Its dominant public profile of foul language, lewd sexuality, and lifestyles appearing simply to be "anti-god"[1] make it difficult for many "religious" individuals to relate and engage with Hip Hop culture. And truly, there is a large element of commercialized Hip Hop culture which is primarily concerned about money, sex, and nihilistic worldviews.[2] But there is something larger at work to which we missiologists must attend: a fundamental attempt to make God and the work of the Holy Spirit more accessible to a people who have been, in large part, ignored by many Christian churches and overlooked by some missiologists.[3]

In my book, *The Soul Of Hip Hop*, I describe how young people aged 14-21 understood God and Christian sacred scripture with deeper meaning from artists such as Tupac, DMX, Lupe Fiasco, and Lauryn Hill because these individuals spoke from their perspective and language (Hodge 2010b, Interviews). Artists such as Tupac also act as natural theologians who interpret scripture and comment upon it no differently than, say, a T.D. Jakes or a Joel Osteen do for their constituents (Dyson 2001). Hip Hop pushes past the traditionalized White, blonde, blue eyed, evangelical social construct of Jesus and asks for a Jesus that can "reach us," be "real" with us, "feel" us, and relate to us – a contextualized deity in a relational stance (Hodge 2010b; Watkins 2011). This type of Jesus is one who can relate to youth in urban settings beyond the standard evangelical model of both mission and church. This type of Jesus also questions authority, seeks to increase social consciousness, validates and acknowledges the social isolation as valid and real to all the 'hood, and every now and then "puts a foot in someone's [butt] to tell a [expletive] he real" (Hodge 2009, Interview). As ethnomusicologist Christina Zanfagna exclaims, "Mainstream hip-hop percolates with unlikely and multifaceted religious inclinations. Despite its inconsistent relationship to organized religion and its infamous mug of weed smoking, drug pushing, gun slinging, and curse spewing, rap music is not without moral or spiritual content... religious messages have always been delivered through a vast array of sounds" (2006, 1). Simply put, Hip Hop provides a contextualized and relevant form of religious discourse, meaning, and identity for urban youth and others who are its listeners. As missiologists and youth workers alike, must give attention to what messages and theological concepts are coming from and out of Hip Hop culture.

There is also no real argument that says society has not changed significantly in the last fort to fifty years. But, what this change means and how it will affect the Christian Church is yet to be determined. Scholars have long argued that we have entered a "post" era and that life, society, religion, and consciousness itself are in flux and disarray of sorts (Bell 1973; Habermas 1988; Soja 2000; Taylor 2007; Touraine 1977). Missiologists David Bosch asserts that, "The 'post-phenomena is not just a fad. We have truly entered into an epoch fundamentally at variance with anything we have experienced to date" (Bosch 1995, 1). This shift and "post"—of sorts—demands that missiologist deconstruct methods of missional engagement. The rise of the "nones" category is reality for the mosaic age group (18-30) [4] and traditional modalities of missional approaches—White, male, from the U.S., Western Christendom as normality—must be challenged and revisited in order to not only "engage" this generation, but develop new methods of cultural exegisis for the Missio Dei and create a contextualized missiology. As Wilbert Shenk reminds us, "A relevant missiology will be one that helps the church embrace its mission fully through clear discernment of the times, together with a vision of what a dynamic missionary response requires" (Shenk 1993, 30). Thus it is imperative for the field of missiology to engage Hip Hop as it is a new, twenty-first century mission field among both urban and suburban youth.

Hip Hop, in its infamous profile of immorality and perceived secular attitudes, provides context, meaning, and a spiritual modus for young people. Hip Hop culture is a complex urban sub-culture which produces a rich theological discourse in which many youth, not just Black and Latino, are able to connect with and relate to. And, while parts of Hip Hop do not reflect any part of a Godly message, this should not discourage the missiologist in engaging this relevant and global culture. In this paper, I will argue that Hip Hop culture, in its spiritual and missional stance, creates a strong missiology for the nones, postindustrial people groups, and young adults. I will briefly historicize the societal change[5] within the last 40 years and how Hip Hop exudes a missiological message, and finally, I will argue that the Missio Dei is fulfilled within Hip Hop's ethos by looking at artists Tupac, Lauryn Hill, and Lupe Fiasco for and to missions among the nones and young adult populations.

Shifting Tides of Culture

Tricia Rose, one of the first scholars to write academically about Hip Hop, observes in *"Black Noise: Rap Music and Black Culture in Contemporary America"* that Hip Hop culture emerged as a source of alternative identity formation and social status for young people within a system that had abandoned them (Rose 1994, 31-33).[6] As Angela Nelson notes, "The racial oppression of black people in many ways has fueled and shaped black musical forms in America" (Nelson 1991, 51). Hip Hop is one of those musical forms. "Contemporary rappers, like early bluespeople, are responding to the 'burden of freedom,' in part by relaying portrayals of reality to their audiences through their personal experiences" (Nelson 1991, 56). Hip Hop culture used rap music to bring definition, value, understanding, and appreciation to the social isolation, economic hardships, political demoralization, and cultural exploitation endured by most ghetto poor communities. So what happened?

Around the late 1950's[7] and early 1960's, the beginnings of the first wave of deindustrialization began to occur (George 2004; Murray 1984; Palen 1981; Sides 2003; Wiese 2004). Businesses began to outsource their work, pay less in benefits, and use cheaper labor, generating larger profits for companies but adversely affecting Black communities. The American economy began to shift away from an industrial economy to one more focused on technology and highly skilled labor – which paid a lot more but required specialized training and education. The result was a fragmentation of the middle class and an upsurge in poverty (Sides 2003; Wiese 2004). Because of historic discrimination in college admissions, many Blacks found it difficult to compete with peers with specialized degrees; jobs in the aerospace industry, for example, did not typically hire Blacks. Moreover, if the applicant did not have the necessary training, there was no point in applying. Todd Boyd notes, "We're not talking about people who had careers. We're talking about people who had jobs. If you have a job you are dependent on *that job*. So when that factory closes, you are in essence 'assed out'" (Peralta 2008, Interview on DVD). By the late 1960's, most of those thriving factories had disappeared. In the wake of this loss, nothing appeared in its place for the thousands of workers now out of a job.[8]

Urban ethnographer Charles Murray (1984) records that deindustrialization brought financial ruin to large swatches of the urban/ inner city community, particularly the young under the age of twenty (Wiese 2004). By the early 1960's, what little capital and access to education Blacks had, began to wither away. By 1968 full deindustrialization emerged, with many corporations leaving the U.S. to go to Mexico, India, and China (Paris 1985; Peralta 2008; Sides 2003; Wiese 2004). The once hopeful and almost cheerful Black middle class was dismantled and beginning to crumble, creating a distinct ghetto ripe with anger and disenfranchised from the rest of American society.[9] The Black generation born during the mid to late 60's was in worse financial and social shape than the predecessor generations. Moreover, these new generations were growing up without Black leaders and visionaries such as Martin Luther King, Bobby Seal, and Malcolm X. What was worse was that there were very few programs that could handle and deal with the significant rise in jobless[10] Black families.[11]

For urban youth during this period,[12] a type of "Great Depression" set in, both financially and emotionally. [13] The new generation of youth was being raised in this ethos of shattered dreams and hopes. They viewed institutions as failed systems and empty promises, In other words, if one system of society has failed and lied to the people such as the government, how much more would a church be at risk for such corruption?[14] They saw that the old way of life was not working for the older generation and this new world they found themselves in was one riddled with double standards, failed promises, destroyed social structures, and a government which seemed almost obtuse and belligerent towards them (Hodge 2010b; Moss 2007; Watkins 2011). Moreover, most affluent churches had left the ghetto for a safer, cleaner, suburban area (Cox 1965, 1984; Rah 2009).[15]

A theological void was apparent for the inner city and many churches, which once could afford helping their community, were now financially hurting themselves. To further this, an attitude and worldview which carried over from nineteenth century missions was that, "...the adjective 'poor' was increasingly used to qualify the noun 'heathen'" (Bosch 1991, 290). Bosch notes that this type of attitude persisted and adopted toward younger churches too; in other words, if tradition and the "right way" was not followed, it was easy to become labeled as heretical and/ or even a heathen (1991, 290-292). A no wonder why urban people groups were disgruntled by Christian theology.

In turn, the age old question of "why do bad things happen to good people" took on new meaning for those in the inner city; why did God "leave" me and my family? How come my family, which happens to be Black and/ or Brown, is in dire straits? These types of questions continued to manifest within inner city people; especially the youth, as they saw their heroes such as Martin Luther King and Malcolm X gunned down. Churches, in general, were not stepping up. Instead, many found solace and safety in the suburbs while the decline of the city continued (Rah 2009, 64-95).

In the mid to late '70's, an angry generation of Black and Brown youth were now culminating within the ghettos around the U.S and Black and Brown youth's social and cultural expressions shifted. In the womb of this shift Hip Hop was forming within the theological void and vacuum of the 'hood (Rose 1994, 34-40). By the time the 1980's arrived, an entire section of America's cites lay in ruin by the degenerate destruction of the crack era (Hodge 2009; Neal 2002; One 2003; Peralta 2008; Quinn 2005; Ruskin 2009). Black and Brown youth had little to no recourse and faced a society that viewed them as thugs, pimps, and societal rejects (Dyson 1996; George 2004; Hodge 2009; Moss 2007). Hip Hop stood up and artists such as Melle Mel told us "The Message":

Broken glass everywhere
People pissin' on the stairs, you know they just don't care
I can't take the smell, can't take the noise
Got no money to move out, I guess I got no choice
Rats in the front room, roaches in the back
Junkies in the alley with a baseball bat

I tried to get away but I couldn't get far
'cuz a man with a tow truck repossessed my car

[CHORUS]
Don't push me 'cuz I'm close to the edge
I'm trying not to lose my head[16]

Run DMC reminded us of "Hard Times":

Hard times can take you on a natural trip
So keep your balance, and don't you slip
Hard times is nothing new on me
I'm gonna use my strong mentality
Like the cream of the crop, like the crop of the cream
B-b-beating hard times, that is my theme
Hard times in life, hard times in death
I'm gonna keep on fighting to my very last breath[17]

M.C. Hammer even told us to "Pray Just to Make it Today" in response to social inequality:

Time and time and time and time again
(That's word, we pray)
I kept on knocking, but
These people wouldn't let me in
(That's word, we pray)
I tried and tried and tried and tried to make a way
(That's word, we pray)
But nothing happened till that day I prayed[18]

And Tupac prompted us to "Keep Our Heads Up":

When you come around the block brothas clown a lot
But please don't cry, dry your eyes, never let up
Forgive but don't forget, girl keep your head up
And when he tells you you ain't nuttin don't believe him
And if he can't learn to love you, you should leave him
Cause sista you don't need him
And I ain't tryin to gas ya up, I just call em how I see em
You know it makes me unhappy (what's that)

When brothas make babies, and leave a young mother
to be a pappy
And since we all came from a woman
Got our name from a woman and our game from a
woman
I wonder why we take from our women
Why we rape our women, do we hate our women?
I think it's time to kill for our women
Time to heal our women, be real to our women
And if we don't we'll have a race of babies
That will hate the ladies, that make the babies
And since a man can't make one
He has no right to tell a woman when and where to
create one
So will the real men get up
I know you're fed up ladies, but keep your head up[19]

These artists, through their music and vernacular, signify two central themes here 1) giving worth, value, and meaning to the suffering, social isolation, and pain so often glanced over when it is experienced from non-dominant people groups, and 2), a message of hope that someone out there knows their struggle and that the person experiencing such issues is not alone.

Even when missiologists were lacking in the inner city, rap artist and "urban prophet"[20] Tupac Amaru Shakur exclaims his own *missio Dei* for urban youth:

So, I feel like I'm doing God's work, you know what I'm saying? Just because I don't have nothing to pass around for people to put in the bucket don't mean I'm not doing God's work; I feel like I'm doing God's work. Because, these ghetto kids ain't God's children? And I don't see no missionaries coming through there. So I'm doing God's work. While Reverend Jackson do his [stuff] up in the middle class and he go to the White house and have dinner and pray over the president, I'm up in the 'hood doing my work with my folks.[21]

In a world which seemed to have lost its sense of "church" God and community, Hip Hop stands in that gap and continues a contextual *missio Dei* for youth in an urban context. These artists are able to connect with young people in manner that is more engaging than a preacher can. The music of Hip Hop has the ability to push past the nonsense and get into what Anthony Pinn refers to as "nitty-gritty hermeneutics" in which simplistic theological responses are not tolerated and a more mature faith is required (Pinn 1995, 113-138). Rap and Hip Hop capture and esteem the ghetto poor existence as valid and real to all ethnic minorities and poor Whites (Hodge 2010b; Smith and Jackson 2005); there is much "God" at work in this process. Let us begin to see Hip Hop as both a valid mission field and a form of Mission to young people[22] in both suburban and urban contexts. Hip Hop is this generations Isaiah and provides a good news message like Jesus Christ (Hodge 2009; Watkins 2011).[23] We cannot ignore this, even if the musical vehicle it is carried in utilizes elements of the profane to make its sacred point (Reed 2003; Spencer 1990; Zanfagna 2006). As the current climate of youth culture continues to evolve, a crucial cultural component of mission will be through Hip Hop. Therefore, we turn to Hip Hop's central theological components, to better understand its sacred quest for God.[24]

Hip Hop & the *Mission Dei*

In this section I will examine two Hip Hop artists who have had a significant effect on Hip Hop Culture and whose names have emerged from interviews, rap music, and Hip Hop scholarship as prophets and "ghetto saints" (Hodge 2013b; Smith and Jackson 2005; Utley 2012). Tupac Amaru Shakur and Lauryn Hill, in an indirect and unintentional way, have radiated a missiological ethos through their music and life. Interviewees have extoled that Hill and Shakur, "spoke God into my life at a time when there was darkness," "created a space for me to learn more about God and his love for me…I was brought into Christianity by folks like Pac and Lauryn Hill." Thus, it is imperative that we, as missiologists, peer into the music and life themes of these two artists.

Lauryn Hill

Let us begin with the great Lauryn Hill.[25] Hill, in one album, *The Miseducation of Lauryn Hill* (1998), Hill created a space for those struggling in relationships, love, faith, and with God to come and connect, meditate, cry, love, and doubt in safety. This opened up the door for some to find a deeper meaning as to who God was. As an interviewee stated:

> Lauryn was like...man...she was like a damn pastor who preached faith in a time of doubt. That album [The Miseducation of Lauryn Hill] was that for me. I use to listen to that when I was going through my divorce. She was my counselor and therapeutic space. Whew. God used her for sure.[26]

Hill was part of the rap group Fugee's and described by many Hip Hop artists as "The Mother of Hip Hop Invention."[27] What Hill created was a space for those who were hurt, disenfranchised and disinherited to find meaning and, essentially, God. She wrestled with God and the pain she had—and still has—in her life within broken promises, failed relationships, questions regarding faith, and the reality of being a Black woman in the U.S..

In her song, "Ex-Factor," she dances with issues surrounding love within a committed relationship:

> It could all be so simple
> But you'd rather make it hard
> Loving you is like a battle
> And we both end up with scars
> Tell me, who I have to be
> To get some reciprocity
> No one loves you more than me
> And no one ever will
> Is this just a silly game
> That forces you to act this way?
> Forces you to scream my name
> Then pretend that you can't stay
> Tell me, who I have to be
> To get some reciprocity
> No one loves you more than me
> And no one ever will[28]

The song goes on to discuss the failures of relationships and the pain associated with those "loves lost."[29] What Hill does to perfection is to dance with the premise of pain, love, and faith. Where is God during these times? This is powerful to listeners because it does not answer fundamental existentialized questions and allows those who listen to grapple with the ambiguity within. This is an essential mantra for the Mosaics: to grapple with the ambiguity of who God is; moving beyond linear step processes to resolution and into an enlightenment of who God is within that ambiguity and doubt; Hill capitalized on this.

Still, Hill did not simply "leave it there." She would take part of that ambiguity and mix it with divinity:

> Father you saved me and showed me that life
> Was much more than being some foolish man's wife
> Showed me that love was respect and devotion
> Greater than planets deeper than oceans
> My soul was weary but now it's replenished
> Content because that part of my life is finished
>
> I see him sometimes and the look in his eye
> Is one of a man who's lost treasures untold
> But my heart is gold I took back my soul
> And totally let my creator control
> The life which was his to begin with[30]

Hill is able to fade into that gray theology in which many—espcially those within urban enclaves—live and reside spiritually. "I Use To Love Him" is a song that interweaves with these issues.

In the song "Doo Wop (That Thing)" Hill, conversely, challenges "backsliders" and "luke warm" believers alike:

> Talking out your neck, saying you're a Christian
> A Muslim, sleeping with the Gin
> Now that was the sin that did Jezebel in
> Who're you going to tell when the repercussions spin?
> Showing off your ass because your thinking it's a trend
> Girlfriend, let me break it down for you again![31]

Here, Hill takes a stance to call out the double talk within religious people and the call to live a higher life—if that is in fact what you are saying you are doing. Hill missiologically calls out the neo-pagan lifestyle[32] in a manner that people will listen. An interviewee notes:

When I heard that song, I was convicted...cause that was me! I was living that lifestyle. I was saying I was Christian and living a life of sin...ya know what I mean? Shit, Lauryn called me out through that album and helped me to live a better life for God...shoot, better than any preacher could ever do

The interviewee went on to exclaim that Hill was instrumental in his faith formation and development; six others also referred to Hill as being their "pastoral guidance" in a theological journey with God.

David Bosch discusses "God Talk in an age of Reason" in his book *Believing In The Future.* Hill takes this God talk to the streets and creates space for those who follow a Nietzscheian worldview and exclaims, "yes! God is still alive, just a bit more complex than Western theology makes him out to be." In this sense, the Missio Dei is in the pain, the suffering, the doubt, and the search for God within all of this. The messier and convoluted it gets with Hill, the greater and more beautiful the Gospel is within that matrix.[33]

Tupac Shakur

Tupac Amaru Shakur,[34] conversely, was notorious for his connection to God and the spiritual realm most did not dare enter; doubt, fear, questions, and the search for God in the profane. Yet, this is what made him one of the most sought after Hip Hop prophets and whose music still lingers as both relevant and applicable to today's societal conditions—quite a feat given the average shelf life in rap music is three to four months. Tupac was iconic. Tupac's life was cut short at the age of twenty five Recalling Tupac's accomplishments at such a young age, Quincy Jones recollects Tupac's death by stating that if Martin Luther King, Jr. had died when he was twenty-five, he would have been a struggling Black Baptist minister; if Malcolm X had died at twenty-five, he would have been a street hustler; and if he himself had died at twenty-five, he would have been a struggling trumpet player; but Tupac died at twenty-five, leaving a legacy of life, love, rage, pain— and theology. "Tupac was touched by God[;] not very many people are touched by the hand of God."[35]

Tupac argues the inadequacy of the previous and existing theologies for the present Crisis—poverty, recidivism rates for young urban males, racism, and classism. Tupac never once questioned, blasphemed, or cursed the name of God or Jesus. What Tupac did do was to call out religious officials, traditionalized churches (churches practicing hyper-traditionalism and adherence to the "letter of the law"), conventional forms of religion, irrelevant theologies, and current methods of evangelism.

Tupac was not a trained theologian, pastor, or evangelist[36] in the way one would recognize from the rigor of the seminary. Tupac did not have the eloquence of a T.D. Jakes or the prowl of a Baptist preacher. Still, Tupac was able to connect God to the streets and give those who had never heard of God a vision for what their life could be like. Lacking formal training never disqualified anyone from doing "God's work." Still, Tupac never really came to any solid conclusions about a theology of the 'hood. He began the discussion, but because of his early death, never finished the mantra of a ghetto Gospel.

> We probably in Hell already, our dumb asses not
> knowin
> Everybody kissin ass to go to heaven ain't goin
> Put my soul on it, I'm fightin devil niggaz daily
> Plus the media be crucifying brothers severely... [37]

This aptly-titled song, "Blasphemy," was a rejection of a form of Black theology that places the pastor at the center of the church, creates a pious stature for him (and it typically is a him), and discourages honest questions and doubts from emerging within the congregation . Tupac not only challenges but shatters the status quo by placing context and reality into his message within this song. He further states:

> The preacher want me buried why? Cause I know he
> a liar
> Have you ever seen a crackhead, that's eternal fire
> Why you got these kids minds, thinkin that they evil
> while the preacher bein richer you say honor God's
> people
> Should we cry, when the Pope die, my request
> We should cry if they cried when we buried Malcolm X
> Mama tell me am I wrong, is God just another cop

waitin to beat my ass if I don't go pop?[38]

Tupac continues his shattering of the status quo of theological "nice answers" by offering up metaphorical comparisons:

They ask us why we mutilate each other like we do
They wonder why we hold such little worth for human
life
Facing all this drama
To ask us why we turn from bad to worse is to ignore
from which we came
You see, you wouldn't ask why the rose that grew from
the concrete had
damaged petals
On the contrary, we would all celebrate its tenacity
We would all love its will to reach the sun
Well, we are the roses
This is the concrete
And these are my damaged petals
Don't ask me why
Thank God, nigga
Ask me how[39]

In one of his greatest theological songs, "So Many Tears," Tupac pushes past the "milk" theology, described by Paul in 1 Corinthians 3:2, and into a mature theological stance on life:

Now that I'm strugglin in this business, by any means
Label me greedy gettin green, but seldom seen
And fuck the world cause I'm cursed, I'm havin visions
of leavin here in a hearse, God can you feel me?
Take me away from all the pressure, and all the pain
Show me some happiness again, I'm goin blind
I spend my time in this cell, ain't livin well
I know my destiny is Hell, where did I fail?
My life is in denial, and when I die,
baptized in eternal fire I'll shed so many tears
Lord, I suffered through the years, and shed so many
tears.[40]

The post soul context of this generation[41] requires one to disembody and deconstruct current theological mantras which continually hold up tradition. Pain, injustice, and racism force the post soulist to look beyond the "standard" and ask God for more. Simplistic answers are rejected and despised: it gets God off the hook too easily to say "just pray about it,"[42] and in times of pain and injustice, everything needs to be on the hook, including God. The procedure is quite simple: have a conversation with God, be real, and do not be afraid to use strong language to describe your pain:

> Was it my fault papa didn't plan it out
> Broke out left me to be the man of the house
> I couldn't take it, had to make a profit
> Down the block, got a glock, and I clock grip
> Makin G's was my mission
> Movin enough of this shit to get my mama out the kitchen and
> why must I sock a fella, just to live large like Rockefeller
> First you didn't give a fuck, but you're learnin now
> If you don't respect the town then we'll burn you down
> God damn it's a motherfuckin riot
>
> I see no changes, all I see is racist faces
> Misplaced hate makes disgrace to races
> We under I wonder what it take to make this
> one better place, let's erase the wait state
> Take the evil out the people they'll be acting right
> Cause both black and white are smokin crack tonight
> And only time we deal is when we kill each other
> It takes skill to be real, time to heal each other
>
> Pull a trigger kill a nigger he's a hero
> Mo' nigga mo' nigga mo' niggaz
> I'd rather be dead than a po' nigga
> Let the Lord judge the criminals
> If I die, I wonder if heaven got a ghetto[43]

For Tupac, the goal was to create a contextualized way in a world that was forgotten (part of the post soul deconstruction process): the 'hood. In his song "Searching for Black Jesuz," Tupac and the Outlawz search for a deity that can relate to them, one who "smokes like we smoke, drink like we drink."[44] In the song "Picture Me Rolling"

Tupac questions whether or not God can forgive him as he asks, "Will God forgive me for all the dirt a nigga did to feed his kids?"[45] In this neo-sacred element, Tupac begins to ask the longstanding theological question: what does forgiveness really look like for sinners?

For the post soulist, this process of searching for God in the mystery, the hurt, the pain, and then finding God in that heinous mixture is a welcome breath of fresh air compared to the avoidance and three-point sermons that so much of evangelical theology has become. It is the heart of dialogue and the very place God is experienced. In fact, almost anyone who has experienced deep loss and pain in which God's hand felt far can relate. For example, "White Man's World" combines Tupac's request for heavenly favor and reprisal in a process similar to the Psalms: "God bless me please...Making my enemies bleed."[46] Within those statements much more is at work—a fundamental attempt to make God accessible in a social structure which has been forgotten and left for dead.

More of the neo-sacred and post soul theology arises in songs such as "Hail Mary." The song suggests a liturgical prayer, beseeching listeners to follow God and to "follow me; eat my flesh."[47] While it might appear that Tupac is asking his listeners to see him as "God," in fact Tupac was acting as a type of pastoral go-between. Tupac, in several interviews from the early 1990s, made reference to people in the 'hood not always having a clear path to God, and that in that absence of such a path, if he was the only pathway, then so be it.[48] Tupac made it clear he was not God or Jesus, but merely a conduit and a beacon to a contextualized Jesuz.[49]

Tupac fills part of the vacancy for those who doubt. In the song "Po Nigga Blues," Tupac poses a question to God which oozes with spiritual doubt: "...I wonder if the Lord ever heard of me, huh, I need loot, so I'm doin' what I do."[50] In other words, will God really forgive me when I am practicing socially unapproved standards of living? Dyson reminds us that "...Tupac's religious ideas were complex and unorthodox, perhaps even contradictory, though that would not make him unique among his believers". Part of that vacancy felt in the 'hood also comes with images of Heaven: streets of gold, mansions, pearly gates, and a God who is "perfect"—these may be too much for the person living on streets riddled with potholes, in project housing, around broken gates, and with White racist images of God. Paulo Freire boldly states that within situations of oppression, the main goal of the oppressed should be to "...liberate themselves from their oppressors."[51] Tupac was helping to create that pathway for liberation[52] and pointing to God; a position we as missiologists cannot ignore.

Conclusion: Hip Hop as Mission

Tupac and Lauryn contextualize a Jesus that youth, the Mosaics, postindustrial people groups, and those estranged from religion can relate to. Not a blonde hair, blue eyed, White embodiment of perfection, but a Christ that both connects and lives among the people; in this case being youth (Cone 1997a, 1997b). For many Hip Hoppers, Jesus is not the "traditional" form of a savior most of us have been taught to believe in (i.e., long wavy hair and hippy garments) Jesus is the multi-racial Jesus. Jesus is the Jesus that can understand the pain and misery of the inner city. Jesus is the one who could relate to the poor, downtrodden, and folks that people set aside (Hodge 2009, 251-256; 2010b, 130-140). Thus, a theology of the Hip Hop Jesuz is a contextualized "version" of Jesuz (Hence the adding of the letter "z" to the name).[53] Further, for Hip Hoppers, life is done in community (Hodge 2010b, 107-124), an aspect to and of missions. Whether those communities are a few people or one hundred, community is still occurring. For example, many of the concerts I have been to reflect Hip Hop's deep desire to engage in community. More importantly, Church happens in that community and the presence of Christ is experienced, thus it stands to reason why a contextualized Jesus would be appropriate.

The reason Tupac and Hill can evoke such a connection with this generation and provide a missiological connection is simple; they:

1. Evoke truth and light within contextual forms of theological inquiries

2. Are multi-ethnic in approach and cultural worldviews

3. Challenge the norms dominant culture and religion

4. Provide ambiguity yet reveal the mystery of who God is within suffering contexts

5. Look for new modes of "church" in a sacred/ profane context while still pointing to God as the ultimate "an-

swer" for life—an aspect that the mosaic generation are interested in

Youth, the Mosaics, postindustrial people groups, and those estranged from religion contexts are not the cultural contexts of fifty years ago. More importantly, with the advent of media, technology, and the age of information, we have a youth culture that is both savvy and technologically creative. For the pastor that is missionally minded, this can present challenges to their theological framework. Hip Hop, while flawed and still human, creates space for those seeking God in alternate ways, to find God and to value the power of what the Bible says in a more relevant contextual form. Hip Hop artists such as Tupac act as theologians who can interpret the Bible for a people who are hurting, in need, and desperate for God's love. As Dyson reminds us, Hip Hoppers "...aim to enhance awareness of the divine, of spiritual reality, by means of challenging orthodox beliefs and traditional religious practices" (Dyson 2001, 204). We must give attention to this global culture and the affect it has on our youth – even more so if they are in our youth groups. For example, in my research, some powerful responses came forth when I asked the question "What does Hip Hop make you feel spiritually, if anything?" Here are just a few: "I can feel God smiling on me when I rap," "I found the bible to be deeper and more real when I listen to Pac," "Hip Hop is our good news...you feel me? I mean, it's like a church and place we can go," and "Hip Hop saved my life. Period. If it wasn't for God working in the rap, I'd be dead now." (Hodge 2009, 2010b). Hip Hop helps the church embrace its mission fully by having a message that youth can and do identify with (Smith and Jackson 2005).

Therefore, missions must look different from what we are used to in order to even begin a conversation with the Hip Hop community, and be what Harvey Cox calls the *laostheou* or "the people of God" in creating a Church (Big C) in which a daily relationship with Christ is at the center—even in the midst of chaos and social inequality (1965, 125). Missions must begin to engage Hip Hop culture as if it were a foreign far off island in the Pacific Ocean and realize that God has been doing something within that culture long before we set foot on its shores.

What is *not* needed is the relationally void[54] style of handing out Christian tracks to complete strangers on the street in hopes that they will "convert" to our belief system.What is *not* needed is this constant "we" and "them" mentality that causes great chasm's between religious and non-religious communities. What is *not* needed is more "religion" for people who need something deeper than just a simple sermon, simplistic five step solutions, and patronizing "I'll be praying for you" statements. What *is* needed is an open mind and an open heart to see where we can be led by those in the Hip Hop community and in turn use the Hip Hop community as a tool for missions in the 21st century and seeing the margins as the center in Christian Mission.

As a concluding comment, missionally engaging Hip Hop is no easy task to be undertaken. Hip Hop is complex and presents not only a Christian theological mantra, but also ones steeped in Fiver Percenters of Nations Gods and Earth, The Nation of Islam, Zulu Nation, and Zionism. Further, as stated prior, there are parts of Hip Hop culture—as there are in any given culture or sub-culture—which do not give homage to God in any way shape or form. However, this should not dismay the mission minded individual; we have a great calling such as Paul did when he was in Athens.[55]

If the Great Commission is truly valued by missiologists – which is so often touted in the literature – then the Hip Hop community is worth the missional pursuit.[56] Scholars studying young people in this era have noted that they are falling away from religion, see God as a good thing and not a personal God, identify with a pluralistic form of church, and see sin as relative to the context (Dean 2010; Kosmin and Keysar 2009). Hip Hop, while not a utopian "evangelizing tool," creates space for youth to engage Jesus without the religious mantras present. Hip Hop gives a much purer God and argues for a relationship with God in context and creates a sense of personal consciousness to be spread, once attained, to the community. Hip Hop is a space for young people to find God on their terms and move beyond the four walls of "church" and into a, as I would argue, much stronger and purer relationship with God as Hip Hop goes beyond simplistic answers (Hodge 2009, 289-293; Watkins 2011, 97-103). Thus, it behooves us as missiologists to grasp the *missio Dei* within Hip Hop in order to better understand 1) Hip Hop culture, 2) current youth culture, 3) the possibilities of mission to a global culture at a time when societally, people are open to hearing about God and spirituality – even if it is in pluralistic circles – a genuine unedited Jesus is more satisfying to people rather than more words regarding "hell" and "sin."[57] The issues of pain, hurt, oppression, and disenfranchisement are crucial literacies for any minister of the Gospel. God is at work in Hip Hop and even if the appearance of it is offsetting, God is still doing a great work within the culture, music, artists, and youth who listen to its messages.

Notes

1   This "anti-god" element cannot be ignored and is a very real element to the culture. Hip Hop scholars have long argued that while Hip Hop is not "dead" it is in critical condition and in need of a cultural "make over." The argument I make here about Hip Hop's spiritual discourse is primarily based upon Hip Hop's cultural roots, research among the Hip Hop community, and Hip Hop's rich underground community which continues to argue for personal and social consciousness. I would also argue that even in the commercialized messages of Hip Hop, God is still at work but seeing this requires cultural exegesis which the length of this article does not permit (Hodge 2010a).

2   At its core, Hip Hop is defined as such: Hip Hop is an urban sub-culture that seeks to express a life-style, attitude, and/or urban individuality. Hip Hop at its core—not the commercialization and commodity it has become in certain respects— rejects dominant forms of culture and society and seeks to increase a social consciousness along with a racial/ethnic pride. Thus, Hip Hop uses rap music, dance, music production, MCing, and allegory as vehicles to send and fund its message of social, cultural, and political resistance to dominate structures of norms (Hodge 2013a).

3   See (Beaudoin 1998; Reed 2003) to see the importance of relevant and contextual messages for people to better understand and come to God.

4   See (Kosmin and Keysar 2009; Logo et al. 2012) as they discuss the data with the rise of "nones"—the rising group of young adults who claim no religious affiliation and a growing disdain toward organized religion.

5   For a detailed examination of the growth and social significance of Hip Hop culture—which this article does not allow me to explore—see (Asante 2008; Boyd 2002; Chang 2005; Kitwana 2003).

6   This includes Christians and missiologists. As was noted in my research (Hodge 2009), respondents who considered themselves Hip Hoppers during the 1970's and early 1980's felt abandoned by Christians; anyone who came into the neighborhood wanted them to change toward their ways rather than accepting the people group as they were and validating their culture.

7   This is also an era that Douglas John Hall argues that Christianity was undergoing a "metamorphosis" and moving into a decline (Hall 1997, 1-3).

8   It is also noted here, however, that during this time period, aptly called the soul era (Neal 2002), that Black churches were still thriving in small communities and the Black church was at the center of the Civil Rights Movement and there for communities in need during this time. Still, the younger generations as noted by (George 1998; Moss 2007; Watkins 2011) were witness to the decline of urban social structure and the fall of many great urban leaders (e.g. King, Malcolm X, Huey Newton). This generation of youth would comprise the first Hip Hop generation (Kitwana 2003) which would give voice to the social isolation felt in many inner cities and the youth which inhabited them (Hodge 2010b). It is also interesting to note that the decline of the Black church as a social entity and power source begins during the late 1960's and early 1970's (Lincoln and Mamiya 1990).

9   Timothy Monsma notes that "children at risk" in cities is an essential element to missionally engaging a people group; particularly when there are notable socio-economic disparities and the unjust use of children as labor (2000, 192-202)

10   On Thursday March 10, 1975, eleven years after the Civil Rights Title IV act, an entire section of the Los Angeles Times entitled "A Ghetto is Slow to Die" engaged this very real phenomenon in the Black community. John Kendall researched families and economic structures from 1963-1975, stating "The fearful live behind protective bars and double locks. High schools are graduating functional illiterates." He also asserted that "Little has changed in the basic conditions of the Black ghetto in 10 years since the Watts riots erupted..." The article was a sobering reality palette which did not give a very promising future for anyone living in ghetto like conditions, but principally for Blacks. Kendall continued, "Some black people have got businesses; some professionals have gotten into significant jobs. But if you talk about the masses or that guy who was in trouble in '65, it is more difficult now." The social manifest that so many Black churches fought to create and instill during the civil rights movement was deduced in one word for life: survival (Kendall 1975). This is significant because, religiously speaking, this era noted as a distinct decline in Black and Brown communities (Lincoln and Mamiya 1990; Pinn 2002) which would in turn effect the next generation of youth in which Hip Hop culture was to be formed in (Hodge 2009; Watkins 2011).

11   More importantly to make mention is the main thrust in mission during this time period was to "send forth and out" (Shenk 1999, 156-169) rather than a push towards domestic missions within the inner city; the idea here was to "evangelize" the world and make this "Big" movement in missions, yet there was plenty of "evangelizing" to be done at home (Rah 2009, 93-97) and among communities ravished just as bad as India, Sudan, and Asia. This is still an ongoing debate within certain missional conversations.

12   It is important to comment that there was a distinct shift in social, theological, philosophical, and even Christological ontology during the late '60's and early '70's; this shift was partly a result from the ensuing economical change for Blacks but also the reality that such societal mantras like "Work hard, and your dreams will come true" were shattered (e.g.Bennett 1993; Boyd 1997, 2002; Cox 1984; Cupitt 1998; George 1992, 2004; Hodge 2010b; Kitwana 2005; Pinn 2002; West 1993); this also would have a significant affect for social institutions such as the church. This article does not have the breadth to cover this issue, but the ensuing effect during this time is still felt according to Eric Lincoln and Lawrence Mamiya (1990).

13   Some have argued that this "shift" in society was the changing from modernity to post modernity. While these terms are applicable in certain ways to the urban, Black, and Latino context, they typically refer to a White, suburban, upper middle class shift and negate and social shifts within the urban, Black, and Latino communities (George 2004; Neal 2002). Therefore, the term post soul is a more relevant term which encompasses social shifts such as The Civil Rights Movement, the messages of Malcolm X and Martin Luther King, the rise of Black popular culture and its effects on mainstream America, the crack era of the 1980's, and the Hip Hop generation; see (George 2004; Taylor 2007; West 1993) for a detailed work on this subject.

14   This type of worldview is significant in understanding contemporary urban youth. The youth in urban settings were raised to distrust social systems and institutions. Church and religion are at the top of those "do not trust" lists. It is important that the missiologist of today understand that their efforts must begin with building trust in this community among youth. Anything outside of that is only inviting distrust (c.f. Shenk 1999)

15   This is also known as "White Flight."

16   (Mel 1980)

17   (Run-D.M.C 1984)

18   (Hammer 1990)

19   (Shakur 1993)

20   This term is better explained in (Dyson 2001; Hodge 2009) where Tupac's life, work, message, music, and theology is examined to create this term "prophet." It is noted, that many of the subjects interviewed in (Hodge 2009) defined Tupac as their "prophet" and "ghetto theologian."

21   Taken from an interview done on BET by Ed Gordon roughly around the mid 1990's.

22   For an examination into this, see (Hodge 2013c) as I discuss the relevance of Hip Hop as a missiological agent.

23   Also see (Dyson 2001, 208-210)where he discusses how rap artists connect with the laments and pessimism of prophets such as David and Jeremiah.

24   In my book, The Soul Of Hip Hop, I argue that Hip Hop has five central theological concepts: A theology of suffering, a theology of community, a theology of social action, a theology of the Hip Hop Jesuz, and a theology of the profane (2010b, chapters 3-7)

25   While Hill is now facing jail time for allegedly not filing back taxes, this does not in any way negate who she is and what her music gave to people theologically. It merely signifies that she is, in fact, human; part of what made and still makes her spiritually attractive to people is that she is human and fallible.

26   Taken from an interview during the research for this paper 2012.

27   During the "golden era" of Hip Hop, roughly 1988-1997, the "invention" term was given to those creative, conscious, and socially forward thinking rappers such as Hill.

28   Lauryn Hill, "Ex-Factor," The Mis-Education of Lauryn Hill (1998).

29   Within the entire album, Hill has interludes where ethnic minority teens are being interviewed and asked about what they think and believe love is; the answers are both amazing and rich and also continue to give voice to a marginalized group; Hill knew this and wanted to have this on her album to have that "youthful voice."

30   Lauryn Hill, "I Use To Love Him," The Mis-Education of Lauryn Hill (1998).

31   Lauryn Hill, "Doo Wop (That Thing)," The Mis-Education of Lauryn Hill (1998).

32   Very similar to what Wilbert Shenk tells us that Visser 't Hooft called for in his five-fold response to neo-paganism in the West (2001, 78-80).

33   This is an ongoing theological discussion in regards to doubt, faith, and the search for God. For a real time look into the power of music within this discussion, see Tom Beaudoin,. 2013. Secular music and sacred theology. Collegeville, Minnesota: Liturgical Press.

34   For an in depth examination into the life of Tupac Shakur see (Dyson 2001; Hodge 2009)

35   Interview taken from the DVD documentary Thug Angel: The Life of An Outlaw (2002).

36   19 of the 20 of the interviews stated that Tupac was their "pastor" and connection to theology. They told me that Tupac was a prophet because of the way he could interpret theological matters and make it "clear" for them, See Hodge, The Soul Of Hip Hop: Rimbs Timbs & A Cultural Theology.

37   Tupac, "Blasphemy," The Don Killuminati: The 7 Day Theory (1996).

38   In this verse we can also see Tupac connecting with mainstream theological thought by asking the serious question of God. In other words, is God just another White, conservative Republican, wanting me to fit in and wear suits and ties like I've been told and have seen? Is there a place for the real nigga and thug in Heaven?

39   "Mama Just A Little Girl" Better Dayz disc one (2002).

40   "So Many Tears" Me Against The World (1995).

41   The post soul context: this is the era which began in the late 1960s
      and early 1970s that rejected dominant structures, systems, and meta-
      narratives which tended to exclude ethnic minorities and particularly
      the 'hood. The post soul era rejects linear functional mantras and
      embraces communal approaches to life, love, and God. The post soul
      context was formed in the cocoon of a social shift which broke open
      the dam to the questioning of authority, challenging the status quo,
      asserting one's self identity in the public sphere, and questioning group
      leaders (George 2004; Hodge 2010b; Neal 2002; Taylor 2007).

42   Anthony B Pinn, Why Lord? Suffering and Evil in Black Theology (New
      York: Continuum, 1995).describes this type of theological process as
      nitty gritty hermeneutics, pushing past the basics of theology and into
      the depths of life to ask God "tougher questions." Acceptance of pain is
      put into context and the hermeneutic moves into the "nitty gritty" of
      life.

43   Lyrics taken from throughout the song "I Wonder if Heaven Got A
      Ghetto" (Original Hip Hop version) R U Still Down disc one (1997).

44   2Pac & The Outlawz,"Black Jesus," Still I Rise, 1999, Interscope Records.

45   Tupac interview with Vibe Magazine, approximately 1995.

46   Tupac Shakur, "White Man's World," Makaveli-Don Killuminati: The
      7-Day Theory, 1996, Deathrow Records.

47   Tupac Shakur, "Hail Mary," Makaveli-Don Killuminati: The 7-Day
      Theory, 1996, Deathrow Records.

48   Tupac interview with Vibe Magazine, approximately 1995.

49   Note the letter "S" has been dropped to demonstrate the
      contextualization of the Christ figure for the 'hood. And the letter Z at
      the end of Jesus' name was added to give a portrait of a Jesus that could
      sympathize and connect with a people that were downtrodden and
      broken. The letter Z is consistent with Hip Hop's vernacular to change
      words and phrases to fit the context and annunciate words for a Hip
      Hop community. The Z also represented a Jesus which was not only
      "above" in theological discussions, but also "below" in reachable form.

The Z gives new dimensions to the portrait of Christ and validates the struggles, life, narrative, and spirituality for many Hip Hoppers. Hodge, The Soul Of Hip Hop: Rimbs Timbs & A Cultural Theology: chapter 6.

50   Tupac, "Po Nigga Blues," Loyal To The Game, 2004, Amaru Interscope Records.

51   Paulo Freire, Pedagogy of The Oppressed, trans. Myra Bergman Ramos (New York, NY: Continuum, 1970), 28.

52   It is interesting to note that within my interviews, a theme of liberation from traditional church arose from the interviewees. "To move away from," "get out from under, "and "move out" were all phrases from respondents, when asked "How has Tupac's music, poetry, and spirituality affected you theologically?" These phrases were part of a larger discussion on how contemporary religion had become corrupted and lost its "edge" in life. Whether or not race was a factor in this response was not analyzed. This would be something for further study, but there is a clear implication here that the interviewees felt they needed to move out from their current theological situation and that Tupac helped them to do just that.

53   Note the letter "S" has been dropped to demonstrate the contextualization of the Christ figure for the 'hood. And the letter Z at the end of Jesus' name was added to give a portrait of a Jesus that could sympathize and connect with a people that were downtrodden and broken. The letter Z is consistent with Hip Hop's vernacular to change words and phrases to fit the context and annunciate words for a Hip Hop community. The Z also represented a Jesus which was not only "above" in theological discussions, but also "below" in reachable form. The Z gives new dimensions to the portrait of Christ and validates the struggles, life, narrative, and spirituality for many Hip Hoppers (Hodge 2010b, Chapter 6).

54   Shaw and Van Engen also tell us that relationships are over communicating any "special" style message or sermon and the receptors—the people group—will typically always respond better to the Gospel when there is a strong relationship intact (2003, 121-122).

55   However this also requires us to be culturally and racially literate in order to breach the spiritual borders and into new "territories."

56   An interesting note here, Daniel Shaw and Charles Van Engen note that to communicate the Gospel message appropriately, one must foster the skill of appropriate communication to the receptors in their context (2003, 114-120). They also follow this with three modes of this communication as well: coupling—which involves connecting a new message with receptors preexisting assumptions, commonality—when message meanings are shared by both the author and the audience alike, and bridging—the authors, or communicators, responsibility to help de-code messages and meanings from the text and or message. Shaw and Van Engen use this in the context of biblical interpretation and communication, yet, the parallels with Hip Hop and Gospel messages also applies (2003, 117-119). Wilbert Shenk asserts that, "...in order to do its work properly, missiology must keep four aspects continually in view: the normative, the historical, the present, and the future" (Shenk 1993, 18). Hence, with this in perspective, the present and the future should be focused—at least in part—to and with Hip Hop and being aware of how one communicates the Gospel is fundamental too. Further, Hip Hop, in its contextual form, embraces John Driver's Messianic Evangelization in which the forming of disciples of Jesus is fundamental(Driver 1993, 199). This was a critical finding in my work when I performed interviews on those between the ages of 13-19 who considered themselves to be "Hip Hoppers." They realized a need for a connection with Jesus and cared less about knowing the "rules" and dogma but more about an actual relationship with Christ.

57   In Knut Alfsvåg's work, the continued debate of the "postmodern" continues. Within those debates the issue of sin and morality typicall surfaces and sin is often defined as a relative and culturally defined term. This has impact on how we in our churches define this word and what it means to actually "sin"(2011).

Works Cited

Alfsvåg, Knut
  2011   "Postmodern Epistemology and the Mission of the Church." *Mission Studies: Journal of the International Association for Mission Studies* no. 28 (1):54-70.

Asante, Molefi K.
  2008   *It's bigger than hip-hop : the rise of the post-hip-hop generation.* New York, NY: St. Martin's Press.

Beaudoin, Tom
  1998   *Virtual Faith: The Irreverent Spiritual Quest of Generation X.* San Francisco, CA: Jossey Bass.

Bell, Daniel
  1973   *The coming of post-industrial society; a venture in social forecasting.* New York: Basic Books.

Bennett, Lerone
  1993   *The Shaping of Black America.* New York NY: Penguin Books.

Bosch, David J.
  1995   *Believing In The Future: Toward a Missiology of Western Culture.* Edited by H. Wayne Pipkin Alan Neely, Wilbert Shenk, *Christian Mission and Modern Culture.* Harrisburg, PA: Trinity Press International.
  1991   *Transforming mission : paradigm shifts in theology of mission, American Society of Missiology series.* Maryknoll, N.Y.: Orbis Books.

Boyd, Todd
  1997   *Am I Black Enough For You? Popular Culture from the 'Hood and Beyond.* Bloomington & Indianapolis: Indiana University Press.
  2002   *The H.N.I.C.: The Death of Civil Rights and the Reign of Hip Hop.* New York: New York University Press.

Chang, Jeff
  2005   *Can't Stop Won't Stop: A History of the Hip Hop Generation.* New York: St. Martin's Press.

Cone, James H.
  1997a   *Black Theology and Black Power.* 5th ed. Maryknoll NY: Orbis Books.
  1997b   *God of the Oppressed.* Maryknoll NY: Orbis Books.

Cox, Harvey
  1965   *The Secular City: A Celebration of its Liberties and an Invitation to its Discipline.* New York: The Macmillan Company.
  1984   *Religion In The Secular City: Toward A Postmodern Theology.* New York: Simon & Schuster Inc.

Cupitt, Don
  1998   "Post-Christianity." In *Religion, Modernity, and Postmodernity,* edited by Paul Heelas, 218-232. Oxford, UK; Malden, MA: Blackwell.

Dean, Kenda Creasy
  2010   *Almost Christian : what the faith of our teenagers is telling the American church.* New York: Oxford University Press.

Driver, John
  1993   "Messianic Evangelization." In *The Transfiguration of Mission: Biblical Theological & Historical Foundations,* edited by Wilbert R. Shenk, 199-219. Scottdale, PA; Waterloo, Ontario: Herald Press.

Dyson, Michael Eric
  1996   *Between God and Gangsta Rap : Bearing Witness to Black Culture.* New York: Oxford University Press.
  2001   *Holler if you Hear Me: Searching for Tupac Shakur.* New York: Basic Civitas.

George, Nelson
  1992   *Buppies, B-boys, Baps & Bohos : notes on post-soul Black culture.* 1st ed. New York: Harper Collins Publishers.
  1998   *Hip hop America.* New York: Viking.

2004 *Post-soul nation : the explosive, contradictory, triumphant, and tragic 1980s as experienced by African Americans (previously known as Blacks and before that Negroes)*. New York, NY: Viking.

Greenway, Roger S., and Timothy M. Monsma
2000 *Cities: Missions' New Frontier*. 2nd ed. Grand Rapids, MI: Baker Books.

Habermas, Jürgen
1988 *Nachmetaphysics Denken*. Frankfurt, Suhrkamp: Philosophische Aufsatze.

Hall, Douglas John
1997 *The End of Christendom and The Future of Christianty*. Eugene, OR: Wipf and Stock Publishers.

Hammer, M.C.
1990 Pray. In *Please Hammer, Don't Hurt 'Em*. Los Angeles, CA: Capitol Records.

Hodge, Daniel White
2009 *Heaven Has A Ghetto: The Missiological Gospel & Theology of Tupac Amaru Shakur*. Saarbrucken, Germany: VDM Verlag Dr. Muller Academic.
2010a "Christ Appropriating The Culture of Hip Hop: The Soul of Hip Hop Pt 2." *Fuller Youth Institute* no. 6 (7).
2010b *The Soul Of Hip Hop: Rimbs Timbs & A Cultural Theology*. Downers Grove, Ill.: Inner Varsity Press.
2013a "Baptized in Dirty Water: A De-Ontological Treatment of Hip Hop's Religious Discourse in Tupac's 'Black Jesuz.'" In *See You at the Crossroads: Hip Hop Scholarship at the Intersections Dialectical Harmony, Ethics, Aesthetics, and Panoply of Voices*, edited by Brad J. Porfilio, Debangshu Roychoudhury and Lauren M. Gardner. A.W., The Netherlands Sense Publishers.
2013b *The Hostile Gospel: Hip Hop's Totemic Post Soul Theology*. Edited by Warren Goldstein, Center for Critical Research on Religion and Harvard University. Boston, MA: Brill Academic.
2013c "No Church in the Wild: Hip Hop Theology & Mission." *Missiology: An International Review* no. XL:4 (4):1-13.

Kendall, John
1975   "A Ghetto is Slow to Die." *Los Angeles Times*, 1975.

Kitwana, Bakari
2003   *The Hip Hop Generation: Young Blacks and the Crisis in African-American Culture*. New York Basic Civitas.
2005   *Why White Kids Love Hip-Hop : Wankstas, Wiggers, Wannabes, and the New Reality of Race in America*. New York: Basic Civitas Books.

Kosmin, Barry A, and Ariela Keysar
2009   American Religious Identification Survey. In *ARIS*. Hartford, CT: Trinity College.

Lincoln, Eric C., and Lawrence H. Mamiya
1990   *The Black Church in the African American Experience*. Durham & London: Duke University Press.

Logo, Luis, Alan Cooperman, Cary Funk, Gregory A Smith, Erin O'Connell, and Sandra Stencel
2012   "Nones" on the Rise: One-in-Five Adults Have No Religious Affiliation. Washington, D.C.: Pew Research Center's Forum on Religion & Public Life.

Mel, Melle
1980   The Message. In *The Sugar Hill Records Story: Disc 2*, edited by Melle Mel Grandmaster Flash, & The Furious Five. Los Angeles, CA: Rhino Records.

Moss, Otis
2007   "Real Big: The Hip Hop Pastor as Postmodern Prophet." In *The Gospel Remix: Reaching The Hip Hop Generation*, edited by Ralph Watkins, 110-138. Valley Forge, Pa.: Judson Press.

Murray, Charles
1984   *Losing Ground: American Social Policy, 1950-1980*. New York, NY: Basic Books.

Neal, Mark Anthony
2002   *Soul Babies : Black Popular Culture and the Post-Soul Aesthetic*. New York: Routledge.

Nelson, Angela S.
    1991   "Theology in the Hip-Hop of Public Enemy and Kool
            Moe Dee." In *The Emergency of Black and the Emergence
            of Rap*, edited by Jon Michael Spencer, 51-59. Durham,
            NC: Duke University Press.

One, KRS
    2003   *Ruminations*. New York: Welcome Rain Publishers.

Palen, J. John
    1981   *The urban world*. 2d ed. New York: McGraw-Hill.

Paris, Peter J.
    1985   *The Social Teaching of the Black Churches*. Philadelphia,
            PA: Fortress Press.

Peralta, Stacy
    2008   Crips and Bloods: Made In America. USA: Verso
            Entertainment.

Pinn, Anthony
    2002   *The Black Church in the Post-Civil Rights Era*. Maryknoll,
            NY: Orbis Books.
    1995   *Why Lord? Suffering and Evil in Black Theology* New
            York: Continuum.

Quinn, Eithne
    2005   *Nuthin' but a "G" thang : The Culture and Commerce
            of Gangsta rap, Popular cultures, everyday lives;*. New
            York: Columbia University Press.

Rah, Soong-Chan
    2009   *The next evangelicalism : releasing the church from
            Western cultural captivity*. Downers Grove, Ill.: IVP
            Books.

Reed, Teresa L.
    2003   *The Holy Profane: Religion in Black Popular Music*.
            Lexington, KY: The University Press of Kentucky.

Rose, Tricia
    1994   *Black Noise: Rap Music and Black Culture in Contemporary America.* Middletown CT.: Wesleyan University Press.

Run-D.M.C.
    1984   Hard Times. In *Run-D.M.C.*, edited by J.Ward, Larry Smith, William Waring and Darryl DMC Mcdaniels. New York, NY: Arista, Profile.

Ruskin, Matt
    2009   The Hip Hop Project. USA: Pressure Point Films; Image Entertainment; One Village Entertainment.

Shakur, Tupac
    1993   Keep Ya Head Up. In *Strictly 4 My N.I.G.G.A.Z.*: Interscope Records.

Shaw, Daniel R, and Charles E Van Engen
    2003   *Communicating God's Word in a Complex World: God's Truth or Hocus Pocus.* Lanham, MD: Rowan & Littlefield Publishers Inc.

Shenk, Wilbert R.
    1993   "The Relevance of a Messianic Missiology for Mission Today." In *The Transfiguration of Mission: Biblical Theological & Historical Foundations*, edited by Wilbert R. Shenk, 17-36. Scottdale, PA; Waterloo, Ontario: Herald Press.
    1999   *Changing Frontiers of Mission.* Maryknoll, NY: Orbis Books.
    2001   *Write The Vision: The Church Renewed, Christian Mission and Modern Culture.* Eugene, OR: Wipf and Stock Publishers.

Sides, Josh
    2003   *L.A. City Limits: African American Los Angeles from the Great Depression to the Present.* Berkeley and Los Angeles, CA: University of California Press.

Smith, Efrem, and Phil Jackson
2005   *The Hip Hop Church: Connecting with The Movment Shaping our Culture.* Downers Grove, Ill.: IVP.

Soja, Edward W.
2000   *Postmetropolis : critical studies of cities and regions.* New York, NY: Blackwell.

Spencer, Jon Michael
1990   *Protest and Praise: Sacred Music of Black Religion.* Minneapolis, MN: Fortress Press.

Taylor, Paul C.
2007   "Post-Black, Old Black." *African American Review* no. 41 (4):625-640.

Touraine, Alain
1977   *The Self-Production of Society.* Chicago, Il: University of Chicago Press.

Utley, Ebony A.
2012   *Rap and Religion: Understanding the Gangsta's God.* Santa Barbara, CA: Praeger.

Watkins, Ralph Basui
2011   *Hip-Hop Redemption: Finding God in the Rhythm and the Rhyme, Engaging Culture.* Grand Rapids, MI: Baker Academic.

West, Cornel
1993   *Prophetic Thought in Postmodern Times: Beyond Eurocentrism and Multiculturalism.* Vol. 1`. Monroe ME: Common Courage Press.

Wiese, Andrew
2004   *Places of Their Own: African American Suburbanization in the Twentieth Century, Historical Studies of Urban America.* Chicago, Ill: University of Chicago.

Zanfagna, Christina
 2006 "Under the Blasphemous W(RAP): Locating the "Spirit" in Hip-Hop." *Pacific Review of Ethnomusicology* no. 12:1-12.

APM

Closing Plenary Address

Cultivating Scholar-Activism in Missiological Eduation

AL TIZON

DOI: 10.7252/Paper.000019

About the Author:
Al serves in a unique joint appoint as Associate Professor of Holistic Ministry at Palmer Theological Seminary of Eastern University, and as co-President elect of Evangelicals for Social Action, both located in King of Prussia, PA. He received his Ph.D. in missiology from the Graduate Theological Union, Berkeley, CA. Al and his family engaged in community development work, ministry to street children, and church leadership development among the poor in his native Philippines for almost ten years as missionaries with Action International Ministries. An ordained minister of the Evangelical Covenant Church, Al served several churches in both the Philippines and the United States as associate and interim pastor for seven years and as lead pastor for five.

Introduction

"The Challenge of the Social in Missiological Education"—if I've understood this year's theme correctly, then I have a potentially helpful story to tell. It's a story that illustrates the way in which social engagement has been incorporated into a seminary's approach to theological education.

More specifically, it's the story of how Palmer (formerly Eastern Baptist) Theological Seminary of Eastern University near Philadelphia has envisioned, designed and implemented a program that reflects an equal commitment to both scholarship/teaching and social engagement/mission.

This program was and is patterned after the seminary's most celebrated professors, Dr. Ronald J. Sider, who has championed holistic mission and gospel-informed, progressive politics for over four decades, pricking and developing the social conscience of the church, particularly in North America, and doing his part in restoring compassion and justice on the global evangelical missionary agenda; this, while preparing seminarians for greater and more effective ministry as a faculty member of Palmer Seminary.

Inspired by the fruit of Sider's scholarship and activism, the seminary began to ask itself in so many words the following question: How can we cultivate scholar-activism in our approach to theological education?

The first part of this paper describes the way in which Palmer has answered that question through the creation of the Sider Center for Ministry and Public Policy and the implementation of the Sider Scholarship Program, in which select seminarians give ten hours a week to engage in work that is related to the Sider Center in exchange for a 50% discount on tuition. The vision and structure of the Sider Center and the implementation of the Sider scholarship program constitute the first part of this paper.

The second part describes how the seminary saw the need to create a special faculty position in order for this scholar-activist oriented program to work. It needed to find a faculty person who was willing to forge the integration of teaching, researching and writing, as well as directing the on-the-ground, holistic ministry efforts of the Sider Center. The position was called the joint appointment, and eventually the seminary found a guinea pig to fill it. Since that guinea pig was me, it seems fitting to be somewhat autobiographical in this section, reflecting upon how the position has worked out these last several years as Palmer Seminary's first official joint appointment.

And lastly, the paper concludes with the newest component of the Sider Center's desire to cultivate scholar-activism—namely, an experiment in an intentional Christian community of students to live out and model the very life that Christian scholar-activism envisions for all, a just and peaceful community enjoying the fruit of life together under the reign of God in Jesus Christ.

The Sider Center: Institutionally Grounding Scholar-Activism

The Sider Center was established in 2005,[1] not only to honor Ron Sider, but to make the organization he founded—Evangelicals for Social Action—an official part of the seminary. Before that, ESA was its own 501c3, its lone institutional connection being that it rented Palmer's basement. The establishment of the center institutionally grounded a basic commitment of Sider and ESA for the last 40 years, namely, scholar-activism.

Scholar-activism can be defined as an approach to theological education that is in the service of practical, grassroots ministry. As such, this approach necessitates remaining directly involved with pastors, missionaries, community organizers, evangelists, lobbyists, and so on; for in this sort of education, the scholarly research, writing and teaching are primarily for their benefit. Another word that describes this kind of theological education is "orthopraxy"—the pursuit of right doing—which I personally like (and still use) but has unfortunately waned in its use as the language of liberation theology in general has waned.

No theological institution would overtly glory in education that is not orthopraxiological, i.e., that is not concerned about the real world. *I'm* not aware of any school that would bear the motto, "We exist strictly for the ivory tower" or "If you're tired of the real, we're the school for you" or some such thing. However, in a culture that thinks dichotomously about theory and practice, theological institutions tend, when they err, to err on the side of theory at the expense of practice. Whether practice is done and done well may or may not be included in the criteria of success for theological education. The establishment of the Sider Center was Palmer Seminary's attempt to cultivate theological education that is in the service of right action in the world.

Furthermore, scholar-activism necessitates popularization; for the picture of effective activism is not simply a seminary graduate who is ready to change the world; it also includes the mobilization of the laity, the grassroots, all God's people, and indeed, all people. Popularized scholarship is education for "ordinary people," for grassroots mobilization. It is education for transformation on the personal, congregational and social levels, and it is key to understanding the vision of scholar-activism.

Kristyn Komarnicki, editor of ESA's *Prism* magazine explains that, "the art of popularizing—distilling complex issues such as global poverty or the social cost of pornography into clear and persuasive stories that the average person can absorb and ultimately act upon—is essential not only to building an informed citizenry but also to transforming individual hearts and minds for Christ."[2] Adding a sense of responsibility to this, Sider argues for popularized scholarship by saying,

> Evangelicalism, especially with its strong anti-intellectual strain, has often . . . been badly served by popularizers and activists with simplistic ideas and superficial solutions. [This will not] change unless more people with good scholarly training become effective popularizers and successful activists.[3]

This is in fact how Sider describes himself. "During my career," he writes, "I have tried to combine the roles of scholar, popularizer and activist."[4] The center at Palmer Seminary, named after scholar-activist-popularizer Ron Sider, seeks to cultivate the same in the lives of seminarians directly, but ultimately for the church and general populace in the service of the gospel.

The Sider Scholars

As a center of a seminary, the Sider Center's direct beneficiaries are its students, especially those who apply for and are awarded the Sider scholarship.[5] Precisely to cultivate scholar-activism, the seminary career of Sider scholars includes social engagement with Sider Center related activities. As Palmer's website describes it, "These scholars will gain valuable experience in research, writing and networking in holistic ministry and/or public policy, as well as a greater understanding of how to merge scholarship with popular writing and organizing for social action."[6]

As stated earlier, Sider scholars give 10 hours a week toward the work of the center in exchange for a 50% discount on tuition. But beyond a mere business transaction, Sider scholars work into their seminary experience an opportunity to be involved in activities, which have included doing research for a book, writing a popular piece for the center's blog or magazine, engaging in rallies against gun violence, helping to organize workshops and conferences, helping a church develop its missional outreach, and so on—this, while fully immersed in classes, working toward the completion of their degrees along with the rest of the student body.

I have managed the Sider scholars under my charge as one of the Sider Center faculty members (more on this shortly) in a particular way; I divide each of their 10 hours in half—five hours toward the efficient operation of the center's holistic ministry efforts, and five hours assigned to one of the center's holistic ministry partners. At different points, Sider scholars under my supervision have served as 5-hours-a-week interns in ministries that include Heeding God's Call, an interfaith organization addressing Philadelphia's gun violence problem; Epiphany House, a ministry of care and adoption services for children with special needs; the ministerium of a nearby first-ring suburb working on ecumenical efforts for community transformation; INFEMIT, an international network of theologians working on issues of holistic mission and contextualization; and Healing Communities, a ministry to prisoners and their families. It may be too early to do this, but in time a study needs to be conducted of how the Sider scholarship has impacted the lives of Sider Center alums.

My preliminary hypothesis for such a study would be that theological education, which involves hands-on activist work alongside a commitment to scholarly growth, will result in graduates who are better equipped to make the transition from seminary to ministry, and thus make a real difference in their communities and beyond for the sake of the gospel.

Gospel for Non-Seminarians

Beyond training seminarians to be world-changers via a commitment to scholar-activism, however, the Sider Center is also committed to educating the populace, or at least non-seminarians, in and through popularized writing and speaking. Books such as Sider's celebrated *Rich Christians in an Age of Hunger, Living Like Jesus* and *Completely Pro-Life*, attest to the center's commitment to providing prophetic, solidly-biblical and well-researched material for seminarians and non-seminarians alike. Resources for churches in holistic ministry and specific social issues are also in production. Moreover, the center has taken advantage of social media and has established its interactive presence in the culture of the Internet. Sider and the other faculty members of the center also maintain a steady speaking schedule in local churches, mission agencies, colleges, universities and seminaries throughout the country and world.

Perhaps the center's best example of popularization is the center's award-winning *Prism* magazine, which features human interest stories and articles that inspire action, undergirded by critical thinking and solid research. *Prism* attests to the Sider Center's desire to popularize "America's alternative evangelical voice," *Prism*'s tagline for many years. *Prism* has fearlessly tackled "hot potato" issues, such as nuclear disarmament, abortion, pornography, racism, gun violence, and environmental abuse to name a few. And despite its small circulation, it has had a remarkable impact. For example, Congesswoman Carolyn Maloney from New York had a life-size poster made of the first page of an article on prostitution from the September/October 2007 issue and had it displayed while Congress deliberated on the Trafficking Victims Protection Act. Through this particular issue of *Prism*, Sider Center/ESA did its part to help pass the Act, which, among other things, has enhanced federal efforts to crack down on prostitution and human trafficking that are happening on America's home front.

The Joint Appointment: Personal Reflections

The Sider scholarship and the popularizing of the gospel attest to the vision and implementation of the Sider Center's commitment to scholar-activism. But in order for the center's ideals to work, a specific kind of faculty had to be recruited; the seminary had to find "Ron Sider types," who were willing to forge an integration of scholarship, activism and popularization. Architects of the position called it boringly "the joint appointment," which indicated the split of duties between teaching, directing a program of the Sider Center, and writing.[7] I was the center's first joint appointment, which in my case combined teaching missional church and holistic ministry and directing the Sider Center's church holistic ministry initiatives. Then three years later, the seminary recruited a second joint appointment, Dr. Paul Alexander, to teach ethics and public policy and to direct the center's public policy initiatives.

A glowing, bright, yellow advertisement appeared in the March/April 2005 issue of *Prism* magazine. Its header read, "Job Opening for Scholar Activist," and the description read as follows:

> Eastern Seminary [the name change hadn't happened yet] and ESA [the Sider Center was not quite established yet] announce a joint position for a tenure-track faculty person who would teach half-time . . . and serve half-time working with Ron Sider . . . and directing ESA's [holistic ministry] program, [which] offers tools, coaching, and programs to local churches seeking to combine evangelism and social ministry.[8]

The requirements of the position included, ". . . passion for holistic ministry; desire to combine academic activities (teaching, research and writing) with activist and popularizing work mobilizing the church for holistic ministry and the society toward justice."[9] I quote this job announcement almost in its entirety because it best describes the nature and intent of the joint appointment—namely, for a faculty person to practically work out scholar-activism in theological education.

The question for the seminary at that point was, "Is this something that only Ron Sider can do because of who he is, or is it replicable with the right person? From a personal standpoint, I certainly didn't know the answer to that at first. But I did write in part in my application, "To teach theology and holistic ministry at Eastern alongside directing holistic ministry is what makes this position unique and personally appealing to me."

And at the seven-year mark of working out the position, I can say that my forecast of the fit between me and the joint appointment has proven true. It has been personally life-giving to occupy a position that has provided the professional space to grow as a scholar, teacher, writer, director and activist.

Beyond a sense of personal fulfillment, however, I would also advocate for scholar/activist-type positions of this sort in all seminaries, though to be a scholar-activist-popularizer is certainly not the call of every faculty member. As Sider has qualified, "I do not mean for a moment to urge most scholars to abandon a life of extended, focused scholarly research in their specific area of expertise. What I have tried is not for everyone."[10] And yet, I'm convinced that scholar-activism should be developed in every institution of higher theological learning in and through those who feel called to this integration.

Based upon my own experience as Palmer's first joint appointment, as well as my own developing thinking about mission and theology, I would like to offer albeit briefly the following reasons why I feel scholar-activism is crucial for theological education in the 21st century.

First, it reinforces the missiological maxim that mission is the mother of theology.[11] When students are missiologically engaged, they have something to theologize about! In other words, the content with which they are interacting comes from both texts and context, from both research and ministry experience. As Gustavo Gutierrez asserted, "Theology is reflection, a critical attitude. Theology follows; it is the second step. . . . Theology does not produce pastoral activity; rather it reflects upon it."[12] Scholar-activism reinforces this notion, that theological education is a response to mission; or if we wish, theological education is ultimately missiological education.

Second, related to the first, scholar-activism invigorates theology. Theology devoid of social engagement/mission ultimately loses its way. It fosters a dry intellectualism that risks becoming uncompelling for students, and worse, irrelevant for both church and society. Today more than ever, students of all disciplines—of which theology is no exception—go to school, yes, to gain new knowledge, which is measured by their report cards, but more importantly to become competent, which is measured by effective and sustained ministry in their neighborhoods and beyond. Scholar-activism puts equal weight on both theological knowledge and competence in ministries of evangelism, compassion, justice and reconciliation.

Third, the world becomes the classroom. For example, I teach a course called, "Current Issues in Urban Mission," which has thus far been the most conducive course to work out scholar-activism. True to its title, the course grapples with issues that are relevant to doing mission in the urban context; but the grappling has not been limited to classroom discussions, as more than half of the sessions are on-location at ministry sites in urban contexts. The classroom is not just a room number on a door, but it is Inter-Varsity Christian Fellowship at Temple University and Urban Promise in Camden, and the Mayor's Office of Faith-Based Initiatives in Philadelphia, and so on. This course is but an example of what I strive to implement—scholar-activism—in all of my courses in one degree or another.

And fourth, scholar-activism deepens the student-teacher relationship in that it involves both thinking and doing together, as opposed to just thinking together. If Yoda's mentoring of Luke Skywalker has any merit at all, then let us remember that the environment, in which the raw Jedi knight learned to use the Force, was a swamp, not a sterile classroom. The result of the training was not just Luke finding himself; it was also a bond that formed between him and his teacher. The value of relational-based ministry has always been important, but I believe ministry grounded in relationship in these postmodern times, where a leader's authority can no longer be assumed, is of paramount importance. And scholar-activism creates situations where the student-teacher relationship can flourish.

Praxis House: Toward a Community of Scholar-Activists

To have spoken of deep relationships segues nicely to the conclusion of this presentation, as I briefly describe the newest piece to the puzzle of Sider Center's quest to grow in scholar-activism—namely, a foray into intentional Christian community.

Even though it is in its embryonic stage, the effort has a tentative name: the Praxis House. "Praxis," which conveys a process of "reflection and action upon the world in order to transform it,"[13] embodies the scholar-activism that the center seeks to cultivate in the lives of students (primarily but not exclusively Sider scholars) by virtue of living together.

Living in community—talking and listening to each other, eating together, studying together, and working together while living under the same roof—can facilitate deeper discipleship; not in an idyllic, problem-free way, as Bonhoeffer reminded us, but as iron sharpens iron.[14] Models of community abound from classic monastic orders such as the Benedictines to new monastic orders among evangelicals such as the Simple Way in Philadelphia and the Rutba House in Durham, North Carolina. Other notable communities that have stood the test of time include the missional community of Jesus People USA in Chicago and the learning community of L'Abri in Switzerland.

Inspired by such models and in light of the ideals of the Sider Center, we asked ourselves, what if we offered a chance for a number of interested and qualified students to live together under the same roof? Having lived in various forms of intentional Christian community through the years, my wife and I decided to make our home the laboratory for this experiment. At the two year mark, there are four students, two who are married with their toddler son, who occupy the house with me, my wife and our high school senior daughter—so eight people in all. Word has gotten out in the Palmer/Eastern University community that such a place exists, and as a result, we receive regular inquiries and requests from students to join us. Clearly, the Praxis House can grow, but because of the size of our house, we cannot take in anymore students. So we are on the market now for a bigger house to accommodate the community of students outgrowing the present house.

I asked David Fuller, a Sider scholar who lives in the Praxis House, to share briefly what his experience has been like. This is in part, what he wrote in response:

> When Al and his wife, Janice, approached my wife and I a year and a half ago about the idea of living in the same house, my ears pricked up immediately. But the reason had nothing to do with cultivating scholar-activism—I just wanted cheap rent. I never once thought about how committing to life-together with other Christians could so profoundly impact my seminary education. Living in a diverse house— in terms of gender, ethnicity and stage-of-life—has proven to be almost like a seminary lab course.
>
> As many of you know, seminary is a profound phase of life. New ideas are being incessantly bounced around and old ideas are continually questioned. It is an exciting and stimulating environment to be immersed in. I would not change it for the world. But I've found that in seminary it is easy to lift theologizing out of a concrete context and become lost in a world of abstract ideas and thesis statements that you yourself can form any way you want to. It becomes a place where as long as you can describe an idea in semi-comprehensible English words, it has seemingly unquestioned merit.
>
> My experience in Praxis House has been to ground my theological exploration. Two theologian-types in one house can get carried away, but the beautiful thing about Praxis House is that we have "regular folk," who are really theologians in their own right (they don't hide behind the fancy language of the academy or the thin veil of "proper theological method"). These "theologians" keep us grounded in the reality of changing diapers, walking the dog, doing the dishes, singing, praying, watching TV, and just celebrating the constantly changing phases of life.
>
> For example, I can talk in the classroom about biblical and theological support (or not) for nonviolent direct action, and then go home to interact with a seasoned

gun law activist and gun shop protestor. I can debate the question of original sin and the age of accountability with my unmarried, childless seminary professor, and then go home to discuss the idea with a middle-aged mother of four as she cooks supper for me...and my two-year-old. The ethical issues surrounding sex, contraception, sexually transmitted infections take on a whole new level of urgency and pragmatism in a house with a nurse practitioner working in clinic in one of Philly's most troubled neighborhoods and a high school senior at one of Pennsylvania's largest high schools.

Something I appreciate about Praxis House is that all of these interactions occur organically. We don't hold special theological discussion times or let's-see-if-the-seminarian-can-apply-the-mystery-of-the-Trinity-to-this-real-life-situation quizzes. It is simply the result of doing life-together.

The most profound effect Praxis House has had on my seminary education has been the chance to live with one of my professors. A single course provides very little opportunity to really get to know your professors. But messy-haired, pre-coffee (think drunken stupor) encounters immediately peel away false pretense or rigid formality. Such a close relationship allows deep theological conversation to take place without the need to use all the right language or all the right "paradigmatic lenses." Living with Al gives me the chance to go deeper into subjects that were only briefly touched upon in class. Whenever I feel confused or am unsure how to reconcile idea A with idea B, Al becomes a wise sounding board; not to tell me what to think or to prove to me his opinion is the best, but to responsibly navigate the complexities of these issues.

I had no idea what I was getting myself into when I moved my family into the Praxis House a little over a year ago. There is no denying that it has difficulties; community never claims to be anything but. More than once I've daydreamed about what it would be like to have my own apartment with just my own family. But it never seems to last long, as I remind myself of why I love the Praxis House and the value it brings to my life and my education.

I consider it a great privilege to be a part of this small experiment and hope that what we have attempted to pioneer at Palmer will be able to be tried, and improved upon in other places across the globe.

Experiences like David Fuller's attest to the fruit of scholar-activism being cultivated in the rich soil of Christian community. Earlier I stated that although I would advocate for scholar-activism to be a part of all institutions of higher theological learning, it is not the calling of all theological educators. But it certainly is for some. Something similar should be said about living in intentional Christian community: it is not for everyone, but it certainly is for some.

This intent of this paper/presentation was simply to affirm the scholar-activist approach to theological education by sharing how it has, and is being, worked out in the Sider Center for Ministry and Public Policy at Palmer Theological Seminary. If it generates any thinking among us around possibilities of cultivating such an approach in other institutions, then to have told this story will have been worth it.

<u>Notes</u>

1   2005 was the year that it was officially and legally established, as ESA merged with Palmer Seminary of Eastern University. But it was already functioning several years before.

2   Kristyn Komarnicki, "Popularizing a Call to Sexual Justice," in Following Jesus: Journeys in Radical Discipleship (Oxford et al.: Regnum, 2013), 111.

3   Ronald J. Sider, "Needed: A Few More Scholars/Popularizers/Activists: Personal Reflections on my Journey," Christian Scholar's Review XXXVI (2): 159.

4   Ibid., 161.

5   The Sider Center also oversees other scholarships such as the scholarship, named after another scholar-activist and friend of Sider, Jim Wallis. The Wallis scholarship functions in the exact same way as the Sider scholarship.

6   "Sider Scholarship," Evangelicals for Social Action http://www.evangelicalsforsocialaction.org/about/who-we-are/sider-center/ (accessed 10 June 2013).

7   The joint appointment also indicated shared responsibility of financing the position—60% funded by the seminary and 40% by the Sider Center.

8   "Job Opening for Scholar Activist," Prism March/April 2005, 12(3), 39.

9   Ibid., 39.

10   Sider, "Needed: A Few More Scholars/Popularizers/Activists," 166.

11   David Bosch credits theologian Martin Kahler for this in Transforming Mission, 20th Anniversary Edition (Maryknoll, NY: Orbis, 2011), 15-16.

12   Gustavo Gutierrez, A Theology of Liberation, 15th Anniversary Edition (Maryknoll, NY: Orbis, 2007), 9.

13   Paulo Friere, Pedagogy of the Oppressed (New York, NY: Continuum, 1970), 36.

14   Dietrich Bonhoeffer, Life Together (New York et al.: Harper & Row, 1954), 26-30.

APM

Conference Proceedings

Conference Program

Social Engagement: The Challenge of the Social in Missiological Education

Registration in hallway of Science Building
Meets in Buyse Lecture Hall in Science Building

Thursday, June 20

4:00 – 6:00pm Registration
5:00 – 6:00   Dinner

7:00   Welcome and Introduction to the Conference
7:15   Worship – Sean Gladding
7:45 – 9:00   David Fenrick, Northwestern College Missional
                    Experiential Education for Social Action

                    Kendi Howells Douglas, Great Lakes Christian College
                    Undergraduate Service Learning: Urban
                    Mission Minor Program

9:00   Evening Reception

Friday, June 21

7:30 – 8:20am Breakfast

8:30   *Worship – Sean Gladding*

9:00 – 10:30 Working Sessios

Group A: SB 129 Participatory Learning	Group B: SB 131 Curriculum Models for Mission Education	Group C: SB 143 Missiology in the Social-Cultural Context	Group D: SB Buyse Hall Issues in Social Engagement
Karen Parchman Duane Brown Travis Myers	Kathryn Mowry Christopher James Dwight Baker	Larry Caldwell Benjamin Beckner Thias Kgatla	Daniel Scott Daniel White Hodge Sheryl Ryan

10:30   *Break*

11:00   *Gary Simpson, Luther Theological Seminary*
                 Missional Congregations, Civil Society and
                 Social Theory: How a Turn to the Social Helps
                 Widen Our Vision for Research, Teaching and
                 Guidance for Mission

12:00 – 1:00   *Lunch ("Orientation Lunch" for first-timers)*

1:15   *Al Tizon, Palmer Theological Seminary/Evangelicals*
                 for Social Action
                 Cultivating Scholar-Activism in Missiological
                 Education

2:15 – 3:00   *Business Meeting and Conclusion*

Business Meeting Agenda

1. Call to Order – Greg Leffel, President

2. Noting of the 2012 Minutes – David Fenrick, Secretary-Treasurer

3. Secretary-Treasurer's Report – David Fenrick

4. Venue for Future Annual Meetings (with ASM) – David Fenrick

   2014 – Northwestern College, Minneapolis MN

   2015 – To be arranged (Wheaton or Northwestern)

5. Executive Committee's Report –Greg Leffel and Madge Karecki, 1st Vice President

6. New Business and Announcements – Greg Leffel, Robert Danielson

7. Election of Officers – Madge Karecki

8. Recognition of New President – Greg Leffel

9. Adjournment – Madge Karecki

Secretary-Treasuer's Report

	Credit	Debit	Balance
Opening Balance: June 14, 2012			2760.59
Receipts			
Membership Dues Received	390.00		
Transfer from ASM (Less Conference Expenses)	1215.70		
Gift from InterVarsity/Urbana	750.00		
Grant from APM Executive Meeting	1289.37		

	Credit	Debit	Balance
Expenses			
APM 2012 Meeting Honorarium		150.00	
APM 2012 Reception		71.20	
Mission Studies Renewal		197.00	
Gift to IAMS		300.00	
Total	3645.07	718.20	

Balance at Wells Fargo Bank, Minneapolis, MN,
as of June 19, 2013:   **$5687.46**

Respectfully Submitted,

David E. Fenrick, Secretary-Treasurer

Executive Committee Report

June 21, 2013

The Executive Committee met three times in 2012 – 2013 (in June 2012 at Techny Towers; January 2013 at Perkins Theological Seminary; June 2013 at Wheaton College) to implement recommendations presented at the 2012 Business Meeting and to consider additional incremental improvements to APM's activities. The focus of our discussions was building capacity to strengthen the association's ability to sustain growth, maintain organizational health and develop a wider constituency.

I. The following actions were taken during 2012 – 2013:

Mid-Year Leadership Retreat:

The EC met together with the Advisory Committee for a day-long retreat at Perkins Theological Seminary/Southern Methodist University in Dallas. The meeting was hosted by APM past-president Dr. Robert Hunt and transportation and housing costs were generously funded by the Grimes Foundation with support from the Chicago Archdiocese and One Horizon Institute.

The retreat was followed by a public seminar hosted jointly by APM and Perkins for about 40 Dallas-area pastors, church leaders, mission committee members, and seminary students. The quite successful seminar raised awareness of the value of mission studies for local churches and created a stimulating interaction between missiologists and leaders of mission-sending churches.

The leadership retreat provided a much-needed venue for in-depth discussions of APM's organizational challenges and its future growth and development. Given the value of these discussions, we decided to continue them annually each January for the next three years. A new three-year grant from the Grimes Foundation was received to support them along with the public mission seminar.

Advisory Committee:

The six-member AC, proposed in 2012, provided valuable support to ASM as we experimented with it for the first time this year. Beyond providing a seasoned perspective and continuity from year-to-year, the committee also multiplies the ability of APM's leadership to implement new initiatives. We decided to continue the committee for three additional years and invite it to each EC meeting including the Mid-Year Leadership Retreat.

If, after a three-year cycle, the AC continues to show its value, the EC will recommend to the members that it be constituted as a formal board of directors for the association.

Administrative Organization:

As APM grows, adds more programs where needed, and as the annual APM/ASM meeting continues to become more complex to administer, it is necessary to diversify leadership responsibilities and in particular to take pressure off of the President. It is also important in a voluntary organization to create more opportunities for members to serve and to gain leadership experience. Several improvements were made to APM's administrative organization as follows:

The "Leadership Checklist": Based on the experience APM leadership over the last several years, a detailed list of duties for each member of the EC was drawn up to create a "job description" for each role. The duties were discussed and proportioned to ease the work load in each position. The Leadership Checklist will be revised from year-to-year to keep up with APM's development. It is available for members to review from the Secretary-Treasurer.

Program Committee: A panel of at least three, chaired by the Second Vice President will implement the President's vision for the Annual Meeting by taking responsibility for promoting the meeting, soliciting papers and panel presentations and organizing the program schedule and logistics.

Nominating, Leadership and Membership Committee: A panel of at least three, chaired by the First Vice President will be responsible for creating and maintaining a database of APM current and inactive members, create a plan for developing future leaders and for enhancing diversity among our members and leaders, create a plan for publicly promoting APM to recruit new members, and present a slate of officers for election at the Annual Meeting along with recommendations for new AC members. New member recruitment may be split off in the future as its own committee (but our discussion this year was inconclusive). A special emphasis for the next year will be outreach to Roman Catholic constituents.

"First Fruits" Open-Access Press:

For many of its early years APM self-published the papers presented in the Annual Meeting, often in mimeograph form. This year we renewed our tradition by making the breakout session papers available on-line prior to our Annual Meeting. This allows our members to review the papers and come to the sessions ready for discussion. We will also publish all of this year's presentations in a permanent on-line volume called The 2013 Proceedings of the Association of Professors of Mission. Our ability to do this is provided at no cost by "First Fruits," the on-line, open-access press facility of Asbury Theological Seminary. "First Fruits" provides APM with a stable and permanent URL to support its online publishing. Special thanks go to Dr. Robert Danielson at Asbury for initiating this service and organizing it for our use in the years to come.

II. The following recommendations were made by the EC for discussion by the members in 2013 (they will be presented as "new business" at the business meeting).

This year our EC/AC discussions about APM's unique mandate to advance missiological education brought to light a number of challenges our association faces to support our members and to respond to the opportunities presented by globalization and online education. These challenges include 1) the fact that a substantial minority (perhaps 40%?) of our members work alone in institutions without support from a missiological faculty; 2) that many of our former students now work around the world in a global missiological "diaspora," developing coursework or whole curricula, often working alone or in challenging circumstances; 3) colleagues around the world have approached APM members about how to facilitate collaboration; and 4) that it is desirable for APM to model best practices and remain ahead of the curve in non-geographical, online education services and the opportunities they present for supporting our members. In addressing at least some of these issues the EC/AC will pursue two recommendations in 2013 – 2014 in support of APM's educational mission and the interests of its members.

Member Services (Steering Committee):

Building on opportunities provided by Asbury's "First Fruits" program, Dr. Danielson presented to the EC/AC a proposal for an expanded suite of member services. Possible services could range from (very hypothetically) sharing syllabi (an existing APM tradition) and subject area bibliographies to online, publishing of open access books and papers, archiving, preserving historical publications, accreditation support, funding advice, course-sharing between institutions, member discussion groups, and global open-access course offerings. Such a wide-scope of services obviously is only conceptual at this point, but Dr. Danielson proposes that as services are added they can be organized around a online root structure hosted by "First Fruits" and titled (in concept) the "APM Handbook for Missiological Education." APM members will contribute materials for the handbook and can work in a "wiki-style" collaboration.

The "Handbook" proposal merits more thought and exploration. We propose creating a steering committee (inviting interested members) to examine the idea and recommend further steps toward implementing it. Dr. Danielson has agreed to chair it. We are also looking for grant funds to support an initial steering committee meeting later in 2013.

"Internationalizing" APM (Steering Committee):

Several members have pointed out that other groups or associations of mission scholars meet outside of North America and have expressed interest in mutually supportive contacts with APM. In addition we have received inquiries about how scholars from the global South may contact North American mission educators for collaboration and mutual support. All of this has raised the question of whether APM desires or is in a position to expand its vision to support missiological education outside of North America. Although APM traditionally has only served members from the United States and Canada, our constitution does not restrict us to work in any particular location. In light of the fact that most of our members work internationally or have substantial international working relationships, does it make sense for APM to look for global opportunities to support missiological education?

This question is open-ended at this point and requires more detailed discussion. We propose creating a steering committee to look into it and make recommendations at the 2014 business meeting.

The 2012 – 2013 Executive Committee

Greg Leffel, President

Madge Karecki, First Vice President

Ben Hartley, Second Vice President

David Fenrick, Secretary-Treasurer

2013 Business Meeting Minutes

1. The APM business meeting was held at Wheaton College, Wheaton, IL. The meeting was called to order and opened with prayer on Friday, June 21, 2013, 2:36 p.m. by Greg Leffel, President.

2. The minutes for the 2012 meeting were submitted by David Fenrick, Secretary-Treasurer, and approved.

3. The Secretary-Treasurer's financial report was submitted and approved.

4. David Fenrick announced the 2014 APM Annual Meeting location – University of Northwestern, St. Paul, MN. He also reviewed the process and decision regarding the future venue for annual APM (with ASM and AETE) meetings. He represented APM on the ASM committee that looked at potential sites. The ASM executive committee chose the following two sites for final consideration. Members will participate in the final selection by providing feedback on each site.

    • 2013 – Wheaton College, Wheaton, IL

    • 2014 – University of Northwestern, St. Paul, MN

    • 2015 – Either Wheaton or Northwestern

5. Greg Leffel, President, and Madge Karecki, First Vice President, presented the Executive Committee's Report, reflecting the mandate given by the APM membership at the 2012 Annual Meeting. (See 2013 Executive Committee Report)

a. The discussion from the APM 2012 meeting in regards to long-range strategic planning. The Executive and Advisory Committees held three meetings this past year. Of particular importance was the strategic vision and planning meeting at the Perkins School of Theology in Dallas, TX, January 22-23, 2013. Through Robert Hunt at the Perkins School of Theology, the Grimes Foundation has extended its grant to facilitate future meetings for the next three years. This allows the APM Executive and Advisory Committees to meet, as well as its members to provide education for pastors and lay-leaders in parallel seminars.

b. A plan was presented that seeks to further the organization by (1) providing a template to expand the capacity of APM in terms of participants, member support and services, resources, and collaboration, and (2) clarify the identity, vitality, growth, vision, and future of APM.

c. Executive Committee job descriptions, including specific roles, responsibilities and check-lists, were presented.

d. A motion was made and approved to accept the Executive Committee's report.

6. New Business and Announcements:

a. Robert Danielson presented a proposal for member services. Robert has agreed to chair this steering committee. One service is a partnership with First Fruits Press at Asbury Theological Seminary. This would include online and paper publication of the proceedings and papers presented at APM annual meetings, as well as an APM handbook which will include guidance on developing curricula and course syllabi. The 2013 APM Annual Meeting reports and paper presentations will be available from First Fruits.

b. Greg Leffel reviewed on-going discussions for international outreach, connections, and partnerships since the APM's organizational identity does not restricted its membership or interests to a limited geographical area.

c. Madge Karecki reviewed the challenge, as well as opportunities, to engage Roman Catholic missiologists and scholars in APM, particularly in leadership.

d. David Fenrick extended an invitation to the APM from the Christian Community Development Association to its annual conference in New Orleans, Sept. 11-14, 2013.

e. Madge Karecki invited APM members to attend the Midwest Fellowship of Professors of Mission Annual Meeting in Chicago on November 16.

f. Steve Bevans announced the Global Ecumenical Theological Institute where 170 seminarians and young theologians from all regions of the world and all Christian backgrounds will be invited to participate, October 25 – November 9, 2013 in South Korea, alongside the World Council of Churches' 10th Assembly. Funding for participation is from the Luce Foundation.

g. Greetings were extended from APM to the Association of Professors of Mission in Brazil.

h. APM noted the deaths of the following colleagues this past year, and their unique and enduring contributions to the field of missiology and the proclamation of the Gospel:

   a. Richard Twiss, President of Wiconi International and North American Institute for Indigenous Theological Studies.

   b. Richard H. Drummand, University of Dubuque Theological Seminary.

   c. Dean Gilliland, Fuller Theological Seminary.

7. The report of the Nominating Committee regarding the election of officers was submitted by Madge Karecki, First Vice President.

   a. David Fenrick, University of Northwestern, St. Paul, MN, was reelected Secretary-Treasurer.

   b. Madge Karecki (Roman Catholic), Office for Mission

Education and Animation, Archdiocese of Chicago, IL, was elected President.

c. Ben Hartley (Concililar), Eastern University, PA, was elected First Vice President.

d. Nelson Jennings (Independent), Overseas Ministry Study Center, New Haven, CT, was elected Second Vice President.

8. Greg Leffel presented the new members of the APM Advisory Board:

- Sarita Gallagher, George Fox Seminary

- Paul Kollman, University of Notre Dame

- Kevin (Kip) Lines, Hope International University

9. Greg Leffel thanked the Executive and Advisory Committees for their hard work on the Executive Report and contribution to the Annual Meeting. He also introduced the new APM President, Marge Karecki.

10. Outgoing President Greg Leffel and the Executive Committee were thanked for their outstanding work in organizing an excellent and memorable conference, as well as Greg Leffel's leadership in directing the APM toward the development of a long-range strategic plan.

11. Madge Karecki closed with prayer at 3:46 pm.

Respectfully Submitted,

David E. Fenrick

Secretary-Treasurer

2013-2014 Leadership Roster

Executive Committee:

President
> Sr. Madge Karecki, SSF-TOSF, D.Th.
> Office for Mission Education and Animation, Archdiocese of
> Chicago, Chicago, IL

First Vice President
> Benjamin L. Hartley, Th.D.
> Palmer Theological Seminary, Philadelphia, PA

Second Vice President
> J. Nelson Jennings, Ph.D.
> Overseas Ministries Study Center, New Haven, CT

Secretary-Treasurer
> David E. Fenrick, Ph.D.
> Northwestern College, Minneapolis, MN

Advisory Committee:

Steven Bevans	Catholic Theological Union
Robert Danielson	Asbury Theological Seminary
Sarita Gallagher	George Fox Seminary
Paul Hertig	Azusa Pacific University
Paul Kollman	Notre Dame University
Kevin (Kip) Lines	Hope International University
Lisa Beth White	Boston University

Plenary Speaker Biographies

David E. Fenrick, Ph.D., Northwestern College

David Fenrick is the Director of the Center for Global Reconciliation and Cultural Education, and teaches Intercultural Studies and Communication at Northwestern College in St. Paul, MN. David earned his Ph.D. in Intercultural Studies from Asbury Theological Seminary.

David has lived and studied in Zimbabwe, Palestine and Israel, and has led numerous educational travel seminars around the world. He also served as a United Methodist minister in Virginia, receiving Excellence in Ministry Awards from both the Commission on Race and Religion, and the Board of Global Ministry.

Kendi Howells Douglas, D.Miss., Great Lakes Christian College

For thirteen years Kendi has served as Professor of Cross Cultural Ministry at Great Lakes Christian College in Lansing, MI. She received her D.Miss. from Asbury Theological Seminary, Wilmore, KY. Her passion is in the area of urban mission and her dissertation documented the history of the Christian Churches/Churches of Christ in the cities of North America. She enjoys research in other areas as well including: women in mission, mission history, and mission biographies.

Kendi is associate editor of *New Urban World Journal*, co-editor of a new book series entitled *Urban Missiology in the 21st Century*, and a founding member of International Society for Urban Mission. She has designed and directs a unique field-based, fully accredited minor program toward a Bachelors Degree in Urban Mission in partnership with United Neighbors of Hope in Thailand and Australia.

Gary M. Simpson, Th.D., Luther Seminary

Following fourteen years in pastoral ministry in the Lutheran Church, Gary was named Associate Professor of Systematic Theology at Luther Seminary, St. Paul, MN in 1990 and Professor of Systematic Theology in 1998. He is the author of numerous articles in English and German and several books and edited volumes including *Critical Social Theory: Prophetic Reason, Civil Society, and Christian Imagination* and the forthcoming edited volume *The Missional Church and Global Civil Society.* He has also edited and served on the editorial boards of several journals including *dialog: A Journal of Theology* and *Word and World: Theology for Christian Ministry.*

Gary received his M.Div. and Th.D. from Christ Seminary-Seminex, St. Louis, MO. He has served in executive leadership in civil society organizations including the Ecumenical Ministries of Oregon Witness and Life Commission, the Jewish-Christian Association of Oregon, the Oregon Holocaust Resource Center, and the Oregon chapter of the National Conference of Christians and Jews. He also served as the moderator of the board of Snowcap Church-Community Action Program (Portland, Ore.) and chaired the Oregon Governor's Task Force on Hunger.

Al Tizon, Ph.D., Palmer Theological Seminary

Al serves in a unique joint appoint as Associate Professor of Holistic Ministry at Palmer Theological Seminary of Eastern University, and as co-President elect of Evangelicals for Social Action, both located in King of Prussia, PA. He received his Ph.D. in missiology from the Graduate Theological Union, Berkeley, CA. Al and his family engaged in community development work, ministry to street children, and church leadership development among the poor in his native Philippines for almost ten years as missionaries with Action International Ministries. An ordained minister of the Evangelical Covenant Church, Al served several churches in both the Philippines and the United States as associate and interim pastor for seven years and as lead pastor for five.

Al is the author of *Transformation After Lausanne: Radical Evangelical Mission in Global-Local Perspective*; co-author of *Linking Arms, Linking Lives: How Urban-Suburban Partnerships Can Transform Communities* with Ron Sider, John Perkins and Wayne Gordon; *Missional Preaching: Embrace, Engage, Transform*; co-editor of *Honoring the Generations: Learning with Asian North American Congregations* with Sydney Park and Soong-Chan Rah; and co-editor of *Following Jesus: Journeys in Radical Discipleship – Essays in Honor of Ronald J. Sider* (forthcoming) with Paul Alexander.

Sean Gladding, Worship Leader

Originally hailing from Norwich, England, Sean has made his home in the U.S. for the last two decades, where he has served in various forms of pastoral ministry including seven years at Houston-based Mercy Street. He has also served in leadership at Communality, a missional community in Lexington, Kentucky. He received his M.Div. from Asbury Theological Seminary where he first encountered the concept of the metanarrative of scripture, an experience that has deeply shaped his life.

Sean's first book, *The Story of God, the Story of Us*, had its origins in a Bible study he developed while co-pastor of Mercy Street, a church for people in recovery from addiction and from bad church experiences – often both. His book was named one of *Relevant Magazine's* Top Ten books of 2010. His second book, *Ten: Words of Life for an Addicted, Compulsive, Cynical, Divided and Worn-Out Culture*, is forthcoming this fall.